I0793766

NO NEUTRALS THERE

US LABOR, ZIONISM, AND THE STRUGGLE FOR PALESTINE

Jeff Schuhrke

Haymarket Books
Chicago, Illinois

© 2025 Jeff Schuhrke

Published in 2025 by
Haymarket Books
P.O. Box 180165
Chicago, IL 60618
www.haymarketbooks.org

ISBN: 979-8-88890-455-8

Distributed to the trade in the US through Consortium Book Sales and Distribution (www.cbsd.com) and internationally through Ingram Publisher Services International (www.ingramcontent.com).

This book was published with the generous support of Lannan Foundation, Wallace Action Fund, and Marguerite Casey Foundation.

Special discounts are available for bulk purchases by organizations and institutions. Please email info@haymarketbooks.org for more information.

Cover design by Jamie Kerry.

Printed in Canada by union labor.

Library of Congress Control Number: 2025938260

10 9 8 7 6 5 4 3 2 1

MIX
Paper | Supporting responsible forestry
FSC® C103567

Praise for *No Neutrals There*

"*No Neutrals There* tells the shameful story of how US labor leaders supported and helped fund the century-long Zionist project of colonization, occupation, and the ethnic cleansing of Palestine. But it is also a history of labor anti-Zionism, Palestinian labor politics, and the promise of working-class internationalism. There are no neutrals under colonialism and genocide, just as there are no neutrals in the class struggle."

—**Robin D. G. Kelley**, author of *Hammer and Hoe: Alabama Communists During the Great Depression*

"A damning indictment of the way American trade unions betrayed Palestinians by aiding the colonization of their homeland. This soul-searching journey is needed so that American trade unions, and the Western Left as a whole, can help to rectify a historical injustice that is a century old. This book covers an untold history that needed to be exposed for the sake of the struggle for freedom in Palestine."

—**Ilan Pappé**, author of *The Ethnic Cleansing of Palestine*

"*No Neutrals There* is a vital and unflinching account of the deep entanglement between the US trade union movement and Zionist settler colonialism. It dismantles the myth of union neutrality on Palestine and exposes the cost of silence. This book is a critical resource for all workers organizing toward genuine internationalism and justice."

—**Rafeef Ziadah**, coauthor of *Resisting Erasure: Capital, Imperialism and Race in Palestine*

"Historian Jeff Schuhrke—author of the 'go-to' book on US labor and foreign policy during the Cold War—explains why the AFL-CIO and other US unions' elected leaders have long provided unquestioning support for Israel. This despite the fact that the global working class watches in horror as millions of Palestinians starve and believes they deserve what all humans want: peace, equal rights, and justice. To understand the contradiction at the heart of US foreign policy, read Schuhrke's book."

—**Peter Cole**, author of *Dockworker Power: Race and Activism in Durban and the San Francisco Bay Area*

"When some American unions began to call for a ceasefire in Gaza, they were widely criticized in the political mainstream for venturing beyond their proper domain. This crucial, illuminating book shows that nothing could be further from the truth. The US labor movement has been entangled deeply with Zionism since long before Israel's establishment."

—**Gabriel Winant**, author of *The Next Shift: The Fall of Industry and the Rise of Health Care in Rust Belt America*

CONTENTS

They say in Harlan County
There are no neutrals there.
You'll either be a union man
Or a thug for J. H. Blair.

—Florence Reece,
"Which Side Are You On?" (1931)

In today's world no one is innocent, no one a neutral. A man is either with the oppressed or he is with the oppressors.

—George Habash,
founder of the Popular Front for
the Liberation of Palestine (1970)

THE AFL-CIO IS NOT NEUTRAL. WE SUPPORT ISRAEL.

—AFL-CIO Executive Council,
full-page advertisement
in *The New York Times* (1982)

ABBREVIATIONS

AALD American Alliance for Labor and Democracy
ADC American-Arab Anti-Discrimination Committee
AFL-CIO American Federation of Labor and Congress of Industrial Organizations
AFSCME American Federation of State, County, and Municipal Employees
AFT American Federation of Teachers
AHC Arab Higher Committee
AIPAC American Israel Public Affairs Committee
AJTUCP American Jewish Trade Union Committee for Palestine
AWC Arab Workers' Congress
AWS Arab Workers' Society
BDS Boycott, Divestment, and Sanctions
DCI Development Corporation for Israel
GSP Generalized System of Preferences
IAM International Association of Machinists
IDF Israel Defense Forces
ILGWU International Ladies' Garment Workers' Union
ILWU International Longshore and Warehouse Union
JLC Jewish Labor Committee
LCOME Labor Committee on the Middle East
LIUNA Laborers' International Union of North America
NLCP/NCLI National Labor Committee for Palestine (pre-1948)/ National Committee for Labor Israel (post-1948)

NYCLAW	New York City Labor Against the War
PA	Palestinian Authority
PAWS	Palestine Arab Workers' Society
PCP	Palestine Communist Party
PFLP	Popular Front for the Liberation of Palestine
PGFTU	Palestinian General Federation of Trade Unions
PLAN	Palestine Labor Action Network
PLL	Palestine Labor League
PLO	Palestine Liberation Organization
SEIU	Service Employees International Union
TAA	Teaching Assistants Association
UAW	United Auto Workers
UE	United Electrical Workers
UHT	United Hebrew Trades

INTRODUCTION

On October 16, 2023, nine days into Israel's total war on the two million civilians trapped inside the besieged Gaza Strip, a coalition of Palestinian trade unions issued an international call to action directed at labor movements around the world. "This urgent, genocidal situation can only be prevented by a mass increase of global solidarity with the people of Palestine and that can restrain the Israeli war machine," the plea stated. "We need you to take immediate action—wherever you are in the world—to prevent the arming of the Israeli state and the companies involved in the infrastructure of the blockade."[1]

Specifically, Palestinian unionists urged their counterparts in other countries to refuse to manufacture or transport weapons and equipment for the Israeli military and to pass motions within their unions to this effect. Over the next several days and weeks, in countries like Belgium, Spain, Italy, India, Turkey, the United Kingdom, Colombia, Japan, and Australia, unions of workers at airports, seaports, railways, coal mines, factories, and other workplaces publicly pledged to honor the call to action in solidarity with the Palestinian people. In doing so, the members of such unions vowed not to allow their labor to be used in the service of genocide and ethnic cleansing.

In the United States—the nation that supplies Israel with the vast majority of its imported armaments—unionists first answered the Palestinian call only two days after it was issued. At the October 18 meeting of the central labor council in Olympia, Washington, the board members voted unanimously to pass a resolution expressing opposition "in principle [to] any union involvement in the production or transportation of weapons destined for Israel" and committing "to investigate ways our member unions may be participating in this war."[2] Representing unions in the counties of Thurston, Lewis, and Mason, the labor council was the local arm of the American Federation of Labor and Congress of Industrial Organizations (AFL-CIO), the national labor federation comprising most of the country's unions. Accordingly, the council's resolution also urged the AFL-CIO to "publicly support an immediate ceasefire and equal rights for Palestinians and Israelis."[3] Immediately after it was approved, the measure was posted on the labor council's website and social media accounts to make their stance known to all.

But five days later, an AFL-CIO senior field representative informed the council's board members that their resolution was null and void because it did not conform to the national federation's official policy. He pointed to a press release issued by the AFL-CIO's top officers on October 11 vaguely calling for "a swift resolution to the current conflict" but not mentioning a ceasefire and not opposing the production and shipment of weapons for Israel. By differing from the AFL-CIO's stated position, the field representative explained, the council's resolution violated a governance rule stating that, as chartered organizations of the AFL-CIO, all labor councils must conform their policies to those of the national federation.[4]

Soon after, the resolution was deleted from the Thurston-Lewis-Mason Central Labor Council's website and social media accounts—as if it had never existed. About a week later, AFL-CIO president Liz Shuler sent a memorandum to all local labor councils and state labor federations across the United States telling them that "the national AFL-CIO is the only body that can render an official public position or action on national or international issues." Without explicitly referencing the unfolding carnage in Gaza, she was all but telling the federation's local and statewide bodies they were not allowed to stand in solidarity with Palestine.[5]

Still, the AFL-CIO's individual member unions—which, unlike central labor councils, operate as autonomous affiliates of the federation—were free to take their own positions. Beginning with the American Postal Workers Union and United Auto Workers (UAW), over the following weeks and months several of them formally joined the growing chorus of international voices demanding a ceasefire in Gaza—as the nonstop horrors inflicted on the people of the coastal enclave were livestreamed before the global public—culminating in the establishment of a new union coalition dubbed the National Labor Network for Ceasefire.[6] The AFL-CIO itself eventually came out in favor of a "negotiated cease-fire" in early February 2024, after at least twenty-five thousand Palestinians had already been killed.[7]

Despite these positive developments, the AFL-CIO and its affiliated unions at the national level still failed to answer the explicit Palestinian call to refrain from building or shipping weapons for Israel. (Importantly, however, some of the unions' local branches passed statements endorsing the call, including UAW Local 4811—composed of graduate student workers, postdoctoral researchers, and other academic employees at the University of California—which also staged an extraordinary Palestine solidarity strike between May 20 and June 10, 2024).[8] With US unions representing at least tens of thousands of workers in the weapons manufacturing industry and thousands more in the logistics sector, the American labor movement appeared to be well positioned to hamper the Israeli war machine by honoring the Palestinian trade unions' request for solidarity. Yet most national labor officials were either hesitant about or outright hostile to any workplace activity that might materially obstruct the Gaza genocide.[9]

This became viscerally apparent in early October 2024, as the genocide reached the one-year mark. Approximately forty-five thousand members of the International Longshoremen's Association—the traditionally conservative union of dockworkers servicing ports along the US East Coast and Gulf Coast—staged a three-day strike to secure raises and protections from automation in their new collective bargaining agreement. Although the work stoppage seriously hindered the movement of commercial goods, the union's leadership pledged to continue handling military cargo. This meant that despite their own strike, the longshore workers kept on loading armaments presumably bound for Israel to be used for slaughtering civilians.[10]

§

There were several reasons for US labor's general unwillingness to take tangible collective action in solidarity with Palestine at such a crucial moment. For one, national union presidents and AFL-CIO officials believed it to be both necessary and advantageous to maintain a good relationship with the US government—especially with Democratic President Joe Biden, a labor advocate as well as a staunch Israel ally. Although respectful and limited disagreement with the administration's Gaza policy could be voiced, doing anything that might *physically* impede Washington's aims in the Middle East would risk souring that relationship and inviting the government's wrath in the form of legal restrictions on unions' ability to operate.

Another reason was that many union leaders and members had conflicting attitudes about Palestine and were convinced—at least initially—that Israel's assault on Gaza was somehow a justified act of "self-defense" after the deadly Hamas attack on

October 7, 2023. For union members in military-related industries, whose jobs are ultimately tied to the perpetuation of armed conflicts, such attitudes would deter any potential eagerness to engage in solidarity action with Palestine, especially if it might jeopardize their employment.

Similarly, there was an aversion among some unionists to take risky and possibly illegal action over a seemingly "remote" foreign policy issue. Indeed, in trying to organize their unions to act in solidarity with Palestinians, rank-and-file workers often must contend with arguments that the labor movement should keep quiet and remain neutral because, it is argued, Palestine has nothing to do with US unions and weighing in on the issue only invites unnecessary controversy.

But, in reality, unions in the United States have never been silent or neutral on the question of Palestine.

This gets to the underlying and most significant reason for American labor's widespread disinclination to answer the Palestinian trade union call to action: the more than one hundred–year alliance between US union officialdom and Zionism—the settler-colonial movement that served to dispossess Palestinians in the twentieth century and continues to suppress their elemental human rights and freedom in the name of Jewish nationalism.

Although it asserts the supposed right of Jews to control Palestine, Zionism is by no means driven exclusively by Jewish people, nor should the term *Zionist* be mistaken as a synonym for "Jew." Indeed, throughout the history of Zionism, Jews have been among its most vocal and dedicated opponents. What's more, non-Jews—particularly Christians—have always been essential players in the Zionist movement. European Protestants were issuing apocalyptic calls for the Jewish "restoration" of Palestine centuries before Jews themselves began advocating Zionism. The largest Zionist organization in the modern United States is Christians United for Israel, an Evangelical group boasting approximately ten million members, which is more than the total number of Jewish Americans. President Biden, a Catholic, repeatedly referred to himself as a Zionist during his time in the White House.[11]

Similarly, US labor officials—among whom Jews have always been a minority—have long been proponents of Zionism and the State of Israel. There are two fundamental reasons for this.

One is AFL-CIO leaders' traditional ideological commitment to Labor Zionism, the particular current within the wider Zionist project that centers the role of Jewish workers in laying the economic foundations for building and maintaining the Israeli state. Prior to the 1955 establishment of the AFL-CIO, the American Federation of Labor and the Congress of Industrial Organizations were separate entities, each generally representing different strands of US unionism. Founded in 1886, the AFL espoused a vision of nonradical, "pure and simple" trade unionism that proclaimed loyalty to American capitalism in exchange for limited gains and protections for the most skilled workers (especially English-speaking white craftsmen). The CIO, which was launched after several unions broke away from the AFL in 1935, put forward a comparatively progressive agenda of using the collective power of all workers to create a more humane economy and more egalitarian society.

Labor Zionism, which emerged in the early 1900s and came to dominate the broader Zionist movement by the 1930s, appealed to both of these differing approaches to US trade unionism. AFL leaders could easily sympathize with Labor Zionism because, like their own brand of unionism, it substituted class struggle with class collaboration in the service of nationalism. For their part, the CIO's more liberal and progressive unionists were drawn to Labor Zionism because its followers in Palestine were putting certain socialistic ideas into practice, such as establishing cooperative enterprises and implementing social welfare programs. Support for

Labor Zionism was one area where AFL and CIO officials were in complete agreement well before the 1955 merger. Awed by how it rapidly delivered material benefits and political power to Jewish workers in Israel—which seemed especially laudable and impressive after the horrors of the Holocaust—important figures within the merged AFL-CIO continued approving of Labor Zionism from the 1950s onward.

But Labor Zionism's apparent successes were always premised on the dispossession and exclusion of Indigenous Palestinians, whose own plight was both misunderstood and deliberately ignored by US union leaders and many rank-and-file members. This points to another way that Labor Zionism struck an ideological chord with influential American laborites. During the US labor movement's formative years in the early to mid-nineteenth century, some of its loudest champions called for lands in the western "frontier" region of the continent to be settled by white workers so they could establish farms and escape the toil and drudgery of wage work—a vision that ultimately depended on the expulsion of Native Americans. The US labor movement, like US society more broadly, continued to be inspired by mythical stories of courageous and hardworking pioneers who moved west, braved attacks by "savages," plowed "virgin soil," and transformed "empty" lands into a booming modern economy by the sweat of their brow—myths that served to dehumanize American Indians by rendering their whole existence as either invisible or an obstacle to "progress."

Even leftist elements of the American labor movement, who have acknowledged the key role of capitalist exploitation in the country's economic development, have often failed to similarly acknowledge the centrality of settler colonialism in that story. The song "Solidarity Forever," first sung in the 1910s by members of the radical Industrial Workers of the World and now the unofficial anthem of the US labor movement, proudly declares that "it is we who plowed the prairies, built the cities where they trade / dug the mines and built the workshops, endless miles of railroad laid."[12] But what goes unrecognized in the lyrics is that those prairies, cities, mines, workshops, and railroads were plowed, built, dug, and laid very shortly after the lands on which they sit were taken from Indigenous nations through merciless violence and intimidation.

US labor's close connections to the history and ongoing legacy of settler colonialism in North America served to make many of its leaders ideologically receptive to Labor Zionism and its own myths of "making the desert bloom" that were premised on the dehumanization and violent dispossession of another Indigenous people.

In addition, Labor Zionist leaders in Palestine intentionally cultivated personal relationships with US union officials in the early to mid-twentieth century with the aim of securing financial and political support. Many of these same Labor Zionists later became high-ranking figures in the Israeli government after 1948, including multiple prime ministers. In those roles, they remained close friends of US labor leaders.

The other fundamental reason for American labor's long-standing alliance with Zionism and the State of Israel is that it has historically been crucial to the AFL-CIO's larger goal of supporting US imperialism around the globe. Throughout the nineteenth and twentieth centuries, capitalists in the United States regularly painted organized labor as an unpatriotic, foreign conspiracy as a way to turn workers and the government against unions. Relatedly, unions routinely faced state repression whenever organizing or striking to demand higher wages, shorter hours, and better working conditions. In response to all of this, many officials in the AFL and later AFL-CIO believed that the safest and most pragmatic path forward for the labor movement would be to demonstrate patriotism, loyalty, and animosity toward foreign enemies. This particularly meant drumming up working-class support for US military operations abroad and officially pledging that unions would not obstruct production by going on strike during the two world wars.

During the Cold War, in which the United States staged numerous imperial interventions and wars around the world to "contain" the spread of communism and other leftist movements, AFL-CIO leaders became even more enthusiastic supporters of US empire because of their own obsessive anticommunism. Many of these labor officials had personally tangled with American communists for control of their unions in previous decades and, as the victors, saw themselves as indispensable experts in helping Washington destroy radicalism in foreign labor movements. They often regarded themselves as more dedicated, consistent, and effective anticommunists than their government counterparts. Also, after the anti-union attacks associated with the Red Scare in the late 1940s and early 1950s—which prompted the CIO to expel eleven of its communist-led unions and then merge with the more conservative AFL—union officials had internalized the belief that exhibiting jingoism and obedience to the established order was vital to organized labor's survival. Beyond this, they thought that an international capitalist economy dominated by the United States would mean steady employment and good wages for American manufacturing workers, who were then at the center of the US labor movement.[13]

As the Cold War took shape, the newly established State of Israel became a crucial US ally in staving off Soviet influence in the geostrategic and oil-rich Middle East. Though it briefly received critical diplomatic and military aid from the Soviet bloc in the late 1940s, by the mid-1950s, Israel was more squarely in the Western camp. This was not a surprising development given that the state was violently founded by European settlers at the same moment when Europe was losing its long-held colonial possessions in and around the Middle East.

From Israel's founding, the AFL-CIO's veteran anticommunists were eager to promote the invaluable service they thought the new state could provide as a US ally in the Cold War. They especially pointed to Israel's labor-centered economic development model, which could be held up as a successful example of noncommunist "nation-building" to be emulated across the emergent Third World, as well as in the United States itself.

AFL-CIO cold warriors believed that securing the political and ideological loyalty of labor movements in Asia, Africa, and Latin America would be decisive to whether the countries of those regions moved into the Soviet camp or not. Israel's Labor Zionism appeared to provide living proof to Third World workers' movements that a newly independent state outside of Europe could achieve impressive economic growth and simultaneously reward workers without embracing communism or aligning with the Soviets. Anticommunist US labor leaders therefore championed a full-fledged alliance between the United States and Israel.

After the Cold War ended with the dissolution of the Soviet Union in 1991, imperial considerations continued motivating American labor officials, along with their counterparts in the US government, to strongly support Israel. Now, instead of being described as a bulwark against communism in the Middle East, the Zionist state was celebrated as a rampart against the encroachment of secular dictators like Iraq's Saddam Hussein and revolutionary Islamic movements like the one that attained power in Iran.

The US foreign policy apparatus argued that as the "only democracy" in the region, Israel was in dire need of significant military and diplomatic support so it could quash such threats before they overran the Middle East. This meant allowing (and enabling) Israel to continue systematically subjugating Palestinians even after supposedly committing to a two-state solution in the 1990s. Still eager to showcase their patriotic loyalty and commitment to the US empire to remain in Washington's good graces, a new generation of AFL-CIO officials put their support behind this unwaveringly pro-Israel policy, or at the very least did not openly dispute it.

Enamored with Labor Zionism and determined to bolster American foreign policy objectives, from the early twentieth century onward, US labor officialdom helped build and sustain the State of Israel. It did this by taking the same type of meaningful, committed action it now refused to take in solidarity with Palestinians at the outbreak of the Gaza genocide, including enthusiastically donating hundreds of millions of dollars from union treasuries (for Zionist colonization and Israeli nation-building); relentlessly pressuring US elected officials (to supply economic and military aid to Israel); occasionally boycotting foreign cargo (that of Israel's Arab rivals); and repeatedly issuing forceful public statements, holding mass rallies, and staging limited work stoppages (to demonstrate popular support for Zionism at critical moments in history).

Indeed, perhaps nowhere else have US unions demonstrated so much international solidarity than in Palestine, but almost exclusively in favor of its Zionist settler population and nearly always at the expense of the Indigenous Palestinian people. It is therefore disingenuous to argue that US labor should now suddenly be silent on Palestine or suggest that it is somehow implausible for American unions to take concrete action around Palestine. If anything, given the historic role its top leaders have played in one-sidedly bolstering Israel, the US labor movement has a special responsibility to stand with Palestinians in their struggle for liberation.

This book tells the story of why and how US labor became one of Israel's most stalwart defenders and generous benefactors throughout the Zionist state's tumultuous and controversial history. Importantly, this is also the story of the Palestinian trade unionists and various rank-and-file US union members—including Arab Americans, anti-Zionist Jews, Black radicals, and anti-imperialists—who, despite the odds, courageously organized in support of Palestinian freedom and dignity over the years and to whom today's pro-Palestine labor activists can look for inspiration.

§

The question of international worker solidarity with Palestine is far from an academic one. Ostensibly represented by the AFL-CIO, the US labor movement could conceivably bring much of the national economy to a standstill if ever it were so inclined, including those areas of the economy that help sustain Israel's brutal occupation and war-making abilities.

To be sure, organized labor in the United States has been taking a beating for at least the past four decades—and it is only getting worse under the second administration of right-wing US President Donald Trump. Because of antiworker laws, corporate union busting, a rigged global political economy, and cautious attitudes among many labor leaders, unions currently represent just below 10 percent of the overall US workforce (down from a historic high point of 35 percent in the late 1940s). Though severely and irrefutably weakened, the ranks of organized labor, it must be recognized, still amount to around fourteen million unionized workers, many of them in crucial sectors of the economy like transportation, communications, energy, construction, health care, and education.

What's more, thanks to the efforts of a younger, more class-conscious generation, in recent years even this relatively small labor movement has demonstrated its ability to secure better livelihoods for workers by confronting corporate power head-on. With a noticeable uptick in the number of unionization campaigns and strikes, the labor movement in recent years has demonstrated renewed vitality and the (still unrealized) potential for growth.

Given capital's ability to flow freely across borders—with multinational corporations setting up shop wherever they can exploit workers the most—a rejuvenated US labor movement would, by necessity, have to be an internationalist labor movement. Workers cannot allow themselves to be pitted against each other along nationalist lines in the global race to the bottom, but instead need to stand together and coordinate their activities to raise living standards for all. Further, given the critical role played by the US foreign policy apparatus in facilitating and protecting the ruling class's accumulation of capital around the globe, such working-class internationalism would also have to be anti-imperialist to be truly effective. In other words, American unions should not shy away from vigorously challenging Washington's foreign policy agenda, regardless of whether Democrats or Republicans are in power.

Similarly, with a trillion dollars of taxpayer money being thrown to the Pentagon and its private contractors every year (including at least $3.8 billion per year in military aid to Israel), a reenergized US labor movement should prioritize shrinking and dismantling the criminally wasteful and destructive military-industrial complex.

As they continue organizing new workers, unions could also use their political influence—which derives from their mass memberships and ability to disrupt the economy—to demand the government reallocate the bloated military budget toward education, health care, housing, and green infrastructure. If properly funded, these sectors would not only provide the kinds of services and social benefits that would greatly improve the quality of life for working-class communities, but would also create far more jobs than Pentagon spending currently does.

Organized labor could simultaneously push the government to implement an industrial policy that ensures a just transition for weapons industry workers so they can maintain remunerative union jobs producing socially useful, civilian products like medical equipment, machine tools, electric locomotives, green energy components, and mass transit vehicles.

Internationalism, anti-imperialism, and antimilitarism on the part of American unions could go a long way toward helping Palestinians achieve safety, dignity, freedom, and self-determination. This could take several specific forms. Besides engaging in work stoppages or slowdowns to disrupt the flow of weaponry for the Israeli war machine, unions and labor bodies could divest their own pension money from Israel and companies that profit off of its occupation and blockade of Palestinian lands and instead donate funds and resources to Palestinian worker organizations. They could honor consumer boycotts organized by the Palestinian-led Boycott, Divestment, and Sanctions movement and cut ties with the Histadrut—Israel's Zionist labor federation that has a long tradition of discriminating against Palestinian workers. Unions could turn to contractual protections, labor laws, and strength in numbers to defend pro-Palestine activists against employer and state repression (and recently, several have been doing so).

American unions could also put genuine pressure on presidential and congressional candidates by withholding endorsements, campaign contributions, and get-out-the-vote efforts unless those candidates commit to using the enormous leverage the US wields over Israel to stop thwarting Palestinian liberation. Unions could do substantially more political education for their own members about the history and realities of Palestine and Israel, including by sponsoring delegations of Palestinian unionists to speak to workers in the United States or organizing delegations of US unionists to listen to workers in occupied Palestine.

None of these types of activities are without precedent. Although there is undeniably an ugly history of anticommunist US labor officials working hand in hand with the State Department and Central Intelligence Agency to undermine left-wing, democratic, worker-led movements around the world in the name of Cold War "containment," there are also numerous historical examples of more progressive elements in US labor taking meaningful action in opposition to fascism, colonialism, and apartheid. Targeting foreign regimes like Nazi Germany, Fascist Italy, Imperial Japan, Franco's Spain, Pinochet's Chile, apartheid South Africa, and the military dictatorships of Central America, such activities included organizing consumer boycotts, refusing to handle cargo, divesting pension funds, and engaging in political lobbying. US unions also gave material assistance and moral support to the peoples such governments were oppressing.

§

In examining this often-overlooked history, it is necessary to start in the early twentieth century, when US labor first began its close partnership with the American foreign policy establishment during World War I and simultaneously started providing material aid to Labor Zionists in Palestine. In seeking the support of US unions, Labor Zionists first approached Jewish American trade unionists despite their traditional aversion to Zionist aims, gradually winning them over by emphasizing principles of worker solidarity more than nationalism. At the same time, to demonstrate their approval of the US government's stated rationale for entering World War I, in 1917 AFL officials endorsed calls for the national self-determination of European peoples, including Jews. Specifically, and explicitly, this meant formally approving the Zionist goal of establishing a Jewish "homeland" in Arab Palestine.

Later, during the crises of the Great Depression and World War II in the 1930s and 1940s, the US labor movement grew to unprecedented size and strength with substantial help from the federal government, cementing the relationship between union officialdom and the state. These were the same decades when antisemitic persecution in Europe escalated into outright genocide, with six million Jews murdered at the hands of the Nazi regime. This monstrous crime gave further impetus to the Zionist project, with the State of Israel founded in 1948 by way of another hideous crime against a humanity: the violent expulsion of some 750,000 Palestinians from their homes. Now at the historical high point of its power, the US labor movement—under the direction of officials who, in the preceding decades, had come to champion both Labor Zionism and US global ambitions—used its economic and political muscle to bolster the creation of Israel and simultaneous destruction of Indigenous Palestine.

Throughout the 1950s and 1960s, leaders of the AFL-CIO intensified their material and political support for Israel to an astonishing degree, motivated by both their dedication to Labor Zionism and their Cold War desire to stymy the spread of communism among workers in the nascent Third World. After the Six-Day War of 1967, in which Israel quickly conquered the remaining Palestinian territory it had failed to take in 1948 and humiliated Soviet-backed Arab nationalist governments in Egypt and Syria, Washington officials gave up any lingering reservations about whether the Zionist state was worthy of complete backing and uninterrupted military aid. But at the same time, a younger generation of Americans—many of whom were already opposing white supremacy and the US war on Vietnam—began openly questioning the Zionist project and expressing solidarity with oppressed Palestinians.

A blend of unfavorable political and economic forces between the 1970s and 1990s served to weaken the union movement in the

United States and sideline Labor Zionism in Israel. In these same decades, the cause of Palestinian liberation increasingly garnered international sympathy, including among segments of the American working class. Amid this changing context, US labor officialdom struggled to legitimize its ongoing alliance with Zionism, especially as more and more rank-and-file workers organized in solidarity with Palestinians and protested their own unions' complicity in Israeli occupation and apartheid. In the early decades of the twenty-first century, despite the best efforts of many pro-Zionist labor officials, broad-based support for Palestinian freedom and human rights began to crystallize within several US unions, as it did within the wider US population.

By exploring this century-long story, we can see the myriad ways that racism and imperialism frequently undermined opportunities for worker solidarity and collective liberation and how the theft of land and denial of self-determination are inextricably tied to the exploitation of labor. Studying this history can therefore help today's US unionists understand why it is imperative that they and their organizations not try to remain neutral (or worse) on Palestine, but rather take a bold and principled stand—especially amid the Gaza genocide.

The systematic, eliminationist violence inflicted on Palestinians today—not by Israel alone, but also by the United States, United Kingdom, Germany, and other Western countries—at once serves as a horrifying reminder of the worst atrocities carried out by the racist and colonial regimes of the twentieth century and as a grim preview of what nightmares may be in store for the remainder of this century as global economic inequality and the devastating effects of climate change collide with rising fascist political movements and new technologies of social control and mass murder.[14]

This is why the cause of Palestinian liberation is the cause of all who believe in justice, freedom, and human dignity—the same fundamental principles that have historically animated the international labor movement. As illustrator Walter Crane famously put it in 1894, "the cause of labor is the hope of the world." If, with labor's help, freedom can be achieved in a place and for a people long plagued by imperial machinations, colonial domination, racial and religious oppression, ecological degradation, and worker exploitation, then there can be hope for the world. It is no wonder that Palestine solidarity activists in the United States and around the globe have adopted the slogan "Palestine will free us all."

CHAPTER 1

LAYING THE FOUNDATIONS

On October 7, 1897, under the cover of the High Holidays, thirteen working-class men and women representing various Jewish socialist groups in Lithuania, Belorussia, and Poland held a clandestine meeting in the attic of a worker's house in Vilnius, Lithuania. There, they collectively agreed to unite their discrete groups into a single revolutionary organization called the General Jewish Labor Bund. The Bund (a word meaning "union") would be at the center of many of the anticzarist rebellions in the Russian Empire at the dawn of the twentieth century.

A very different kind of meeting, with very different objectives, had taken place just over a month earlier in Basel, Switzerland. There, more than two hundred middle- and upper-class Jews from across Europe publicly convened to found the Zionist Organization. Their chief aim, as stated in the platform they approved at the gathering, was to establish a legally protected home for the Jewish people in the Middle East, specifically in Palestine.[1]

At this time, the majority of the world's Jews lived in Eastern Europe. They were largely confined to a region of the Russian Empire known as the Pale of Settlement, extending from the Baltic Sea in the north to the Black Sea in the south. There, they faced discrimination, exploitation, and *pogroms*—the Russian term for state-sponsored antisemitic riots. To escape this systemic violence, and in the hopes of finding a better life, some 586,000 Jews fled Eastern Europe and came to the United States between 1882 and 1900.[2]

As industrial capitalism penetrated the Pale in the late nineteenth century, Jews came to comprise a significant proportion of a nascent urban proletariat in cities like Vilnius, Warsaw, Minsk, Białystok, and Grodno, where they became well-versed in modern ideas like nationalism, democracy, and socialism. It was these ideas—along with the harsh realities of antisemitism—that inspired the establishment of both the Jewish Labor Bund and the Zionist Organization.[3] Though they were each the product of European modernity, the Bund and the Zionist Organization embodied different answers to antisemitic oppression. While the former represented a proletarian Jewish movement dedicated to liberation through class struggle and socialism, the latter was a more bourgeois configuration that sought Jewish emancipation through nationalism and settler colonialism.

Eventually, an attempt would be made to reconcile these competing movements in the form of Labor Zionism, which would have an important influence on union officials in the United States right as they coincidentally started seeing themselves as partners in realizing Washington's foreign policy objectives.

BUNDISTS AND ZIONISTS

In the first several years after its 1897 founding, members of the General Jewish Labor Bund put forward a universalist vision of revolution tied to Marxist ideas of class struggle, while at the same time recognizing the particular forms of oppression and discrimination endured by Jews in Eastern Europe. As essayist Abraham Brumberg succinctly explained upon the Bund's centennial anniversary: "The Bund placed its faith in a socialist revolution that would free both Jew and non-Jew and liberate humankind from economical, political, and national oppression—including antisemitism."[4]

In czarist Russia, Bundists secretly printed and distributed socialist propaganda, held underground reading and discussion circles to promote Yiddish culture, organized strikes among urban Jewish workers, and led self-defense efforts against antisemitic pogroms.[5] They were instrumental in the creation of the revolutionary Russian Social Democratic Labor Party in 1898, but broke from it in 1903 due to the party leadership's preference for a centralized body over a more federated one that would tolerate an autonomous suborganization like the Bund. The party itself would famously split into the Menshevik and Bolshevik factions, with the latter eventually transforming the Russian Empire into the communist Soviet Union.

Amid social unrest, mass strikes, and revolutionary activity in Russia—all of which sparked more violent antisemitic backlash—another 1.4 million European Jews emigrated to the United States between 1900 and 1914.[6] Many of them were young radicals associated with the Bund who had led the way in challenging Russia's czarist regime in the unfinished revolution of 1905 and were forced to escape the resultant political repression. They came to cities like New York, Philadelphia, and Chicago ready to similarly take on US capitalism.

The earlier wave of Jewish immigrants in the 1880s and 1890s—many of them also socialists—had largely found work in the needle trades. In 1888, a group of them in New York City formed the United Hebrew Trades (UHT) to be an umbrella group directing and coordinating efforts by Jewish immigrants to establish and sustain local unions. Nine years later, UHT members founded the *Jewish Daily Forward*, a pro-union, Yiddish-language newspaper led by working-class intellectual

Abraham Cahan. Then in 1900, with support from the UHT and the *Forward*, Jewish immigrant workers in the women's clothing industry spearheaded the founding of the International Ladies' Garment Workers' Union (ILGWU).[7]

The young Bundists who arrived in America in the early 1900s brought new vitality to these various Jewish-led worker institutions. They helped grow the ILGWU and led historic strikes to improve conditions in sweatshops. Many participated in the New York-based Workmen's Circle, a fraternal organization that provided mutual aid to working-class Jewish immigrants and promoted Yiddish literature and culture.[8] By 1906, there were already sixty US branches of the Bund with a total of three thousand members.[9]

As in Russia, Bundists in the United States were dedicated socialists who believed in uniting the entire working class, but they did not wish to lose sight of their Jewish identity. In the words of historian Steve Fraser, the Bundists "accepted almost everything about socialist ideology except for the logic of universal proletarian assimilation."[10] Still, resistance to assimilation did not mean that Bundists—in the United States or Europe—automatically sympathized with fellow Jews if they belonged to a different social class. After all, many of the sweatshop employers they squared off against were Jewish, but nevertheless were identified as class enemies.

Sidney Hillman exemplified the energy and vision that the new wave of Jewish immigrants brought to the US labor movement. As a Bund activist in Lithuania, between 1903 and 1906, a teenage Hillman organized typesetters, led public demonstrations, and participated in the 1905 Russian Revolution. He was imprisoned for his activism twice and, facing escalating political repression and pogroms, was forced to flee to England before eventually making his way to the United States in 1907. Only three years later, as a cutter at Chicago's Hart, Shaffner & Marx menswear company, Hillman helped lead a strike of forty thousand garment workers in the Windy City. Veterans of that strike would establish a dynamic new union in 1914 called the Amalgamated Clothing Workers of America, with the 27-year-old Hillman serving as the union's first president.[11]

Under the leadership of Hillman and other Bundists, the Amalgamated Clothing Workers championed "social unionism," which meant empowering union members and working-class communities beyond the workplace by building affordable cooperative housing, offering unemployment insurance, and establishing a workers' bank.

§

In stark contrast to members of the Bund, Zionists contended that Jews would never be allowed to live peacefully in non-Jewish societies and therefore needed their own territorial state. Rising antisemitic violence in Europe seemed to prove and give urgency to this argument. Emulating the many nationalist movements that emerged in Europe's decaying empires during the nineteenth century, Zionists argued that Jewishness should be defined as a national identity more than a religious one.

But unlike the other newly assertive national groups of Europe—which were concentrated in specific geographic areas where they constituted majorities—Jews were a diasporic people, scattered around the world and thus a minority wherever they lived. Zionists therefore could not hope to establish a Jewish state where they already resided in Europe, but would instead have to look elsewhere. Therefore, by necessity, Zionism not only sought to mimic Europe's other nationalist movements of the nineteenth century, but also to copy the efforts of European empires to build settler colonies in other parts of the world.[12]

"By imitating the colonial ventures of the 'Gentile nations' among whom Jews lived, the 'Jewish nation' could send its own colonists into a piece of Afro-Asian territory, establish a settler-community, and in due course, set up its own state," Palestinian scholar Fayez Sayegh would explain in the 1960s. "For Zionism, then, colonization would be the instrument of nation-building, not the by-product of an already fulfilled nationalism."[13]

To Zionists, Palestine seemed the ideal location to carry out their nationalist, settler-colonial program.

Considered the "Holy Land" to the Abrahamic religions of Judaism, Christianity, and Islam, the Middle Eastern area of Palestine (a word dating back to ancient Greek) serves as the principal setting for most of the stories depicted in the Bible. Though its understood precise boundaries have repeatedly changed throughout history, Palestine has generally been regarded as the territory between the Jordan River Valley and Mediterranean Sea. A yearning for Palestine, a place known to Jews through the Bible as Eretz Yisrael (the Land of Israel), was a religious tradition dating back centuries and tied to a Jewish belief in the coming of the messiah at the end of times. From at least the dawn of the Protestant Reformation in the sixteenth century, some Christian theologians in Western Europe had espoused the physical "restoration" of Jews to Palestine as part of their own apocalyptic beliefs in the return of Christ.

But Zionism, which began crystalizing as a political movement among European Jews in the early 1880s, was a thoroughly modern and secular project—not a religious one. Indeed, the leading advocates for Zionism at the time were secular atheists. Reform rabbis vehemently opposed Zionism for how it attempted to change Judaism from a religion to a national identity. Orthodox rabbis similarly rejected it by arguing that colonizing Palestine would be meddling with God's will. Ironically, however, Zionists pointed to biblical stories of Eretz Israel as justification for their project. As Israeli historian Ilan Pappé writes, "[T]hough they did not believe in God, He had nonetheless promised them Palestine."[14]

The Zionist Organization founded in 1897 was the brainchild of Theodor Herzl. Born, raised, and educated in the Austro-Hungarian Empire, Herzl was a middle-class journalist. He would later claim that he was inspired to embrace Zionism when he was a foreign correspondent in Paris during the notorious Dreyfus affair, in which a French military officer of Jewish descent was wrongfully convicted of espionage and treason. In early 1896, Herzl published his highly influential pamphlet, *Der Judenstaat*. In it, he called for the creation of a state for Jews in Palestine—or, if that was impossible, then in remote parts of southern Argentina—as the answer to European antisemitism.

The following year, Herzl organized and presided over the First Zionist Congress in Basel. He had initially hoped to hold the gathering in Munich, but was forced to change plans after the city's Reform and Orthodox rabbis united in protest over their opposition to Zionism.

Bundists also opposed Zionism, which they saw as a bourgeois fantasy that sidetracked the all-important class struggle. As socialists, they were prone to be suspicious of nationalist projects, but their critique of Zionism went further. The Zionist belief that Jews could never thrive in Europe and the fixation on emigration as the sole answer to antisemitism, Bundists argued, only played into the hands of antisemites.

Bundists instead championed the notion of *doykayt*—or "hereness"—which meant focusing Jewish political struggle wherever Jews lived in the diaspora. "Zionism cannot be the solution for the whole Jewish people," said Isaac Leib Peretz, a Polish Jewish writer with ties to the Bund. "We have grown in the diaspora. And the diaspora is our battlefield. We do not run away from the battlefield." Literary figures like Peretz also disliked Zionism because many of its adherents promoted the use of Hebrew over Yiddish, undermining the kind of cultural identity Bundists sought to foster.[15]

Most importantly, the Bund dismissed Zionism as completely impractical. For one thing, Palestine was under the control of the Ottoman Empire, and Herzl's stated plan to woo the Ottomans into ceding territory (or get other imperial powers to convince the Ottomans to do so) seemed as unrealistic as it was unsavory. Further, Bundists said, Palestine's underdeveloped rural economy would simply be unable to absorb millions of newly arriving immigrants from Europe.

Most critically, they pointed to the obvious fact that Palestine's Indigenous population would not take kindly to a massive influx of European settlers looking to colonize their home.[16]

PALESTINE AND THE BEGINNING OF LABOR ZIONISM

Palestine was part of the Arab and Islamic world from the seventh century onward, recognized as a distinct region known as Filastin (Palestine). Muslims constituted the vast majority of its population, living alongside Christian, Druze, and Jewish minorities. During the Middle Ages, European Christians repeatedly attacked and tried conquering Palestine and its valuable position in global trade routes in a series of bloody, religiously fueled wars called Crusades. Starting in 1516, the region became part of the Ottoman Empire, which was centered in modern-day Turkey.

Palestine was home to a mostly rural society of *fellaheen* (peasants). Living in villages that were typically self-contained social worlds and self-sufficient economies, fellaheen families practiced subsistence agriculture. They grew wheat, barley, citrus fruits, and olives; raised sheep and poultry; and produced handcrafted goods like pottery, reed mats, and homespun cloth. They were compelled to pay taxes and provide army conscripts to the Ottoman Empire, which ruled locally through a small number of elite Palestinian families who lived in cities like Jerusalem, Nablus, Nazareth, Jericho, and Hebron.

By the close of the nineteenth century, Palestine was undergoing dramatic social and economic change. Aiming to compete with the Western European empires by centralizing state administration and modernizing the economy, the Ottomans imposed legal reforms introducing private ownership of large landholdings by absentee landlords. For the first time, fellaheen tenants could be evicted if the lands they traditionally farmed were sold off. A small number of urban notables began buying up agricultural lands in the countryside, with many fellaheen transformed into sharecroppers and wage laborers in the process. Meanwhile, trade with Europe increased, allowing commercial agriculture for exports to take root in and around coastal towns and cities like Jaffa, Haifa, and Acre. Such changes were accompanied by new educational opportunities and a growing press as part of the modernizing reforms of Ottoman rulers.

Thus, Palestine was seeing the emergence of new classes of proletarians, merchants, professionals, and intellectuals. Accompanying these various transformations was the beginning of an Arab nationalist consciousness desiring political and cultural independence from the Turkish-dominated Ottoman Empire.[17]

§

Even before Herzl launched the Zionist Organization, a small number of Eastern European Jews had already begun moving to Palestine in the 1880s. Like the much larger wave of Jews emigrating to the United States during the same period, they hoped to escape antisemitism and make a new start. But unlike their more numerous counterparts who headed for America, those who moved to Palestine were also motivated by a proto-Zionist Jewish nationalism. This wave of immigration would later be called the First Aliyah (a Hebrew word meaning "to ascend" and used to describe waves of Jewish immigration to Palestine).

On the eve of the First Aliyah, Palestine had an estimated 455,000 inhabitants. Of these, approximately 400,000 were Muslim, 40,000 were Christian, and 15,000 were Jewish.[18] The Palestinian Jews were mainly Mizrahi (native to the Middle East and North Africa) and Sephardic (descendants of Jews expelled from Iberia by Spain's Catholic monarchs in the fifteenth century). "In spite of marked religious distinctions between them and their neighbors," writes historian Rashid Khalidi, Palestinian Jews "were not foreigners, nor were they European settlers: they were, saw themselves, and were seen as Jews who were part of the indigenous Muslim-majority society."[19]

Unlike the native Palestinian Jews who primarily lived in cities, the Jewish immigrants who began coming from Europe in the late nineteenth century moved to the countryside and established agricultural colonies. This served to create tension with the native fellaheen—who were already experiencing economic pressures brought on by Ottoman land reforms—especially because the newly arriving European settlers often ignored and violated local customs. For example, as political scientist Muhammad Muslih writes, "[A]fter establishing their colonies, they blocked the customary pasture rights to adjacent villages, rounded up trespassing flocks and fined the Arab peasants who owned them, and paid no heed to Ottoman civil law and courts."[20]

As the First Aliyah began in the 1880s, some European Jewish socialists took issue with the idea of "reclaiming" the Holy Land, just as the Bund would criticize Zionism a few years later. The Russian Jewish revolutionary Ilya Rubanovich, for example, warned that such a project would inevitably involve violently supplanting Indigenous Palestinians. "What is to be done to the

Arabs?" Rubanovich asked in 1886. "Would the Jews expect to be strangers among the Arabs or would they want to make the Arabs strangers among themselves?" He ultimately answered his own questions by presciently arguing that Zionism would lead European Jews to ally with imperial powers to displace the Palestinians, who in turn would feel forced to defend themselves by any means necessary.[21]

Some proto-Zionists themselves understood that native Palestinians could not simply be ignored, most notably Russian thinker Asher Ginsberg—better known by his pen name, Ahad Ha'am. After visiting Palestine in 1891, he wrote a landmark essay titled "The Truth from the Land of Israel," in which he reported that the Palestinian Arabs were not "desert savages" but rather a civilized, "cunning" people with "sharp intellect" who "would not easily yield their place" to make way for a Jewish state. Ahad Ha'am also criticized the labor practices of early Zionist settlers, who were purchasing agricultural lands from absentee landlords, establishing their own private farms, and using newly landless fellaheen as their exploited labor force. He would later argue that Palestine should serve more as a "spiritual center" for Jews than a political state.[22]

For his part, Herzl also recognized the "problem" Indigenous Palestinians posed to the Zionist vision. Echoing the same justifications as European colonizers of the era, he argued in *Der Judenstaat* that Europe's Jews would bring modernity and economic development to Palestine from which the native Arab population would prosper.[23]

But Herzl privately admitted that for his dream of a Jewish state to be realized, at least some of Palestine's native inhabitants—particularly the poorer and supposedly less productive elements—would need to be removed. In an 1895 diary entry, he wrote about "gently" expelling Indigenous Arabs and taking their lands. "We shall try to spirit the penniless population across the border by procuring employment for it in the transit countries, while denying it employment in our own country," he wrote. "Both the process of expropriation and the removal of the poor must be carried out discreetly and circumspectly."[24]

Herzl only visited Palestine once, in 1898. The following year, he received a remarkable letter from Yusuf Diya al-Din Pasha al-Khalidi. A member of one of Palestine's notable families, Yusuf Diya had gotten a Western-style education in Malta and Istanbul. He was a respected scholar and Ottoman government official who had served as mayor of Jerusalem.

Very much aware of Zionism, and sympathetic to the plight of European Jews, in March 1899, Yusuf Diya wrote to Herzl to say that Zionism's ideals were "natural, beautiful and just" and conceded that Palestine was the historical homeland of the Jews. But he added that the "brutal force of circumstances must be taken into account." Palestine, Yusuf Diya reminded Herzl, was already "inhabited by others," and the Zionist plan to take it over would inevitably result in violent strife. "[I]n the name of God, let Palestine be left alone," he concluded.[25]

Herzl responded quickly, but dismissed Yusuf Diya's concerns. Repeating his colonial justifications for Zionism, he wrote that European Jews would bring "their intelligence, their financial acumen and their means of enterprise to the country, no one can doubt that the well-being of the entire country would be the happy result."[26]

§

Herzl died in 1904 at the age of forty-four. A year earlier, he had ignited controversy at the Sixth Zionist Congress in Basel when he proposed setting up a Jewish homeland in British East Africa instead of Palestine. The proposal stemmed from an offer by the British government for territory in modern-day Kenya, then part of colonial Uganda. With renewed pogroms underway in Russia, Herzl urged the Zionist Congress to seriously consider it, at least as a temporary answer to escalating antisemitism. But most of the delegates hated the idea and, accordingly, it went nowhere.

Instead of heading to East Africa, over a million Eastern European Jews moved to the United States between 1904 and 1914.[27] At the same time, inspired by Zionism, about forty thousand Jews went to Palestine—a wave of immigration known as the Second Aliyah. Most of them settled in cities like Jerusalem, Haifa, and Jaffa, as well as the new town of Tel Aviv (founded by Jewish settlers near Jaffa), while others purchased agricultural lands from absentee Arab landlords, evicting still more Indigenous Palestinian fellaheen. Land was frequently bought and leased by the Jewish National Fund, a nonprofit real estate entity created by the Zionist Organization in 1901 to acquire land in Palestine exclusively for Jewish settlers.[28]

In what would prove to be a significant development, an increasing number of left-wing Jews broke from the Bund after the failed 1905 Russian Revolution, attempted to reconcile their socialist beliefs with Zionism, and emigrated as part of the Second Aliyah. Political activist and self-described Marxist theorist Dov Ber Borochov argued that the ongoing poverty and economic exploitation of Eastern European Jews—despite years of revolutionary activity—was directly tied to the absence of a Jewish national state.[29] He and his adherents viewed both the "political Zionists" epitomized by Herzl and the anti-Zionist Bundists as their ideological rivals. They coalesced into an independent movement called Poale Zion (Workers of Zion), which aimed to fuse the dream of a Jewish homeland in Palestine with the vision of a worker-led socialist society.

Unlike Herzl's political Zionists, Borochov's Labor Zionists argued that Jews should not wait for the imperial powers to generously grant them a homeland in Palestine. Instead, they believed that such a homeland would need to be built from the ground up through "Hebrew Labor"—the physical exertion of Jewish settlers themselves. This was especially appealing to middle-class and intellectual socialists who did not have much experience doing physical labor and eagerly wanted to "proletarianize" themselves. In the process, they believed, Jewish social and economic life would be transformed in Palestine by centering manual and agricultural labor instead of bourgeois professions.

Under the slogans "the conquest of labor" (kibush avoda) and "the conquest of land" (kibush hakarka), Labor Zionists aimed to create a new Jewish working class in Palestine they imagined would function as the workforce for a nascent, self-sufficient Jewish economy that would systematically exclude native Arab workers. As it developed, such an economy would, it was hoped, be able to absorb millions of new Jewish immigrants, allowing Palestine to be colonized and providing the material basis for an eventual Jewish state.[30]

With its worker-centered approach to settler colonialism and nation-building, Labor Zionism would eventually win adherents among trade unionists in the United States, both Jews and non-Jews.

§

Indigenous Palestinians, especially the increasingly landless and unemployed fellaheen, were becoming ever more concerned by the growing Zionist colonization associated with the Second Aliyah. "It did not require the difference of their Jewishness, nor any religious or racial fanaticism on the part of the peasants, to make the latter feel that the immigrants posed a threat to them," writes anthropologist Rosemary Sayigh. "[W]hat they feared, and with reason, was the intrusion into their relationship with the land" by the settlers.[31]

Many Arab notables and intellectuals were also getting worried, pleading with the Ottomans to put a stop to further European immigration. In 1914, the year World War I broke out and halted the Second Aliyah, poet and journalist Isa al-Isa, editor of the newspaper *Filastin*, wrote that Palestinian Arabs constituted "a nation threatened with disappearance by the Zionist tide" and "a nation which is threatened in its very being with expulsion from its homeland."[32]

THE AFL, WORLD WAR I, AND THE BALFOUR DECLARATION

Influenced by the Bund, most members and emerging leaders of Jewish-led unions in the United States like the ILGWU and Amalgamated Clothing Workers opposed Zionism during the first two decades of the century. The most prominent labor leader in the nation at this time, Samuel Gompers, also expressed doubts about Zionism. Cofounder and president of the American Federation of Labor (AFL), Gompers was born into a Sephardic Jewish family in London in 1850. Receiving a brief education at the Jewish Free School, he moved to New York with his parents at age thirteen to escape poverty. Gompers would eventually become a cigar maker and union official before helping found the AFL and becoming its first president in 1886, a role he would remain in until his death in 1924 (with the exception of one year).

Though initially drawn to socialism in his youth, after witnessing the harsh repression that greeted US labor radicals, Gompers gradually came to believe that practicing "pure and simple" trade unionism was a more pragmatic path forward for the labor movement than striving for fundamental social and economic transformation. This meant prioritizing the most highly skilled, white workers and demanding limited—though still important—objectives like higher pay and shorter hours, but never challenging capitalism itself. Gompers contended that what was good for the US economy was good for American workers, as long as they could have a seat at the table. He was therefore constantly preoccupied with achieving respectability for organized labor and recognition of the AFL as the legitimate partner of business and government in the maintenance of the capitalist order.[33]

Despite his heritage, Gompers never publicly identified as a Jew, nor did he observe Jewish religious traditions. In a 1913 speech to the United Hebrew Trades in New York City, the AFL president expressed disagreement with Zionism and echoed the Bundist principle of doykayt, arguing that the ideal of a Jewish home should be more a "condition, a relation that may be established in any land where the heart and spirit are free" than a literal territorial state in Palestine.[34]

A year after this speech, World War I began in Europe. The conflict pitted an alliance of the British, Russian, and French empires against a rival alliance led by the empires of Germany, Austria-Hungary, and the Turkish Ottomans. Though sympathetic toward the British and French, the US government under President Woodrow Wilson remained formally neutral for the first three years of the war. The United States officially entered the fray with a declaration of war on Germany in April 1917, though it would be months before American troops arrived in Europe.

Wilson brought the country into the conflict despite strong antiwar sentiment within the US labor movement. Working-class socialists—including many Jewish unionists in New York's needle trades—justly considered the war a futile, interimperial conflict spurred on by capitalists at the expense of workers being sent to kill each other. The presence of US unions in key industries like mining, steel, meatpacking, and shipbuilding meant organized labor was well situated to potentially impede the war effort.

Ever eager to prove to the government that the AFL could be a valuable partner and thus secure a degree of legitimacy, Gompers promised labor's full support for the war and called on unions to forego strikes and other actions that might hinder industrial production. Wilson appointed Gompers to the prestigious Council on National Defense, where he rubbed elbows with several high-ranking government officials and powerful industrialists to plan ways to ramp up wartime production.

Needing to convince skeptical union members to get behind the war, Gompers also partnered with Washington to establish the American Alliance for Labor and Democracy (AALD). Funded by the Committee on Public Information—the US government's new pro-war propaganda agency—the AALD would produce and disseminate literature trying to convince rank-and-file unionists that the war's purpose was not to prop up Western European empires as many of them believed, but rather, in President Wilson's words, to heroically "make the world safe for democracy."[35]

In particular, Wilson argued that the war was being fought to achieve self-determination for European nations living under the oppressive empires of the Germans, Austro-Hungarians, and Turks. Zionism thus appealed to him because, as political scientist Richard Ned Lebow explains, it "proposed to uproot Turkish tyranny and replace it with democratic government and to offer a haven to Jews suffering under the yoke of oppression." As a devout Christian and elder in the Presbyterian Church, Wilson was also personally intrigued by Zionism for religious reasons. "To think that I, the son of the manse [minister's house], should be able to help restore the Holy Land to its people," he mused to Rabbi Stephen Wise.[36]

Under Gompers's stewardship, the AALD held its founding convention in Minneapolis in September 1917. Only about 170 delegates attended, most of them AFL bureaucrats and pro-war socialists and social democrats, who traveled to the convention on a specially chartered train dubbed the "Red, White, and Blue Special." At the gathering, resolutions were passed pledging the labor movement's loyalty to the US government and full backing of the war effort, while denouncing antiwar activists for being the stooges of Germany.[37]

One especially noteworthy resolution addressed "the general problem of dealing with small nations"—echoing President Wilson's calls for self-determination of European nations—which explicitly endorsed Zionist aims:

> The American Alliance for Labor and Democracy expresses its unqualified approval of the avowal of President Wilson that one of the motives for America's entry into the war is to secure for the small nationalities the right to live their own lives on their own soil and to develop their own culture under free national auspices.
>
> Inasmuch as among all these small nationalities the Jews alone have no homeland of their own, we urge upon the President and the international congress which will negotiate terms of peace, the legitimate claims of the Jewish people for the reestablishment of a national homeland in Palestine on a basis of self-government.[38]

At least five representatives of the Zionist Organization of America were on hand to push for passage of this resolution. They thought it might be a tough sell, but the measure easily passed with a reception that was "so enthusiastic as to be startling," according to one of the Zionist representatives there.[39]

Although Gompers had expressed doubts about the idea of a literal Jewish homeland in Palestine as recently as four years earlier, he now seemed to accept it. This does not appear to be because he had a sudden change of heart about Zionism. Indeed, it is unclear whether Gompers had given much thought to Zionism at all in the intervening four years. What mattered most to him and other top AFL officials at this moment was showcasing their patriotic support for Wilson's war program, as they believed this would grant the AFL the respectability among the establishment they so keenly wanted.

One significant way to do this was by publicly encouraging Wilson's calls for the creation of new, democratic nation-states inside the crumbling empires of America's wartime enemies. This included the establishment of a democratic Jewish "homeland" inside a region of the Ottoman Empire—Palestine—even though such a proposal ignored and threatened the vast majority of Palestinians' own rights to democracy and self-determination.

§

As World War I raged on, government officials in the United Kingdom considered ways to secure more allies while they simultaneously planned to use the war to expand the reach of the British Empire. Driven by the antisemitic belief that Jews secretly wielded enormous international influence, along with the equally antisemitic belief that all Jews were Zionists, in early 1916 some UK Cabinet ministers suggested that a crucial way to win the war would be offering up Palestine for Jewish colonization. With their troops battling the Ottoman Turks for control of the Middle East with the help of an Arab nationalist rebellion, Britain's imperialists already considered Palestine's political future to be within their purview.[40]

After Russian revolutionaries finally succeeded in overthrowing the czar in early 1917, British officials rightly surmised that Russia would soon pull out of the war. They also worried that, despite Gompers's assurances, the vital US industrial war machine might be obstructed by rebellious American workers who opposed US entry into the conflict. Deludedly thinking that the Jewish minority populations of Russia and the United States were uniformly Zionist and held outsized sway, the UK Cabinet believed the time was right to forge an alliance with Zionism. Such an alliance was encouraged by one of Britain's leading Zionists, chemist Chaim Weizmann, who actively lobbied UK foreign secretary Arthur Balfour to make a public statement promising to hand over Palestine to the Jewish people. Besides exaggerating the influence of the international Zionist movement, Weizmann couched his appeal in the language of racism and Western chauvinism—quite familiar to Balfour, a white supremacist and antisemite—by arguing that Palestinian Arabs were too backward and duplicitous to be trusted with a state of their own.[41]

The only Jew in the UK Cabinet, Edwin Montagu, advocated against creating a Jewish national home in Palestine. Specifically, he contended that doing so would only exacerbate antisemitism around the world by causing governments to question the loyalty of their Jewish citizens. "Jews will hereafter be treated as foreigners in every country but Palestine," Montagu wrote in an August 1917 memorandum. "Palestine will become the world's Ghetto. . . . When the Jews are told that Palestine is their national home, every country will immediately desire to get rid of its Jewish citizens." He further noted that for Zionist aims to be realized, Palestine's "present inhabitants" of Muslims and Christians would need to be driven out, forced "to make way for the Jews" with Jews being "put in all positions of preference."[42]

But Balfour and the other Christians on the UK Cabinet ignored Montagu's counsel. In what would come to be known as the Balfour Declaration, on November 2, 1917, the foreign secretary sent a highly consequential, carefully worded letter to the president of the British Zionist Federation. In it, Balfour explained that the UK government favored "the establishment in Palestine of a national home for the Jewish people," promising Britain's "best endeavors to facilitate the achievement of this object."[43] But he added that "nothing shall be done which may prejudice the civil and religious rights of existing non-Jewish communities in Palestine"—in other words, the Indigenous Muslim and Christian Arabs who comprised a whopping 94 percent of the population.[44]

Balfour and the Cabinet made sure to include that last clause in a weak attempt to avoid alienating Britain's Arab allies in the ongoing war against the Ottomans, but it failed to explicitly name the Palestinian Arabs and to positively affirm their own right to national self-determination, instead seeming to falsely present them as a minority group who should simply not face prejudice. The letter was made public on November 9, with Zionists rejoicing at having won the official support of the British Empire, which was already poised to take control of Palestine upon the war's conclusion.

§

Only one week after the Balfour Declaration was made public, the AFL held its national convention in Buffalo, New York. Gompers hoped to give his recently created, pro-war American Alliance for Labor and Democracy an added boost by having the AFL delegates formally endorse its jingoistic platform, which included the plank on establishing a Jewish "national homeland" in Palestine. American members of Poale Zion—the Labor Zionist movement started by Ber Borochov—were among those in attendance asking delegates to vote in favor of the pro-AALD measure.

A debate broke out on the convention floor, sparked by a minority of antiwar delegates from the ILGWU, United Mine Workers, and Seattle Central Labor Council. They questioned why organized labor should get behind a government-funded propaganda organization like the AALD. One of the most forceful opposition voices on the convention floor was a young Jewish shirtwaist maker named Sarah Shapiro of ILGWU Local 25 in New York. Referencing the growing government repression against antiwar dissenters, Shapiro argued that the AALD's purpose was to "take away the rights of the workers and to give them into the hands of the few who claim to be patriots." A frustrated Gompers derided her as "a little girl," while saying that anyone who opposed the AALD was a traitor to both the United States and the labor movement.

Not wanting to be branded as traitors, the convention delegates overwhelmingly passed the measure. By ensuring the AFL's formal support for US participation in World War I, the vote cemented labor officialdom's newfound partnership with Washington. To make this partnership even clearer, President Wilson came to Buffalo and addressed the convention delegates—the first time a US president had ever participated in a national labor gathering—and thanked them for their patriotic loyalty.

The vote also effectively meant that the AFL backed the idea of a Jewish national homeland in Palestine, which carried special meaning coming as it did in the immediate aftermath of the Balfour Declaration. As historian Sheila Stern Polishook later wrote, "The Buffalo Convention initiated the first stage of organized labor's long standing commitment to Zionism."[45]

§

Interestingly, nearly all the no votes in Buffalo came from the predominantly Jewish ILGWU delegation. But this had more to do with the socialist garment workers' opposition to the war than it did with their attitudes about Zionism. Only six months later, at its own annual convention, the ILGWU would pass a resolution in favor of "the rehabilitation of Palestine as a physical center of Jewish life and culture."[46] The resolution was directly inspired by the Inter-Allied Labor and Socialist Conference, a recent gathering in London of the Socialist and Labor parties of Britain, France, Belgium, and Italy—all of which had come around to supporting World War I.

The Inter-Allied conference met in February 1918 and passed several measures in favor of national self-determination for subjugated European peoples. One such resolution called for Jews to have equal rights in all countries, for Palestine to "be set free from the hard and oppressive Government of the Turk" (i.e., the Ottomans), and for a "free State under international guaranty" to be formed in Palestine where "such of the Jewish people as desire to do so may return and may work out their own salvation free from interference by those of alien race or religion."[47] Although the measure did not explicitly call for the creation of a "Jewish homeland" in Palestine, it also noticeably made no reference to Palestinian Arabs whatsoever.

When the ILGWU convention was held in May, the primarily socialist delegates passed their own resolution "heartily" endorsing and concurring with the Inter-Allied conference's Palestine measure. That same month, the Amalgamated Clothing Workers—also led by Jewish socialists, but not affiliated with the AFL—similarly voted to endorse the Inter-Allied conference's statement on Palestine at their national convention.[48]

Another noteworthy resolution was passed in January 1919 at the First Jewish Labor Congress, a meeting in New York of representatives from the United Hebrew Trades (UHT), ILGWU, Amalgamated Clothing Workers, and other Jewish-led unions in the needle trades. The congress was convened by the National Workmen's Committee on Jewish Rights, a group formed by the UHT a few years earlier to raise awareness about antisemitism in Europe, which claimed to represent 500,000 working-class Jews in the United States. The delegates debated

Zionism and passed a measure that, in line with the Bundist tradition, rejected the idea of an explicitly Jewish state in Palestine. Instead, the resolution called for the establishment of "a free, independent republic in which no nationality, whether a minority or majority people, shall have any special rights," but where Jews would have "the possibility of free development and of a free, unhindered national life," as well as "the right of free immigration and colonization."[49]

As these resolutions indicate, though many Bund-inspired Jewish American trade unionists did not consider themselves Zionists, by the end of World War I they were beginning to accept the idea of Jewish settlement and colonization of Palestine. This was in part because, thanks to the Balfour Declaration, the idea was starting to seem less far-fetched than it had previously. It was also partly because many of their allies had already endorsed Zionist goals, including Western European socialist parties, the AFL, and pro-labor US intellectuals like Supreme Court Justice Louis Brandeis. But perhaps the most important factor in this gradual shift was the formation of a new Jewish workers' organization in Palestine led by Labor Zionist settlers.

THE HISTADRUT AND US LABOR

Palestine had been hit hard by World War I, experiencing food shortages and destruction caused by the intense fighting between British and Ottoman forces. By 1918, the year the war ended, the region was under British military occupation. The defeated Ottoman Empire—to which Palestine had belonged for four hundred years—would be dismantled within four years.

Struggling to cope with these shocks, the Indigenous Palestinian population (including the native Jews) only slowly came to learn of the Balfour Declaration. Already facing dispossession from Zionist settlement before the war, Palestinian Arabs were terrified and outraged to learn that their new British rulers intended to facilitate further colonization of their lands by foreigners.

In 1922, the United Kingdom formalized its control over Palestine under the aegis of the new League of Nations, which issued a mandate for British administration of the region. The League's mandate echoed the Balfour Declaration in recognizing and encouraging the nationalist aspirations of Jews in Palestine while completely disregarding the right to self-determination of the territory's overwhelming Arab majority. The mandate designated the Jewish Agency—an executive body associated with the Zionist Organization—as the official political representative of the Yishuv, the Jewish community in Palestine. The Jewish Agency would function as a de facto government for the Yishuv, working closely with the British authorities.

In Mandatory Palestine, the nascent Palestinian Arab nationalist movement that had begun emerging in the latter years of the Ottoman Empire now crystallized in direct response to British occupation and Zionist colonialism, which were fused together. Throughout the 1920s, urban notables held a series of Palestine Arab congresses to demand independence, majority rule, and limits to Jewish immigration and land purchases. Politically distant from the fellaheen and Arab working class, and not wanting to jeopardize their relationship with the British authorities, the Palestinian elites who participated in these congresses made their appeals in solely legalistic and diplomatic terms without trying to organize mass action. The UK government ignored them, even while granting limited concessions to other Arab nationalist movements in places like Syria, Egypt, and Iraq.[50]

Meanwhile, in Eastern Europe, a new round of brutal anti-Jewish violence began amid the civil war in Russia that followed the Bolshevik Revolution, spurring tens of thousands of Jews to emigrate. With the United States enacting antisemitic and xenophobic immigration restrictions, and with Zionist aspirations becoming ever more viable due to the Balfour Declaration and British Mandate, Jewish immigration to Palestine skyrocketed in the 1920s. Through two new waves of migration—the Third and Fourth Aliyot—Jews went from constituting about 6 percent of Palestine's population in 1918 to 18 percent by 1926.[51]

Labor Zionist settlers continued building a Jewish-only economic sector to absorb the incoming immigrants. Before World War I, they had begun establishing new types of egalitarian rural settlements—*kibbutzim* (collective farms) and *moshavim* (cooperative villages)—which multiplied in the 1920s. Not only evicted, the Indigenous fellaheen who had traditionally lived and worked on these agricultural lands were also purposely excluded from employment on the new settlements as part of the Labor Zionists' twin vision of the "conquest of labor" and "conquest of land."

Dispossessed and unemployed, poor and working-class Palestinian Arabs became increasingly resentful of this growing foreign encroachment, aided by British imperialism. As the British dismissed the nationalist desires articulated by Arab elites, they simultaneously repressed attempts at peaceful protest. In this context, riots targeting Zionist settlers broke out three times during the decade—in 1920, 1921, and 1929—spontaneously carried out by Arab peasants and workers without coordination or leadership from the notables. As Zionism's early critics had predicted decades earlier, the colonization of Palestine was naturally being met with violent resistance by the Indigenous population.[52]

§

In 1919, a group of Labor Zionists in Palestine formed Ahdut Ha'avoda (Unity of Labor), a new political party that explicitly prioritized Jewish nationalism over socialist revolution. This development was the result of a controversy within the Poale

Zion movement over whether to move to the left by joining the new, Moscow-based Communist International (Comintern) or lean rightward by participating in the bourgeois-led Zionist Organization and partnering with the British Mandate authorities. Ahdut Ha'avoda came down on the more anticommunist, pro–class collaboration side of this debate. In June 1920, two months after Arab riots in Jerusalem, Ahdut Ha'avoda founded the Haganah, a paramilitary organization ostensibly meant to defend Zionist settlers from native attacks.

Part of why Ahdut Ha'avoda's members chose to ally with the Zionist Organization—despite previously setting themselves apart as socialist workers—was that they needed the financial support it brought to bear. The goal of Labor Zionists was the creation of a Jewish proletariat in Palestine that could lay the foundations for a Jewish state. But this could never come to fruition without the creation of a thriving Jewish economy in Palestine. There could be no working class unless there was sufficient work to be had in the first place.

Labor Zionists, led by Ahdut Ha'avoda, therefore took it upon themselves to spearhead economic development as the only way to generate the conditions for a Jewish workers' movement in Palestine to exist. Doing this would require massive capital investment from abroad, which the Zionist Organization and Jewish National Fund—with their middle- and upper-class networks around Europe and the United States—could help deliver. It would also require cooperation with Palestine's pro-Zionist British rulers.

Class struggle and anti-imperialism would thus take a back seat to collaborationism for the sake of economic development. And because the envisioned economy would need to be exclusively Jewish to avoid labor market competition with native Palestinian Arab workers, class solidarity would be abandoned in favor of nationalism and settler colonialism.

With this economic development agenda in mind, representatives of Ahdut Ha'avoda and other Labor Zionist groups gathered in Haifa in December 1920 to establish the General Organization of Hebrew Workers in the Land of Israel, better known as the Histadrut ("the Organization"). The Histadrut would function as a federation of Palestine's nascent Jewish trade unions, similar to the role of the AFL in the United States, but—much more importantly—it would also drive and direct the construction of a Jewish-only economic sector. As a report by pro-Zionist American labor officials would explain years later, "Labor movements in other countries devoted their efforts to organizing workers in existing industries. Histadrut had first of all to create the working class and the industries to employ it."[53]

Besides only trade unions, then, the Histadrut also established kibbutzim and moshavim, new industrial enterprises, housing and construction companies, a transportation network, a workers' bank (Bank Hapoalim), and workers' sick fund (Kupat Holim). All of these would deliberately deny any job opportunities or social services to native Palestinian workers to further edify "Hebrew Labor." The paramilitary Haganah was also folded into the Histadrut.

Managing a variety of essential economic activities, organizing workers, and even having its own militia, the Histadrut thus served as a kind of proto-Jewish state in Palestine. Although the Jewish Agency was the official governance body of the Yishuv, it was the Histadrut that carried out all the practical activities of settler colonialism. Its founders would eventually orchestrate the mass expulsion of Palestinian Arabs and become the first political leaders of the State of Israel.[54]

Meanwhile, the relatively small number of leftist Labor Zionists—those who sided with the Comintern and decried Ahdut Ha'avoda's class collaborationism—abandoned Zionism and formed the Palestine Communist Party (PCP) in the 1920s.

They argued that the Histadrut should end its Jewish-exclusive policy and organize Palestinian Arab workers for the sake of class solidarity, but were expelled from the Histadrut for taking this position. The PCP's members envisioned a society in Palestine where Jewish and Arab workers would live together in dignity, equality, and freedom. Comprised almost entirely of Jews at first, by the end of the decade, the PCP would set out to bring large numbers of Palestinian Arabs into the party at the Comintern's urging, a program called "Arabization."[55]

At the same time, the number of Arab proletarians in Palestine was beginning to rise in the 1920s. Evicted from their agricultural lands and denied rural employment by Zionist settlers, many Palestinian Arabs began moving to cities in search of new economic opportunities. Especially in the coastal cities of Haifa and Jaffa, they found jobs in industries run by the British Mandate authorities, including transportation (railways and ports), communications (telephone and telegraph lines), and public works.

Recognizing that key industries like the railways had mixed Jewish and Arab workforces, by the mid-1920s, the Histadrut formulated a policy of organizing Arab workers in such industries—but only into segregated unions. This was also part of a calculated (and largely unsuccessful) effort to get the growing Arab working class to turn against the urban notables who were openly asserting Palestinian nationalism. The Histadrut's leaders hoped that under their paternalistic instruction, Palestinian Arab workers would come to see Zionists as more friendly and beneficial to them than Arab elites.[56]

§

For the Histadrut to realize its nation-building mission, it would need enormous amounts of foreign investment, whether from groups tied to the Zionist Organization or other sympathetic actors. One potential helping hand identified early on was the US labor movement.

Organized labor in the United States was no stranger to the settler colonialism and racial exclusion practiced by Labor Zionists in Palestine. In the mid-nineteenth century, US labor reformers like George Henry Evans led the "free soil" movement, which called on the federal government to give working-class people plots of land in the American West—despite the reality that these lands were already home to numerous Native American nations. This would ostensibly allow impoverished white workers in the growing cities of the East to escape wage labor and instead become prosperous independent producers, thus fulfilling Thomas Jefferson's vision of the United States as an egalitarian republic of yeoman farmers.[57] The "free soil" demand was supported by the New York Industrial Congress, a short-lived umbrella group of over ninety local trade unions and reform groups in the nation's largest city.[58]

Settling western lands by violently removing Native Americans—whom whites defined as racially inferior and therefore undeserving of self-determination—also functioned as a "safety valve" to relieve the class tensions emerging in eastern cities between the nascent proletariat and bourgeoisie. Rather than fight bosses and property owners for the fruits of their labor, white wage earners were encouraged to go west and fight "savage" Indians for territory. As historian Greg Grandin writes, "[I]nstead of waging class war upward . . . [working-class white Americans] waged race war outward, on the frontier."[59] By presenting settler colonialism to workers as a substitute for class struggle, the "safety valve" argument in some ways prefigured Labor Zionism.

The popular, labor-led demand for "free soil" eventually culminated in President Abraham Lincoln's signing of the 1862 Homestead Act, which distributed 270 million acres of federally held western lands to 400,000 settler families. Of course, the land was not really "free." To facilitate settlement, the US military would spend the next thirty years violently dispossessing the Indigenous peoples of the American West and forcing them onto reservations. And, in the end, it was a handful of wealthy capitalists and speculators who gained ownership of most of the western lands for their own private gain.[60]

Instead of escaping wage labor, then, most working-class white settlers continued facing exploitation in the west at the hands of elites who now owned the newly established railroads, mines, bonanza farms, and cattle ranches. But in many cases, they blamed their economic woes on Chinese immigrant workers instead of on the rapacious greed of capitalists. Viewing Chinese workers as racially inferior, overly docile competitors for jobs, most white-led labor organizations that took shape in the 1870s and 1880s explicitly excluded them from membership and successfully lobbied Congress to suspend further Chinese immigration.

By the 1890s, when US society broadly recognized that the western frontier was now "closed," the AFL emerged as the nation's leading trade union body, declaring at its 1893 convention that the Chinese brought with them "nothing but filth, vice, and disease." The labor federation's president, Gompers, championed continued Chinese exclusion, saying in 1901 that "every incoming coolie [a derogatory term for imported Asian workers] means . . . so much more vice and immorality injected into our social life."[61] Many of the AFL's affiliated unions adopted similar racist and xenophobic policies, advocating against any further immigration and often refusing to admit African American workers into their ranks (or only organizing them into segregated union locals).[62]

Thus, by the 1920s, the Histadrut's own racist practices were already quite familiar—and not particularly troubling—to the US labor movement's dominant current, embodied by the AFL.

§

In 1921, a delegation of three Histadrut officials arrived in the United States on a mission to raise money for their labor-centered settlement activities in Palestine. For nearly two years, they traveled around the country trying to sell shares of Bank Hapoalim and raise funds for the Haganah.

They especially focused on securing financial support from Jewish-led US unions, couching their appeals in the language of international worker solidarity. But the Histadrut representatives received a mostly chilly reception from Bundist-aligned Jewish trade unionists, who opposed Zionism.

Nevertheless, the delegation garnered sympathy from some Jewish American union officials. Although not Zionists, these unionists considered the Histadrut to be a legitimate socialist workers' organization and were open to supporting it as a matter of international labor solidarity. The fact that the Histadrut consciously excluded or segregated Indigenous Arab workers did not appear to disturb them.

One US labor leader who sympathized with the Histadrut was Max Pine, secretary of the United Hebrew Trades in New York. Pine had emigrated to the United States in 1890, cofounded the influential *Jewish Daily Forward*, and unsuccessfully ran for local and state office as a socialist. Joseph Schlossberg and Jacob Potofsky, both socialist immigrants from Russia and respectively the secretary-treasurer and assistant general secretary-treasurer of the Amalgamated Clothing Workers, were also intrigued by the Histadrut's vision of building a worker-centered society. Although the Amalgamated Clothing Workers' president, Sidney Hillman, traced his political roots back to the anti-Zionist Bund, by the 1920s he was becoming detached and indifferent to Jewish politics as he consciously tried to assimilate into mainstream US society. Hillman therefore did not stand in Schlossberg and Potofsky's way as they advocated cooperation with the Histadrut's Labor Zionists.[63]

In August 1923, Pine convened a meeting of like-minded Jewish American trade unionists, including Schlossberg and Potofsky, to form the National Labor Committee for Palestine (NLCP). The NLCP's purpose was to serve as a permanent body of US unionists raising money for the Histadrut and its various economic development activities. Besides Pine, Schlossberg, and Potofsky, the committee included officials from other New York–based, Jewish-led unions like the ILGWU and the Cloth Hat, Cap and Millinery Workers union.

Months after its founding, the NLCP launched a national fundraising drive dubbed "the Gewerkschaften campaign." The German word for trade unions, *Gewerkschaften*, was what the UHT was called in Yiddish. Throughout the spring of 1924, Pine crisscrossed the United States and Canada, holding events with local Jewish trade unionists to raise money for the Histadrut and to raise awareness about the Labor Zionist movement in Palestine. The campaign brought in $51,165. In 1926, the NLCP led a second Gewerkschaften drive, organizing support committees in twenty-five states and this time raising around $113,000 for the Histadrut's cooperatives, clinics, and educational facilities. Though Pine would die of pneumonia in 1928, the fundraising campaign he started became an annual tradition.[64]

Growing xenophobia in the United States gave added impetus to these pro-Histadrut efforts. In 1921 and again in 1924, Congress passed new restrictions on immigration from Eastern and Southern Europe, which meant that European Jews trying to flee antisemitic persecution increasingly had little choice but to go to Mandatory Palestine. Though opposed by Jewish-led unions like the Amalgamated Clothing Workers and ILGWU, the anti-immigrant legislation of the 1920s was supported by the AFL leadership.[65] With the Histadrut providing basic services and economic opportunities to new Jewish arrivals in Palestine, some Jewish American unionists gave money to the organization out of humanitarian concern.

Meanwhile, the Histadrut scored another crucial US ally: longtime *Forward* chief editor Abraham Cahan, one of the most respected figures on the Jewish American Left. Much like the cofounders of the NLCP, Cahan was a non-Zionist who increasingly came to accept the reality of Jewish immigration to Palestine in the 1920s. In the fall of 1925, the 65-year-old Cahan visited Palestine and was warmly welcomed by Labor Zionists, who understood the political and intellectual weight he carried in the United States. He was impressed by the Histadrut's agricultural communes and by Tel Aviv's vibrant Jewish life and culture.[66]

Cahan returned home a dedicated supporter of the Histadrut. At a mass gathering in New York to launch the NLCP's third Gewerkschaften campaign in 1927, he gave an address in which he declared, "I am not a Zionist in the accepted term, but I sympathize with them." Cahan continued, "I will do all in my power to help Palestine [Jewish] Labor, to lighten its burden. They hunger too much and work too hard and have too little sunshine in their lives, except for their spiritual sunshine."[67]

With the editor of the *Forward* and several Jewish union leaders strongly urging support for the Histadrut in the 1920s, the first cracks in what had previously been an anti-Zionist consensus among working-class US Jews began appearing. Despite the prior existence of Labor Zionist entities like Poale Zion and Ahdut Ha'avoda, scholar Adam M. Howard writes, it was "only the formation of Histadrut [that] provided the inspiring labor organization capable of winning over non-Zionists in the United States."[68]

Non-Jewish labor officials like AFL president William Green, a Protestant Christian who had succeeded Gompers upon the latter's death in 1924, recognized the growing popularity of the Histadrut among Jewish union leaders and lent their voices to the NLCP's fundraising drives. For example, Green formally endorsed the third Gewerkschaften campaign, sending a telegram with a message of encouragement to the participants at the same mass meeting in 1927 where Cahan spoke. As journalist and author Melech Epstein noted, showing up at the Histadrut fundraisers gave Green and other non-Jewish labor leaders a platform between annual union conventions, with their speeches at these events gaining widespread media attention at home and abroad. It also obviously signaled that support for the Histadrut was beginning to spread into the mainstream, non-Jewish US labor movement, which was in line with the AFL's World War I-inspired endorsement of Zionist aims.[69]

By 1928, the Gewerkschaften campaigns had raised a total of around $400,000 for the Histadrut. While NLCP leaders noted that this amount was "small and woefully out of proportion to the needs and hopes of our class colleagues in Palestine," they were content that "tens of thousands of Jewish workers in the United States and Canada have been won over to the cause, and that the army of willing hands is steadily growing, making each succeeding campaign for funds much easier sailing. And bigger in volume."[70]

§

In August 1929, riots broke out in multiple Palestinian cities in which Arabs attacked Jews and vice versa. Although the violence was blamed on a religiously fueled conflict over access to Jerusalem's Western Wall—a sacred site for both Muslims and Jews—British Mandate authorities recognized that the root causes were Arab grievances over continuous Zionist intrusion and the Histadrut's racist policies. A year after the riots, the UK's colonial secretary recommended limitations on further Jewish immigration to Palestine.

Zionists and their allies around the world, who viewed the Palestinian Arab riots as nothing other than antisemitic pogroms, condemned the recommendation. American labor officials joined the international voices expressing disapproval, with NLCP leaders signing onto an open letter of protest sent to the British Labour Party. For his part, AFL president Green wrote letters to President Herbert Hoover and leaders of the British Trades Union Congress criticizing the proposed immigration restrictions in Palestine. Hypocritically, Green and the AFL's other non-Jewish leaders had supported quotas that similarly limited Jewish immigration to the United States, which suggests they preferred European Jews being channeled to the Middle East than coming to America.

The pressure from the international Zionist movement and its supporters ultimately worked. In early 1931, UK prime minister Ramsay MacDonald—leader of the Labour Party—issued a statement effectively countermanding the recommended immigration limits.[71]

CHAPTER 2

HOLOCAUST AND NAKBA

Amid the crises of the Great Depression and World War II in the 1930s and 1940s, millions of previously unorganized American workers formed new unions or joined existing ones and militantly confronted their employers, prompting the US government to play a more active and labor-friendly role in the economy than ever before. In this context, labor leaders greatly strengthened the partnership with Washington they had first started forging during World War I. By cooperating with President Franklin D. Roosevelt's efforts to reshape capitalism at home and defeat fascism abroad, American labor officials achieved unprecedented power and influence by the 1940s—when the United States would fully embrace its position as the most powerful and influential country in the world.

At the same time, the international Zionist movement garnered newfound sympathy in the United States in response to Nazi Germany's genocidal escalation of antisemitism, which would culminate in the murder of six million European Jews. Therefore, as the US union movement grew stronger in these years, so too did its leaders' material and political support for Zionist colonization of Palestine. Although a spirited movement of Palestinian Arab workers emerged in this period to rival Labor Zionism, US labor officials—both Jews and non-Jews—focused their Palestine solidarity efforts exclusively on the Histadrut and its increasingly aggressive efforts to establish a state by violently displacing the Indigenous population.

The growing power of both the US labor movement and Labor Zionism in these pivotal decades, as well as the closer relationship that developed between the two, is in many ways personified by two significant historical figures: International Ladies' Garment Workers' Union (ILGWU) president David Dubinsky and Israeli prime minister David Ben-Gurion.

TWO DAVIDS

Born David Dobnievski in modern-day Belarus, Dubinsky cut his political teeth with the Jewish Labor Bund. Growing up in the Polish city of Łódź—the most important textile manufacturing center in the Russian Empire—Dubinsky was a child witness to the 1905 Russian Revolution, in which local Bundists played a central role in organizing the city's working class. He attended his first Bund meeting at age 14 while working at a bakery. Inspired, he soon became the assistant secretary of his own Bundist bakery workers' union and led a strike for pay raises. In 1908, the young Dubinsky was arrested, imprisoned for 18 months, then sent to a Siberian labor camp as punishment for his activism. While in transit to Siberia, he managed to escape.

Now a fugitive, Dubinsky sneaked out of Russia and decided to emigrate to the United States, reaching New York City in January 1911 when he was nineteen years old. There, he joined the Socialist Party of America and found work in the women's clothing industry, becoming an ILGWU member. Amid intra-union factional disputes in the 1920s pitting union activists from the Communist Party USA against the ILGWU's entrenched bureaucracy, Dubinsky sided with the old guard, having distrusted the more left-wing Bolsheviks since his days in Russia. This allowed him to rise through the union's ranks, eventually becoming the ILGWU's president in 1932 after the communists had all either been expelled or voluntarily exited to build parallel unions.

Combined with the Great Depression, the years of internal strife had left the ILGWU in tatters, but, as union president, Dubinsky was determined to rebuild. Taking full advantage of the labor-friendly policies of Democratic President Franklin D. Roosevelt's New Deal—a set of ambitious laws that aimed to reform capitalism in response to the turmoil and radicalism sparked by the Depression—Dubinsky led the ILGWU in a mass organizing campaign across the East Coast and Midwest that saw the union's membership grow from just 40,000 in early 1932 to 200,000 by spring 1934.

As he leaned into the liberal reformism of the New Deal, Dubinsky abandoned socialism. He was appointed to the American Federation of Labor (AFL)'s Executive Council in 1934, becoming its only Jewish member, as well as its youngest. The following year, he joined Hillman, United Mine Workers president John L. Lewis, and the presidents of five other AFL-affiliated unions to form the Committee for Industrial Organization (CIO). The CIO aimed to take advantage of Roosevelt's New Deal reforms to rapidly unionize millions of unorganized workers in mass industries like steel and auto. Its leaders called on the AFL to abandon the craft union tradition in favor of industrial unionism. This meant organizing all workers in a particular industry into a single union, regardless of their specific trade or skill level, to build greater collective power.

But with William Green and other top AFL officials unwilling to upset organized labor's status quo by embracing the CIO's bold approach, and with Lewis and Hillman determined to move forward with their plan anyway, the AFL suspended the unions that were part of the CIO, including Dubinsky's ILGWU. Uneasy with this labor disunity, Dubinsky attempted to mend the rift, but to no avail. In 1938, when Lewis transformed the seemingly ad hoc "Committee for Industrial Organization" into the "Congress of Industrial Organizations" as a permanent rival to the AFL, Dubinsky withdrew the ILGWU from the CIO and rejoined the AFL two years later.

Meanwhile, the CIO quickly unionized huge industrial corporations like General Motors and US Steel, effectively pushing the AFL to finally ramp up its own organizing efforts to avoid being supplanted by the new labor organization. As a result, millions of hitherto unorganized workers were unionized in only a few years by both the CIO and AFL, helping the US labor movement grow to unprecedented heights. As they became more powerful as a result of this union growth, national labor officials like Dubinsky became important allies of President Roosevelt and his worker-friendly administration.[1]

Despite drifting away from socialism in the 1930s, Dubinsky clung to some aspects of his Bundist origins, including a distaste for Zionism. Still, like many other Jews in the US labor movement, he came to sympathize with the ever-growing Jewish settler community in Palestine out of a practical concern for their well-being, although without explicitly supporting the Zionist aim of establishing a Jewish state. But unlike figures such as Max Pine or Joseph Schlossberg, Dubinsky was extra sensitive about not giving the appearance of endorsing Zionism, at least for a time. When Schlossberg invited Dubinsky to speak at the National Labor Committee for Palestine's 1937 convention, the ILGWU president replied, "I must respectfully decline for reasons which are, I believe, very well known to yourself and to the other leaders of this movement"—namely, his ongoing hesitance to publicly embrace Zionism.[2]

§

During the same years David Dubinsky rose through the ranks of union officialdom and progressive politics to become one of the most important labor liberals in the United States, David Ben-Gurion similarly rose to prominence in the Jewish labor movement in Palestine to ultimately become the political leader of the Yishuv and arguably the most consequential figure in the history of Zionism.

Born David Grün in the Polish city of Płońsk, Ben-Gurion was an ardent Zionist since childhood. Growing up, he did not personally experience antisemitism (Płońsk was a relatively peaceful and prosperous town for Jews), but he was enamored with the idea of building a Jewish homeland and joined the socialist Poale Zion as a teenager.[3] In 1906, at age 20, Ben-Gurion moved to Palestine as part of the Second Aliyah. He was an agricultural laborer for a few years, competing for work with Indigenous Palestinian Arabs, before becoming a journalist for Poale Zion's Hebrew-language newspaper.[4] During World War I, he toured the United States promoting the Zionist cause, then joined the Jewish Legion, a military unit established by the British Army in the months after the Balfour Declaration.

Returning to Palestine after the war, Ben-Gurion cofounded Ahdut Ha'avoda—one of the major Labor Zionist parties formed after Poale Zion fractured—and became the first general secretary of the newly created Histadrut. Starting with a membership of 4,400, the Histadrut quickly grew to 16,000 members by 1922 as new Jewish settlers sought out the employment, banking, and health care services it offered. As the head of this organization, Ben-Gurion had considerable power and influence in the growing Yishuv.

Indefatigable, ambitious, and abrasive, Ben-Gurion saw himself as a "Zionist Lenin," according to biographer Tom Segev. It was not Vladimir Lenin's communist ideology that he admired, but rather Lenin's apparent ability to mold his people's destiny through sheer force of will. As the Histadrut went about colonizing Palestine by building a new, separate economy exclusively for Jewish settlers, Ben-Gurion maintained an iron grip over the organization and its activities. He was also largely in control of the Haganah, the Labor Zionist militia that fell under the Histadrut's purview.[5]

He further served as the architect of the Histadrut's ambiguous approach to Palestinian Arab workers who toiled in mixed Jewish-Arab industries like the railways, organizing them into segregated unions under Zionist tutelage. This was partly to drive a wedge between workers and elites within the Palestinian Arab population, as well as to placate British Mandate authorities wanting to see peaceful relations between Jews and Arabs.[6] As a matter of pragmatism, Ben-Gurion typically sought to stay in the good graces of world powers, namely the United Kingdom and United States. He particularly valued seeing the Histadrut win the financial backing of the US labor movement, writing in 1923 that "the cooperation of the workers' movement in America [is] actually more important than the diplomatic victory of the Balfour Declaration."[7]

Control over an all-encompassing organization like the Histadrut naturally gave Ben-Gurion political clout. In 1930, he was at the center of the merger between Ahdut Ha'avoda and the other main Labor Zionist party, Hapoel Hatzair, resulting in the formation of Mapai (the "Workers' Party of the Land of Israel"). With the Histadrut's support and Ben-Gurion at the helm, Mapai became the Yishuv's dominant political party.

In 1935, after stepping down from leadership of the Histadrut, Ben-Gurion became executive chair of the Jewish Agency—the de facto government of Palestine's Jewish community. Now as the Yishuv's primary political leader, he made it his mission to push for the full realization of Zionism's chief aim: the establishment of a Jewish state.[8] Like other leading Zionists, he was well aware that this goal would require the forced expulsion of Palestine's native population. In 1941, for example, Ben-Gurion wrote that "it is impossible to imagine general evacuation [of the Arab population] without compulsion, and brutal compulsion."[9]

PALESTINIAN ARAB WORKERS AND THE GREAT REVOLT

The Histadrut was not the only workers' organization in Palestine. Beginning in the 1920s, as Arab workers increasingly found employment in emerging sectors like transportation, communications, and public works, they began forming trade unions of their own. In Haifa's railway workshops, a group of skilled Arab workers led by the brothers Abd al-Hamid Haymur and Id Salim Haymur, alongside their colleague Said Qawwas, organized a mutual aid association that by 1925 was called the Palestine Arab Workers' Society (PAWS). Members of PAWS embraced a nationalist outlook, particularly in response to the Histadrut's Jewish-only policies and its attempts to organize Arab rail workers into segregated unions.

In January 1930, PAWS organized the first-ever national congress of Palestinian Arab workers, with the idea of expanding beyond the railroads to workers of all industries and trades. The sixty-one delegates claimed to represent three thousand workers—most of them Haifa railway employees—and called for an eight-hour workday, the right to strike, an end to discrimination against Arab workers, and independence from British rule.

The PAWS congress was supported by the small Palestine Communist Party (PCP), which was led and composed of leftist Jews who, at the urging of the anti-Zionist Soviet Union, had abandoned Zionism in favor of promoting class solidarity between Arab and Jewish workers and anti-imperialism against the British. In the wake of the 1929 riots pitting Arabs against Jews, the PCP was endeavoring to bring more working-class Palestinian Arabs into the party to transform it from a small clique into a mass organization. This program of "Arabization," as the party called it, served as a rebuke to the Histadrut's Jewish-exclusive and segregationist policies. Building a relationship with PAWS was an essential component of this strategy, though it faced obstacles because many of PAWS's noncommunist members opposed an alliance with the Soviet-backed PCP.

In the years following its 1930 congress, PAWS remained strongest in Haifa, organizing Arab workers on the docks, in the quarries, and in the tobacco and petroleum industries. Occasionally, with the encouragement of the anti-imperialist PCP, Palestinian Arab and Jewish workers would go on strike together in rare moments of unity against the British authorities. Overall, Arab unions grew slowly and remained relatively small, in large part because only around 8 percent of Palestinian Arabs were employed in the industrial sector, with the rest working in agriculture.[10]

Meanwhile, to try curbing the influence of PAWS, the Histadrut established the Palestine Labor League (PLL) in 1932. The PLL was an attempt to formalize the Histadrut's earlier efforts to organize Arab workers into segregated unions. Although the PLL was ostensibly a separate organization, it was fully under the Histadrut's control, with policies consistent with Mapai's Labor Zionism. It failed to gain much headway. The approximately 1,100 Arab workers who joined over the next few years did so primarily out of a hope that the PLL's connections to the Histadrut would allow them to secure jobs in the fast-growing Jewish economic sector.[11]

§

Tensions in Mandatory Palestine sharpened significantly in the mid- to late 1930s due to the rapid influx of Jewish refugees fleeing Adolph Hitler's murderously antisemitic Nazi regime in Germany. The Nazis came to power in early 1933, enacting a series of laws that stripped German Jews of their political and civil rights. With tight immigration restrictions still in place in the United States and United Kingdom, many Jews hoping to escape Nazi persecution looked to Palestine.

Soon after Hitler became German chancellor in 1933, Jewish organizations in the United States and Europe organized an economic boycott of German-made goods and services. The Nazi regime responded that August by signing the Haavara Agreement with German Zionist leaders and the Jewish Agency in Palestine. Also known as the Transfer Agreement, the accord enabled middle- and upper-class Jews fleeing Germany to retain a portion of their assets by purchasing German-made goods to be exported to Palestine—thus breaking the boycott. Many Jewish groups around the world, including in the United States, criticized the agreement and continued the anti-German boycott.[12]

Well over one hundred thousand European Jews, mainly from Germany, fled to Mandatory Palestine in the mid-1930s, bringing millions of dollars in assets thanks to the Haavara Agreement. (By comparison, only seventeen thousand Jews were admitted into the United States in the same period due to immigration restrictions.)[13] As a result, the Jewish economic sector in Palestine overtook the Arab one for the first time. As this influx of European capital spurred economic growth, the Histadrut organized a belligerently racist campaign to ensure the new jobs being created would not go to native Arab workers. In the industrial cities of Haifa and Jaffa, the Histadrut sent roving pickets to construction sites and businesses to forcibly expel Arab workers from their jobs, while also circulating flyers and advertisements urging Jews not to purchase any Arab-produced goods, but to instead "buy Jewish." Unemployment among Palestinian Arabs steadily increased.[14]

A new labor organization was founded in 1934 called the Arab Workers' Society (AWS), which demanded the British authorities put a stop to the Histadrut's anti-Arab pickets and strong-arm tactics. While PAWS was based in Haifa, the AWS was strongest in Jaffa. Its leader, Michel Mitri, was an engineer educated in Latin America. As the AWS grew to at least 4,700 members, in early 1936 Mitri began building alliances with PAWS, the PCP, and Arab nationalist groups with the idea of eventually creating an all-Palestine Arab labor federation. The Histadrut reputedly tried bribing Mitri into staying away from the Arab nationalist movement, but he refused.[15]

Meanwhile, in and around Haifa, the Syrian-born Muslim preacher Sheikh Izz al-Din al-Qassam gained a popular following among the poor and unemployed as he called for moral renewal and active resistance to British imperialism and Zionism. He organized a guerilla band of a few hundred men and planned to launch an armed revolt—putting to shame the inaction of the cautious elites who formally led the Palestinian Arab nationalist movement—but was killed in a gun battle with British police in November 1935. Al-Qassam's martyrdom struck a nerve with Palestine's Arab masses, leading to increased anti-British and anti-Zionist protests that crystallized the following April with the launching of a general strike by Arab workers. Thus began what would be remembered as Palestine's Great Arab Revolt.[16]

§

Because it caught Palestinian Arab notables by surprise, the general strike that started on April 19, 1936, has typically been described as spontaneous. But as historian Zachary Lockman notes, the prior organizing efforts by labor leaders like Michel Mitri of the AWS helped lay the groundwork for the mass work stoppage.[17]

For the next six months, Palestinian Arab workers struck at ports, railway workshops, petroleum facilities, and public works. Their main demands were an end to Jewish immigration and land purchases, as well as national independence. At a May Day rally in Haifa, strikers explicitly connected the British Mandate's encouragement of Zionism to their own economic hardships, with a PAWS statement denouncing Zionist colonization for "depriving the [Arab] worker of his job and the peasant of his land."[18]

To try breaking the general strike, the Histadrut mobilized its Jewish members to scab, along with its segregated Arab members in the PLL who were desperate for work. With British troops protecting the strikebreakers, they were able to keep Haifa's port open and the railway running. Further, the British authorized the construction of a new port in the Jewish-majority city of Tel Aviv to keep maritime trade going, especially crucial after Arab strikers shut down Jaffa harbor.

Meanwhile, hundreds of armed fellaheen fanned out across the countryside, attacking oil pipelines, railroads, police stations, and Zionist settlements. Others in rural areas refused to pay taxes to the Mandate authorities as an act of civil disobedience. In response, British troops stormed through villages blowing up or burning down the homes of suspected rebels. For its part, the Palestine Communist Party came out in strong support of the uprising despite having failed to truly "Arabize." The party's mostly Jewish members distributed leaflets to fellow working-class Jews condemning the Histadrut's scabbing and arguing that the revolt was a natural response to colonial dispossession, countering Zionist propaganda that compared the rebellion to the antisemitic pogroms of Eastern Europe. As a result, the PCP achieved a measure of newfound popularity among Palestine's Arab community, particularly the youth.[19]

Despite the organizing of various Arab labor organizations and the PCP, they were not yet unified and strong enough to challenge the traditional leadership of the Palestinian Arab nationalist movement: the wealthy urban notables. These elites, who had no experience organizing the masses, had been indifferent toward al-Qassam's attempted guerrilla revolt the year before. But now they realized that, in the words of Palestinian nationalist writer Ghassan Kanafani, "[I]f they did not try to mount the great wave that had been set in motion by al-Qassam, it would engulf them."[20] They quickly moved to assert control over the uprising by establishing the Arab Higher Committee (AHC), a self-appointed council of notables that claimed to speak on behalf of the workers and peasants.

Hajj Amin al-Husayni, the most prominent Palestinian Arab leader during the Mandate period, served as chair of the AHC. Al-Husayni held the religious title of Grand Mufti of All Palestine, a lofty position invented by British Mandate authorities specifically for him in exchange for his promise to keep Palestine's Arab population in line. As he angled to maintain his leadership role amid the radicalism of the Great Revolt, the mufti would increasingly distance himself from his British patrons and become a more militant advocate for nationalism and independence. He would also work to eliminate leftist and working-class Palestinian Arab leaders whom he perceived as his rivals since they did not answer to him.

By the fall of 1936, the kings of Iraq, Transjordan, Saudi Arabia, and Yemen—all clients of the British Empire—promised Palestinian Arabs that the UK government would address all their grievances if they would first discontinue their revolt. Wanting to maintain control over the situation, the AHC eagerly followed this advice and called for an end to the general strike. The work stoppage and wider uprising came to a halt that October. Two months later, Arab Workers' Society leader Michel Mitri was assassinated by unknown assailants—though it has been speculated that either the British or Grand Mufti al-Husayni orchestrated the killing due to their fears of Mitri's growing influence as the leader of an independent working-class movement.[21]

§

A few weeks after the general strike ended, a British Royal Commission headed by Lord William Robert Wellesley Peel opened a months-long inquiry into the causes of and potential solutions to the social turmoil in Mandatory Palestine.

After hearing testimony from key Arab nationalist and Zionist leaders, the Peel Commission concluded in July 1937 that the British Mandate was no longer workable and recommended partitioning Palestine. Specifically, the commission called for 17 percent of Palestine's territory to go to a Jewish state—a move that, if carried out, would have displaced some 200,000 Indigenous Palestinians from their homes—and for the rest of the territory to be absorbed into neighboring Transjordan, which was ruled by the British-aligned King Abdullah.[22]

Though Zionist leaders were dissatisfied with the proposed borders of the Peel Commission's partition plan, they were willing to accept it on the grounds that it would allow for the establishment of a Jewish state.[23] Palestinian Arabs, on the other hand, were universally appalled that the commission's recommendations completely ignored their desire for national independence. Not only would the partition plan permanently carve out part of their homeland's territory to European colonizers, but it would also merge what remained into a neighboring kingdom rather than give them a state of their own. The Arab Higher Committee rejected the Peel plan, and the Great Arab Revolt was quickly reignited. Guerilla bands of fellaheen once again launched attacks on Mandate personnel and Zionist settlers, targeting British military bases as well as transportation and communications infrastructure.

Former Jerusalem mayor Raghib al-Nashashibi and his politically influential family—who were closely allied with the British and Transjordan's King Abdullah—did not support the armed revolt and pulled out of the AHC. While al-Nashashibi called for conciliation, Grand Mufti al-Husayni became hardened against any compromise, leading to a violent internecine conflict between the rival factions of Arab elites. The British outlawed the AHC and arrested most of its leaders. The mufti escaped to Syria, destined to live out the rest of his life in exile while remaining the most influential Palestinian nationalist leader until 1948.

Using many of the same tactics honed during the Irish War of Independence nearly twenty years earlier—tactics that would also be regularly employed by the Israeli state in future generations—the British military brutally crushed the Arab revolt. Sending in 100,000 troops, the Mandate authorities imposed martial law and detained thousands without trial, demolished the homes of suspected guerillas or their sympathizers, and carried out summary executions. Over the course of two years, from 1937 to 1939, an estimated 14 to 17 percent of the male Palestinian Arab population was either killed, wounded, exiled, or imprisoned. By August 1939, the armed rebellion was defeated.[24]

Zionists like Ben-Gurion welcomed the violent crackdown, believing that a Jewish state could never be realized until the Palestinian Arabs were first forced into submission.[25] "Only after total despair that will come not only from the failure of the disturbances and the attempt at rebellion, but as a consequence of our growth in the country, may the Arabs possibly acquiesce in a Jewish Eretz Israel," Ben-Gurion said. Whether consciously or not, the Mapai leader was echoing his right-wing political rivals, the Revisionist Zionists. Led by Ze'ev Jabotinsky, the Revisionists argued that peace with Palestine's Indigenous population would first require their military domination by an "iron wall."[26]

"We must either suspend our settlement efforts or continue them without paying attention to the mood of the natives," Jabotinsky had written in 1925. "Settlement can thus develop under the protection of a force that is not dependent on the local population, behind an iron wall which they will be powerless to break down."[27] Referring to Zionism as a "colonizing venture," he said that any hope for the establishment of a Jewish state depended on whether the Zionists could muster a powerful army or find a patron to do so for them. "If you wish to colonize a land in which people are already living, you must find a garrison for the land, or find a benefactor who will provide a garrison on your behalf," Jabotinsky wrote.[28]

Britain's vicious suppression of Palestinian Arabs' anticolonial rebellion at the end of the 1930s appeared to be the realization of Jabotinsky's "iron wall" thesis, potentially opening the door to the creation of a Jewish state. But before that could happen, World War II intervened.

THE HOLOCAUST

Back in the United States, trade unionists were closely following events in Germany after the Nazis came to power in 1933. In addition to his antisemitic persecution, Hitler also outlawed unions and imprisoned labor leaders, recognizing that an independent workers' movement would pose a threat to his total control over German society.

At the AFL's national convention that October, the delegates voted to endorse the international boycott of German-made products "until the German government recognizes the right of the working people of Germany to organize into bona fide independent trade unions of their own choosing, and until Germany ceases its repressive policy of persecution of Jewish people."[29]

Among the first US groups to carry out sustained organizing against Nazi Germany were Zionist organizations and the Communist Party USA. New York's leading Jewish trade unionists—many of them former Bundists who identified as neither Zionists nor communists—decided to create their own vehicle to oppose Nazism. In February 1934, they established the Jewish Labor Committee (JLC).

The JLC's founding convention on the Lower East Side was attended by over one thousand delegates from the ILGWU, Amalgamated Clothing Workers, United Hebrew Trades, Workmen's Circle, the *Jewish Daily Forward*, and other working-class Jewish organizations. Noting how antisemitism went hand in hand with antilabor repression in Hitler's Germany, the JLC sought to support both Jewish and non-Jewish unions in Europe, aid socialists and social democrats targeted by fascists, and fight against racial and religious prejudice in the United States and abroad.

David Dubinsky became the JLC's treasurer. In his role on the AFL Executive Council, he convinced the labor federation to get behind the new organization. In 1934, the AFL established the Labor Chest for Relief and Liberation of Workers of Europe, raising $150,000 from affiliated unions to help political refugees and underground movements on the other side of the Atlantic. The Labor Chest was effectively run by the JLC, with most of its funds and staffers coming from the ILGWU and Amalgamated Clothing Workers.

One of the JLC's first priorities was implementing the AFL-endorsed boycott of Nazi Germany by organizing needle trades workers and machinists to refrain from using German-manufactured tools and equipment. When the 1936 Summer

Olympics were held in Berlin, the JLC protested by holding its own World Labor Athletic Carnival (or "Anti-Olympics") on Randalls Island in New York. Over four hundred athletes participated—many of them local rank-and-file union members—and Mayor Fiorello La Guardia attended.

Meanwhile, the JLC also tried advocating for the lifting of US immigration restrictions, but failed to make much progress in the face of rampant xenophobia among policymakers. Even the otherwise sympathetic AFL voted down an ILGWU-backed resolution in 1935 calling for special immigration measures for refugees. The AFL had a long history of championing anti-immigration policies in the name of safeguarding jobs for native-born, white American workers. At the same time, tellingly, the labor federation's non-Jewish leaders would continuously advocate for the unrestricted immigration of European Jews to Palestine.

Faced with such anti-immigrant sentiment, and concerned that a sudden influx of Jewish refugees into the United States amid the ongoing Depression might only exacerbate antisemitism at home, some anti- and non-Zionist Jewish Americans—including those in the labor movement—started seeing mass emigration to Palestine as the only hope for Europe's beleaguered Jewish population.[30]

§

In line with its leaders' Bundist roots, the JLC officially took a non-Zionist position and supported the doykayt concept of "hereness." In its founding declaration, for example, the JLC stated that Jewish American workers "are of the opinion that the Jewish question must be solved in the countries in which the Jews live."[31] As a result, the committee received little enthusiasm or support from Labor Zionists in Palestine. "The

Bundists have fortified themselves there," Ben-Gurion said of the JLC. "Their socialism has almost completely disappeared, but their anti-Zionism has remained intact."[32]

The most vigorous anti-Zionist Jewish American voices of the 1930s were not within the JLC, however, but rather in the Communist Party USA. As scholar Benjamin Balthaser has noted, as many as half of the party's members throughout the decade were Jewish, and approximately 10 percent of all Jews in the United States were party members.[33]

Despite the JLC's official position, some of its members were openly supportive of further colonization of Palestine as an answer to Nazi oppression, including the Amalgamated Clothing Workers' Joseph Schlossberg and United Hatters, Cap and Millinery Workers president Max Zaritsky. In January 1937, as the Peel Commission was investigating the causes of the Palestinian Arab general strike the year before, Schlossberg, Zaritsky, and five other Jewish American trade union officials became the first US labor delegation to visit Palestine, though they did not go on behalf of the JLC. "We owe it to the Jews in Palestine, who carry such a large share of burden . . . of providing homes for victims of race persecution, to come to them at this difficult time, with a message of cheer and solidarity from the great masses of organized Jewish workers in the greatest of the free and democratic countries," Schlossberg said.[34]

Hosted by the Histadrut, the delegation spent a month in the country visiting cooperatives, agricultural settlements, and a technical institute named in honor of the late Max Pine, who had led the charge in getting US unionists to fundraise for the Histadrut. (This would be the first of many Histadrut facilities named after American labor leaders.) The delegates brought a letter from AFL president William Green expressing the labor federation's "immovable" support for the Balfour Declaration and its promise to establish a Jewish homeland in Palestine.

On the way home, the delegation stopped in France, where Zaritsky had a friendly meeting with Jewish socialist prime minister Léon Blum, who supported Zionism. A few weeks after returning to New York, Zaritsky launched the National Committee for a Léon Blum Colony in Palestine with the goal of raising $100,000 to finance a new farming and fishing settlement for Jewish refugees escaping Europe that would be named in honor of the French leader. This appeared especially urgent as Nazi Germany annexed Austria and the Sudetenland in 1938. Between 1938 and 1940, Zaritsky's new initiative held a series of high-profile fundraiser dinners attended by famous individuals like Green, LaGuardia, Senator Robert Wagner, Albert Einstein, and Eleanor Roosevelt. By 1943, enough money had been raised to construct and open the Léon Blum Colony in northern Palestine.[35]

§

By early 1939, the UK government recognized that war with Germany was inevitable. Wanting to shore up their alliances in the Middle East and North Africa, and knowing Jews would have little choice but to support them in a war against the Nazis, the British adopted a new policy that May attempting to placate Arab nationalists. The White Paper of 1939, as this policy was called, limited Jewish immigration to Mandatory Palestine to seventy-five thousand people over the next five years and imposed restrictions on Zionist land purchases.

One of the White Paper's advocates was George Antonius, a Lebanese Christian intellectual who worked for the Mandate government in Jerusalem and sympathized with the Palestinian Arab cause. In his 1938 book *The Arab Awakening*, Antonius made a prescient warning to the world about the immorality of using Nazi antisemitism to justify the dispossession and subjugation of Indigenous Palestinians, writing:

> The treatment meted out to Jews in Germany and other European countries is a disgrace to its authors and to modern civilisation; but posterity will not exonerate any country that fails to bear its proper share of the sacrifices needed to alleviate Jewish suffering and distress. To place the brunt of the burden upon Arab Palestine is a miserable evasion of the duty that lies upon the whole civilized world. It is also morally outrageous. No code of morals can justify the persecution of one people in an attempt to relieve the persecution of another. The cure for the eviction of Jews from Germany is not to be sought in the eviction of the Arabs from their homeland; and the relief of Jewish distress may not be accomplished at the cost of inflicting a corresponding distress upon an innocent and peaceful population.[36]

Although the White Paper hardly met Palestinian Arab demands for national independence, moderates associated with Raghib al-Nashashibi were willing to accept it as a step forward. But in the end, al-Husayni, the Grand Mufti living in exile, made sure Palestinian Arabs rejected it for not going far enough.

Unsurprisingly, Zionist leaders also rejected the White Paper. In the months after the policy's approval by the UK Parliament, outraged Zionist mobs attacked Palestinian Arabs, while the Irgun—a right-wing militia founded by Ze'ev Jabotinsky—carried out a campaign of assassination and sabotage targeting British personnel and property.[37] The new restrictions on Jewish immigration to Palestine appeared especially egregious considering they were being imposed amid the Nazis' escalating attacks on Jews in Europe. For their part, AFL president Green and CIO president John L. Lewis both cabled British prime minister Neville Chamberlain to express their "deep concern" over the White Paper just days after it was announced, calling on him to "carry out the letter and the spirit of the covenant contained in the Balfour Declaration."[38]

Though mostly non-Zionist, the leaders of the Jewish Labor Committee also came out in opposition to the White Paper, mainly out of a humanitarian concern for European Jewish refugees. That September, the Nazis invaded Poland—the country with the largest Jewish population in Europe—officially starting World War II. The JLC now put all its energies and resources toward trying to save Jewish and non-Jewish labor leaders caught in the warzone. Many Polish Bundists managed to escape to Lithuania, while other displaced socialists took refuge in France. Over the next few months, Dubinsky and the JLC compiled a list of 468 families (or 1,380 individuals) hiding out in Lithuania and France and asked the US State Department to provide emergency exit visas for them. The list was presented on official AFL letterhead, and Green personally beseeched President Roosevelt to carry out the request.

In 1940, the situation became even more dire as France came under Nazi occupation and Lithuania was invaded by the USSR as part of the short-lived nonaggression pact between Hitler and Soviet premier Joseph Stalin. The State Department began granting emergency visas to those on the "AFL list" or "Dubinsky list," as government officials called it. At the same time, the JLC wired funds to the refugees and purchased transatlantic tickets for them out of Lisbon, the final point of departure to the United States. By December of 1940, the JLC estimated that it had evacuated 308 individuals from Europe, spending $138,499 on the operation. Hundreds more would be safely brought to the United States over the next couple years, with the JLC claiming to have saved over eight hundred refugees by 1942.[39]

But millions of others targeted by the Nazis were not saved. Despite the exceptions made for those on the "AFL list," the

US government maintained its rigid immigration restrictions during the war. Thousands of desperate Jewish refugees from Nazi-occupied areas were denied asylum in the United States on the flimsy argument that they could be spies. In 1939, the German ocean liner St. Louis, carrying 937 mostly Jewish passengers, was turned away from the port of Miami and was eventually forced to return to Europe, where 254 of the passengers would be murdered by the Nazis.[40]

After invading Poland in late 1939, the Nazis forced the country's 3.5 million Jews into ghettos, then concentration camps. Millions of Jews in other German-occupied countries suffered the same fate. In 1941, the Nazi regime adopted its so-called "Final Solution," altering its antisemitic policy from expelling Jews to exterminating them. Over the next few years, European Jews and others whom the Nazis marked for annihilation—including Romani, Slavs, Jehovah's Witnesses, homosexuals, and people with disabilities—were taken to death camps to be systematically murdered in one of the worst crimes ever perpetrated in world history: the Holocaust.

In response to both the White Paper and the unfolding Holocaust, advocates for a Jewish state in Palestine put forward a more openly ambitious Zionism. This was on display in May 1942 at a conference held at New York City's Biltmore Hotel. The six hundred US Zionists in attendance were addressed by both Chaim Weizmann—the longtime Zionist leader who had been instrumental in securing the Balfour Declaration—and David Ben-Gurion. Although the international Zionist movement under Weizmann's leadership had traditionally promoted the establishment of a Jewish homeland within Palestine, at Ben-Gurion's urging, the delegates at the Biltmore gathering instead called for transforming all of Palestine into a "Jewish Commonwealth" upon World War II's end.[41] This maximalist vision would come to be known as the Biltmore Program.

Alarmed by the Nazis' eliminationist policies but still unwilling to advocate lifting immigration restrictions, many non-Jews in the United States also stepped up their support for Zionism during the war, including non-Jewish labor leaders. AFL president Green and CIO president Philip Murray (who succeeded Lewis in 1940)—both closely allied with President Roosevelt and promising him no strikes during the war—served on the executive council of the American Palestine Committee, a national lobbying organization of prominent Christian academics, government officials, and clergy advocating the creation of a Jewish state in Palestine. Through Green and Murray, the two labor federations also partnered with various Christian groups to cosponsor high-profile events that mustered non-Jewish support for Zionist aims, including the Emergency Conference to Save the Jewish People of Europe in July 1943 and the National Conference on Palestine in March 1944.[42]

With well-known and respected Christian Americans like Green and Murray becoming more vocally sympathetic toward Zionism, non-Zionist Jews—including those in the labor movement—began feeling indirectly pressured to also support the creation of a Jewish state in Palestine as the only appropriate response to the Holocaust.[43]

In all of these advocacy efforts, the question of what would happen to Palestine's Indigenous Arab majority was routinely ignored or side stepped, demonstrating a profoundly racist worldview even in response to Nazi evil.

§

By creating millions of new jobs in war-related industries, World War II pulled the American economy out of the Great Depression. Throughout the war, the US labor movement continued the rapid growth it had begun in the 1930s thanks to ongoing organizing efforts and the Roosevelt administration's pro-union wartime policies. Revolted by early reports of Nazi extermination camps, leaders from both the AFL and CIO used their newfound political and economic influence to continue advocating an end to the 1939 British White Paper and for the establishment of a Jewish state in Palestine.

As Zionists in the United States mobilized public support for the Biltmore Program, sympathetic trade unionists attempted to secure the Jewish Labor Committee's backing. But many of the JLC's leaders remained loyal to Bundist principles and were thus unwilling to endorse Zionism. Effectively going around the JLC, in 1944 pro-Zionist unionists led by Max Zaritsky founded the American Jewish Trade Union Committee for Palestine (AJTUCP). With Green and Murray serving as honorary co-chairs, the AJTUCP declared that "the American labor movement . . . is completely in favor of, and supports the aims of their Jewish co-trade unionists—to help in the rebuilding of Palestine as a Jewish Commonwealth." The committee drafted language to be used in official AFL and CIO messages to world leaders urging them to endorse the Biltmore Program. Not wanting to see the anticommunist wing of the Jewish labor movement split over disagreements on Palestine, the JLC's non-Zionist leaders tolerated this new organization and their own members' participation in it.[44]

Focused on public relations and awareness raising, in the last year of the war, the AJTUCP convinced multiple unions, state labor federations, and local labor councils to adopt resolutions and publish op-eds criticizing the White Paper and backing the establishment of a Jewish state in Palestine as the only moral response to the Holocaust. This included unions that had few Jewish members and mostly non-Jewish leaders, like the powerful United Auto Workers (UAW). In January 1945, for example, UAW president R. J. Thomas wrote an article arguing that "it is in the interest of American workers that in Palestine there should be laid as speedily as possible the foundation for a democratic Jewish commonwealth."[45]

In May 1945, World War II in Europe came to an end with German surrender. That August, Zaritsky traveled to London and personally lobbied the newly elected Labour Party government to revoke the White Paper and support the Biltmore Program. Dubinsky cabled Prime Minister Clement Attlee that October also calling for the end to the White Paper's immigration restrictions. Still a non-Zionist, Dubinsky stopped short of endorsing the establishment of a Jewish state and instead only expressed support for the "extension and growth of the Jewish national community in Palestine."[46]

In the meantime, the true magnitude of the Holocaust—a staggering eleven million murdered, including six million Jews—began to be revealed to the world. Allied forces liberated Nazi concentration camps to find emaciated prisoners barely clinging to life, gas chambers used for committing mass murder, and ghastly piles of corpses. These gruesome discoveries were transmitted to the international public through photographs and newsreel footage, resulting in widespread horror. Beginning in late 1945 and continuing for much of the next year, Nazi leaders were brought before Allied military tribunals and tried for crimes against humanity in the famous Nuremberg trials.

In this context, and in response to mounting pressure, in late 1945 the UK government proposed a joint Anglo-American Committee of Inquiry to study the problems of Palestine and to figure out what to do with homeless European Jews stuck in displaced persons camps. Viewing this proposal as a stalling tactic, AFL president Green demanded "action now!" He added, "Any attempt to prolong the unbearable status quo by instituting new investigations of the plight of Jews in Europe and the possibilities of emigration to *countries other than Palestine* will be regarded by American labor as a cowardly evasion of the issue."[47]

Despite Green's protestations, the proposed joint committee moved forward, convening in Washington and London in early 1946. Hearing testimony from Mandate authorities and both Zionist and Palestinian Arab leaders, the Anglo-American Committee recommended 100,000 displaced Jews be allowed to immigrate to Palestine, effectively ending the 1939 White Paper policy. Importantly, however, the committee explicitly called for neither a Jewish state nor an Arab state in Palestine, but rather a pluralistic state where Muslims, Jews, and Christians would have equal rights. "Because it is a Holy Land," the committee's report declared, "Palestine is not, and can never become, a land which any race or religion can justly claim as its very own."[48]

NAKBA

Although the Anglo-American Committee recommended abrogation of the White Paper, the UK Foreign Office was not willing to move displaced European Jews into Mandatory Palestine. Zionist militias had been waging an armed rebellion against British rule in Palestine since late 1945, and Foreign Secretary Ernest Bevin worried that allowing in Jewish refugees would only pour gasoline onto the fire by outraging the local Arab population.

The Haganah, the Irgun, and the Stern Gang (an extreme right-wing breakaway from the Irgun) all teamed up to attack British personnel and bases in Mandatory Palestine. These assaults culminated in the Irgun's terrorist bombing of the King David Hotel in Jerusalem in July 1946, which served as British military headquarters and housed the central offices of the Mandate government. Ninety-one people were killed in the bombing, mostly civilians.[49]

As these events unfolded, American labor leaders furiously fired off letters and telegrams to the UK's Labour Party government demanding no further delays to bringing the Jewish refugees to Palestine, while also calling on President Harry Truman—who succeeded Roosevelt upon his death in 1945—to pressure the UK government. After British troops raided the Histadrut's offices in June 1946 for harboring weapons, Green, Dubinsky, Murray, and Hillman all cabled Prime Minister Attlee to express their shock and dismay.[50]

§

For their part, Palestinian Arabs had been mostly divided since the Great Revolt of 1936–1939. The notables who constituted the Arab Higher Committee remained in exile during World War II. Now untethered from his former British patrons, Grand Mufti al-Husayni had gone to Nazi-occupied Europe, where he cozied up to Hitler and tried unsuccessfully to convince the Arab world to back the Axis powers.[51]

The Jaffa-based Arab Workers' Society fell apart due to factionalism after the murder of its leader, Michel Mitri, in late 1936. This left the Haifa-based Palestine Arab Workers' Society (PAWS) as the only major Arab labor organization. In the early 1940s, the Palestine Communist Party's official trade union policy was to organize within PAWS, but the latter's noncommunist leaders were hostile to leftist influence. Meanwhile, the PCP suffered growing division between its Jewish and Arab members over disagreements about whether the Yishuv constituted its own national group, whether to ever support Histadrut-led strikes, and whether to organize parallel Arab worker unions outside PAWS. In 1943, the PCP split over these disputes, with its Arab members forming their own communist party the following year called the National Liberation League. Unlike the Jewish-led PCP, which regarded the Yishuv as a distinct national group and therefore proposed a binational state in Palestine, the National Liberation League called for a democratic Arab state where Jews would have equal rights as a minority group.[52]

As an Arab-led party, the League was in a better position to make inroads among Arab trade unionists than the PCP. The League's communist members quickly won the leadership of local PAWS branches in Jaffa, Jerusalem, Gaza, and other cities. But PAWS general-secretary Sami Taha—a noncommunist—remained firmly in control of the organization's Haifa headquarters and most of its rural chapters. Accusing Taha of using undemocratic methods to prevent them from having a real voice in the organization, in August 1945, eleven of PAWS's communist-led branches broke away and, joining with some independent unions, founded the rival Arab Workers' Congress (AWC) in Jaffa. Over the next few years, the AWC and PAWS would compete to be the official representative of Palestinian Arab workers.[53]

Once World War II ended, the Arab Higher Committee was reconstituted and some of its elite members returned to Palestine. Though the mufti remained in exile, he and his loyalists dominated the committee and again presumed to be the leaders of the Palestinian Arab nationalist movement. But the communist National Liberation League and its AWC did not fall in line, instead openly criticizing the Arab Higher Committee as a group of conservative reactionaries.

Unlike the mufti, Palestinian Arab communists recognized the distinction between Zionists and Jews. "In calling for an independent national regime, the Arab workers seek to liberate the broad masses of the people, Arab and Jewish, from the noose of exploitation and Zionism," the National Liberation League's party newspaper explained in 1945, "and they declare that an independent national regime will ensure all just national rights to the Jews and the other minorities in Palestine."[54] In response, the AHC falsely accused Arab communists of wanting to partner with Zionists like Ben-Gurion.

Hoping to co-opt the Arab workers movement, the mufti's loyalists brought PAWS leader Sami Taha into their inner circle. Likely due to pressure from the mufti clique, Taha repeatedly dismissed the leftist Arab Workers Caucus's attempts at a rapprochement with PAWS and even undermined the AWC's strikes by directing PAWS members to cross picket lines.

Despite such divisions, for a brief moment in April 1946, Mandatory Palestine witnessed a rare display of working-class solidarity. Early that month, Arab and Jewish workers at the British-run postal and telephone service went on strike together to demand better compensation in the wake of the war. The strike quickly spread to railway workers and civil service employees, who were also both Arab and Jewish. By April 15, twenty-three thousand public sector workers across Palestine were on strike—members of PAWS, AWC, and the Histadrut. Coming together around their shared economic grievances against the British Mandate authorities, they marched through Jerusalem carrying signs written in Arabic, Hebrew, and English reading "Long Live Unity."[55]

Although the government workers won raises and pensions by the end of the month, the Arab-Jewish unity would, in fact, not be long-lived.

Exhausted with the constant turmoil in Palestine, in February 1947, Britain's Labour Party government announced plans to end the Mandate the following year, opening the door to an even more bitter and urgent struggle between Zionists and Arab nationalists over the future of Palestine. In this zero-sum conflict, the mufti came to regard Taha as an unreliable partner because his leadership of PAWS afforded him a degree of independence. In September 1947, days after he reportedly expressed the opinion that Palestine's Arab and Jewish workers would inevitably need to band together, Taha was assassinated in front of his house. Although the assailant was never identified, the murder was widely believed to have been carried out on the mufti's orders.[56]

Taha's assassination was emblematic of the internecine rivalries and factionalism among Palestinian Arabs in the mid-1940s that would leave them especially vulnerable to the disaster about to befall them.

§

When the British announced their intention to give up control of Palestine, they decided that its political future would be determined by the new United Nations (UN). Questioning the legality of allowing this newly created, foreign-dominated international body to determine Palestine's fate, the Arab Higher Committee boycotted UN hearings on the matter.

On November 29, 1947, the UN General Assembly voted to pass Resolution 181, a nonbinding plan to partition Palestine into Jewish and Arab states. Although Arabs comprised around 75 percent of Palestine's population at this time, the UN resolution granted 56 percent of the territory to Jews. Even within the borders of the proposed Jewish state, Jews at that time owned only 11 percent of the land and constituted a minority in every district. Jerusalem—considered a holy city by Jews, Muslims, and Christians—was to be made a corpus separatum ("separate body") under the international administration of the UN.[57]

Palestine's Indigenous Arabs overwhelmingly refused to recognize the legitimacy of this decision that would give over half their country to a minority of European settlers, considering it a gross injustice. As Palestinian historian Walid Khalidi explained, "The native people of Palestine, like the native people of every other country in the Arab world, Asia, Africa, America and Europe, refused to divide the land with a settler community."[58]

Zionist leaders like Ben-Gurion—who wanted all of Palestine but had settled on asking the UN for at least 80 percent of the land—were disappointed that the resolution did not give them more territory. Nevertheless, they celebrated it as an opportunity to finally establish a Jewish state once the British Mandate was set to end the following May. Further, they would use the Palestinian Arabs' rejection of the UN partition plan as justification to seize territory for a Jewish state beyond Resolution 181's proposed borders.[59]

In a remarkable development, the partition plan only passed in the UN General Assembly thanks to the support of the traditionally anti-Zionist Soviet Union and its new satellite states in Eastern Europe. During the war, the Soviets had begun reversing their long-held opposition to Zionism in the name of building up an antifascist popular front. Now, citing the horrors of the Holocaust and the strife within Mandatory Palestine, and hoping to secure a new ally in the Middle East (a region ruled by conservative, anticommunist, British-backed monarchs), the USSR did a surprise reversal and endorsed the establishment of separate Jewish and Arab states in Palestine. Dutifully following the Soviet government, both the Jewish-led Palestine Communist Party and the Arab-led National Liberation League supported the UN's partition vote despite previously calling for a single state.

Britain, which had promulgated Zionism through the Balfour Declaration thirty years earlier, ironically abstained from the historic General Assembly vote. The UK Cabinet, particularly Foreign Secretary Bevin, knew that partition would only stoke more violent conflict and did not want to have to play the role of peacekeeper.

The United States voted in favor of Resolution 181, but the State Department warned President Truman that partition would spark war between Jews and Arabs as they inevitably battled for territory.[60] Indeed, fighting between armed Zionist settlers and native Palestinians began in December 1947, immediately after the UN partition vote. To try reducing the bloodshed, Truman joined the British in imposing an arms embargo on Palestine. Unable to legally purchase weapons from the West, Ben-Gurion turned to the Soviet bloc. In January 1948, the Jewish Agency purchased thousands of guns and bombs, along with dozens of fighter planes, from communist Czechoslovakia—helping turn the Haganah and Irgun into well-equipped fighting forces.[61]

§

Ben-Gurion, who was both the Jewish Agency's chief executive and defense minister, now pressed forward with a violent campaign of ethnic cleansing.

In March 1948, following two months of sporadic fighting between the Jewish militias and Palestinian Arab guerillas, Ben-Gurion instructed Haganah commanders to adopt Plan Dalet (or Plan D). The plan was a major military offensive that, in the name of "security," called for the conquest and forcible depopulation of Arab-majority villages, towns, and cities. A key part of this strategy involved terrorizing urban populations into fleeing through constant bombardment and sniper attacks, as well as by carrying out massacres in nearby villages to sow fear. One of the most notorious massacres was in the village of Deir Yassin, near Jerusalem, on April 9, 1948. After killing the village's local defenders, the Stern Gang indiscriminately fired machine guns into houses, then rounded up survivors and executed them—including children, women, and the elderly. All told, at least ninety-three civilians were murdered in the attack.[62]

Another such massacre occurred on May 2 in the village of Ayn al-Zaytun, near the city of Safad. There, the elite Haganah unit Palmach rounded up the Arab villagers and—with the help of a collaborator donning a hood to conceal his face—identified a group of men and teenage boys on a prepared list of alleged guerillas. Those individuals were then separated from the rest of the villagers and gunned down in cold blood. Official Haganah documents reported at least seventy killed, but witnesses estimated a higher number. A similar scene played out a few weeks later, on May 22, in the village of Tantura between Tel Aviv and Haifa. Again, villagers were rounded up and suspected militants were identified by a hooded informer from a list prepared by Haganah intelligence, then executed. Other able-bodied men and boys in the village were also reportedly murdered, leaving anywhere from 110 to 230 dead.[63]

At the same time, Plan Dalet saw to the "de-Arabization" of several cities. After shelling Haifa for months, two thousand Zionist troops with Haganah's Carmeli Brigade invaded the city in late April. British soldiers, who had been standing between Zionist forces and Haifa, moved out of the way and left the city's civilian population defenseless except for five hundred untrained Arab volunteers. The attack on Haifa was codenamed "Operation Cleansing the Leaven," a reference to the Jewish tradition of removing bread and flour from homes on the eve of Passover.

"Brutally appropriate, the cleansing of Haifa, in which the Palestinians were the bread and flour, began on Passover's eve, 21 April," writes Israeli historian Ilan Pappé. Carmeli Brigade commander Mordechai Maklef ordered his troops to "kill any Arab you encounter; torch all inflammable objects and force doors open with explosives." Tens of thousands of terrified civilians fled their homes and made their way to Haifa's seaport, bombarded by mortars along the way. Desperate to escape the relentless attack, the crowds rushed onto boats, with many capsizing in the chaos.[64]

Jaffa, which Resolution 181 had carved out as part of a proposed Arab state, was similarly bombarded and ethnically cleansed that spring. So were West Jerusalem, Acre, Baysan, and Safad.[65]

At midnight on May 14, 1948, as the British Mandate officially ended, Ben-Gurion and the Jewish Agency declared independence for what they named the State of Israel. Already by this point, some 300,000 Palestinian Arabs had been driven out of their homes by Zionist militias.[66] The Haganah was now reconstituted as the Israel Defense Forces (IDF), with the Irgun and Stern Gang later folded in.

President Truman announced de facto US recognition of Israel mere minutes after Ben-Gurion's declaration (the US government would grant de jure recognition after Israel's first elections eight months later). The Soviet Union formally recognized Israel on May 17. Thus, the new Zionist state secured instant international legitimacy. But the surrounding states that comprised the Arab League, which were flooded with hundreds of thousands of Palestinian refugees thanks to Plan Dalet, refused to recognize Israel. Now that the British were gone, the neighboring Arab states invaded Palestine.

Transjordanian and Iraqi forces only entered the territory allocated for an Arab state under the UN partition plan. In the previous months, Transjordan's King Abdullah had held secret talks with the Jewish Agency over his desire to annex the UN-proposed Arab territory rather than allow the creation of an independent Palestinian state. Egypt and Syria also invaded, with the Egyptian air force bombing Tel Aviv, killing around 150 people. Meanwhile, Lebanese forces mobilized at the border with Palestine, but did not invade.[67]

In the summer of 1948, the UN dispatched Swedish diplomat Folke Bernadotte to mediate between Israel and the Arab states. During World War II, Bernadotte had negotiated the release of thousands of prisoners from Nazi concentration camps, including Jews. After coming to Palestine and securing a temporary ceasefire, he was assassinated by Zionist terrorists with the Stern Gang.

The fighting would continue until early 1949, with Israel capturing 88 percent of Palestinian territory. Transjordan's elite Arab Legion prevented the Israelis from conquering the West

Bank and East Jerusalem—territory that King Abdullah instead annexed for his now renamed Hashemite Kingdom of Jordan. Egypt similarly assumed administrative control over the Gaza Strip along the Mediterranean coast.

The ethnic cleansing campaign had continued throughout 1948, with more mass expulsions and atrocities. That October, at least 145 Palestinian Arab civilians were murdered in the village of Dawaymeh near Hebron. Zionist soldiers who took part in the massacre confessed to cracking babies' skulls, raping women, stabbing men, and burning people alive in their homes.[68] UN observers reported that same month that Israel was "uprooting Arabs from their native villages in Palestine by force or by threat," noting that conquered areas were being plundered and looted. But the UN secretary general suppressed the report and nothing was done.[69]

All told, between December 1947 and January 1949, an estimated 15,000 Palestinian Arabs were killed and another 750,000 were expelled from their homes, where they and their ancestors had lived for many centuries.[70] The IDF quickly established a military police unit to capture and deport so-called "infiltrators" trying to get back to their farms.[71] To this day, they and their descendants have not been allowed to return.

Approximately 500,000 displaced Palestinian Arabs flooded into the West Bank and Gaza Strip—which were now respectively under the control of Jordan and Egypt—where they joined another half million of their fellow Palestinians already residing in those territories. Another 250,000 fled beyond Palestine's borders to Lebanon, Syria, Egypt, and Jordan, where most would live in crowded refugee camps. Around 150,000 other Palestinian Arabs—many of whom had also been displaced from their native towns and villages—found themselves in areas conquered by the new Israeli state, suddenly becoming a discriminated minority group in their own homeland.[72]

This traumatic uprooting, which continues to unfold well into the twenty-first century, is known to Palestinians as al-Nakba (the Catastrophe).

US LABOR AND THE NAKBA

As historian Marjorie Feld has deftly argued, in the wake of the Holocaust, Zionist leaders successfully imposed a "forced consensus" on the majority of American Jews and their allies that a Jewish state in Palestine was essential to Jewish survival. That argument was further fortified after a 1946 pogrom in Kielce, Poland, killed over forty Jews and seemed to confirm that Eastern Europe would never be safe for them. Still, a vocal minority of Jewish Americans continued to reject Zionism, such as the religious members of the American Council for Judaism, who contended that the Holocaust was being cynically exploited by Zionists to silence any dissent against their nationalist ambitions.[73]

Using the political clout they had amassed during the preceding years of union growth, in 1947 American labor officials lobbied foreign diplomats at the United Nations to create a Jewish state. That spring, Histadrut general secretary Joseph Sprinzak wrote to CIO president Philip Murray to express "deepfelt thanks" for this advocacy, adding that it was "comforting to know that you and your organization have remained faithful to our cause."[74]

Meanwhile, to ensure the US labor movement would "be able to speak with one voice at this critical period, on matters concerning Palestine," the recently formed American Jewish Trade Union Committee for Palestine became an affiliate of the older and larger National Labor Committee for Palestine.[75] Welcoming in non-Jewish labor leaders, the council dropped "Jewish" from its name to become the American Trade Union Council for Histadrut. The group aimed to coordinate all of labor's political lobbying around Palestine while also raising $1 million for the Histadrut.

Reflecting the Soviet Union's reversal on Zionism, communist trade unionists in the United States also began mobilizing support for a Jewish state through a new group of their own called the American Jewish Labor Council. Their support was not welcomed by the anticommunist unionists who had been more sympathetic to Zionism all along.[76]

For its part, the Jewish Labor Committee also became more openly supportive of Zionist aims. In 1947, the JLC established contact with the Histadrut and, for the first time, contributed funds to help settle European Jews in Palestine, specifically $250,000 for some of the 100,000 displaced persons who the Anglo-American Committee said should be allowed to emigrate there.

The JLC's executive secretary at this time was Jacob Pat, a Polish Bundist who had moved to New York shortly before World War II. Despite his long record of anti-Zionism, Pat now said the creation of a Jewish state was "necessary and positive."[77] In contrast, the Bund Organization of New York passed a resolution in late 1947 opposing the UN partition plan and the establishment a Jewish state. Warning that this would only lead to endless conflict with the native Arab population, the resolution instead called for the creation of a single, democratic, binational state in Palestine where Jews could enjoy equal rights.

The New York Bund Organization was a chapter of the International Jewish Labor Bund, which was established after World War II by veteran socialists across the diaspora hoping to revive the Bundist tradition. In June 1948, only a month after the State of Israel was declared, the World Coordinating Committee of the new international Bund passed a measure condemning the "psychosis of Zionist-Messianic illusions" and arguing that the "Jewish community is more important than the

Jewish state" and that the "interests of the community are in peace, but the path to a state is war." But many Bundists, like the JLC's Pat, vehemently disagreed with this position. After years of debate, by the mid-1950s the International Bund would officially accept Israel as an actually existing haven for Jewish people and culture, even while remaining ambivalent about the Zionist settler colonial project itself.[78]

In accordance with the JLC's changing position on Jewish settlement in Palestine, its treasurer, ILGWU president David Dubinsky, began speaking at pro-Zionist events in 1947. This disturbed some of the JLC's non-Zionist officials, including Louis Nelson, manager of ILGWU Local 155. On December 3, 1947, just days after the United Nations partition vote, Nelson resigned from his position as JLC vice chair. He alleged the JLC—which endorsed the UN decision—had "deviated from it's [*sic*] original program" and was allying "with political forces which are chauvinistic and nationalistic."[79]

A few days later, Dubinsky wrote Nelson admitting that his recent appearance at a Histadrut fundraiser in New York "marked a departure" from his previous opposition to Zionism. "I have never been a Zionist, as you know," Dubinsky explained, "but there are large and important elements within our organization who are devoted to that cause and I would consider it a violation of my duty as [ILGWU] President to place my personal views above those of the organization and to commit the organization to those personal views."[80]

§

In December 1947, as the war for Palestine began, the Histadrut cabled the CIO's Murray to warn that the US/UK arms embargo was creating the conditions for a massacre of Palestine's Jewish population by "Nazifascist [*sic*] forces" led by the Hitler-aligned mufti. While British authorities were allowing Arabs to "carry arms openly," Histadrut leader Mordechai Nemirovsky alleged, Jews had no means of self-defense. "We appeal [to the] CIO to call upon [the] British labour movement [to] influence its Government to desist from [its] present policy . . . [and] urge [the] CIO [to] lend its weight to help carry out [the] decision adopted by [the] United Nations . . . and give [the] Jewish worker and Palestine Jewry legal possibilities for selfdefence [*sic*] and maintenance of order and security in Palestine," Nemirovsky wrote.[81]

Echoing these appeals, the American Trade Union Council for Histadrut called on fellow US unionists to pressure Truman to allow for "the immediate arming of [the] Palestine Jewish community defending itself against Arab aggressors incited by Nazi collaborators."[82]

These urgent messages failed to mention the Jewish Agency's major arms deal with Czechoslovakia, which provided the Haganah with fighter planes and thousands of guns, nor did they convey Ben-Gurion's intention to exploit the uncertainty caused by the rapid British exit to seize as much territory as possible—beyond what was designated by the UN partition plan—while permanently expelling native Palestinians.

On March 1, 1948, as the Haganah was preparing to implement Plan Dalet, some 7,500 ILGWU members held a rally at the Manhattan Center to demand the immediate lifting of the US arms embargo, which "deprives the Jews of weapons to defend themselves while Arab terrorists freely obtain them elsewhere." At the direction of union leadership, the garment workers collectively walked off the job an hour earlier than usual to attend the event, with four thousand gathering inside the building and an overflow crowd of 3,500 standing on West 35th Street listening to the speeches inside through loudspeakers.[83]

Among the speakers was Golda Meir, a Jewish Agency official who was on a two-month US fundraising tour. Meir, who would later serve as Israel's prime minister, had spent much of her early life in Milwaukee before emigrating to Palestine in 1921 and becoming a Histadrut leader and Mapai politician.

Three weeks after this rally, Truman responded not by ending the arms embargo, but rather by proposing a temporary UN trusteeship over Palestine to stop the bloodshed and allow time for a peaceful and orderly implementation of the partition plan. Although the proposal was praised by Judah Leon Magnes—a high-profile American rabbi who had lived in Palestine for several years and cofounded Jerusalem's Hebrew University—US Zionists and their allies, including in the labor movement, blasted it as an attempt to delay Jewish statehood.

The White House was flooded with telegrams and letters from unions, state labor federations, and central labor councils protesting Truman's trusteeship proposal and again calling for an end to the arms embargo.[84]

§

On April 9, 1948, the same day as the Deir Yassin massacre, leaders of the American Trade Union Council for Histadrut met in Manhattan to plan an afternoon work stoppage and mass rally of all New York City's needle trades workers for the following Wednesday.

Endorsed by the AFL, CIO, ILGWU, Amalgamated Clothing Workers, and United Hatters, the purpose of the demonstration would be to dramatically express organized labor's support for the UN partition plan and opposition to Truman's trusteeship proposal—demanding the establishment of a Jewish state in Palestine without further delay. One hundred thousand postcards had already been mailed out to local union members inviting them to participate.[85]

At 2:00 p.m. on April 14, around thirty thousand workers in New York's garment district participated in the work stoppage, boarding subway trains north to the Bronx to attend the rally at Yankee Stadium despite a spring storm. Speakers included spokespersons for Green and Murray, as well as various officials from the AFL, CIO, and needle trades unions.[86]

The ILGWU's Joseph Breslaw read a statement on behalf of Dubinsky, who said the UN partition plan had been "trampled and sabotaged by bloody Arab aggression."[87] A speech by Ben-Gurion, cabled to New York from Palestine, was also read at the rain-soaked rally. "It is unbecoming of a non-American to question the motives of the American Government in this astonishing reversal of policy," he said of Truman's trusteeship proposal. "But my life-long connection with large sections of the American people has imbued me with a deep faith in the decency and moral strength of your great people."[88]

Truman was also facing criticism from the New York Liberal Party. Founded a few years earlier by anticommunist progressives, the statewide Liberal Party was led by Dubinsky and other prominent Jewish unionists in New York. The presidential election was only six months away, and Truman's victory was far from assured.

Disappointed in the president's trusteeship proposal for Palestine, the Liberal Party openly debated whether to endorse Truman or somebody else. This was especially bad news for Truman because his Republican opponent in the upcoming general election would be New York governor Thomas Dewey, meaning the president would need as much support as possible in New York (then the most populous state in the nation) if he hoped to win its forty-seven electoral votes.

Feeling the pressure, and understanding the need to shore up support from organized labor and Jewish voters in a tight election, Truman broke with his own State Department by de facto recognizing the State of Israel immediately after its independence was declared on May 14. This, combined with his (albeit overruled) veto of congressional Republicans' anti-union Taft-Hartley Act the previous year—a law that imposed substantial new legal restrictions on union activity—earned Truman the endorsement of most labor officials and New York's Liberal Party. He would go on to win the presidential election that November, though still narrowly losing in New York state.[89]

Although they continued calling on Truman to lift the arms embargo through the remainder of 1948, US labor leaders homed in on a new target of protest: the UK's Labour Party government. While providing weapons to its client Arab states like Transjordan, Britain was still refusing to so much as recognize Israel. At the United Hatters convention in late May, Zaritsky gave a speech excoriating the Middle East policy of UK Foreign Secretary Ernest Bevin, who had previously served as the longtime head of Britain's large Transport and General Workers' Union. "I hang my head in shame that Mr. Bevin claims to be a man of labor, the head of a Labor government and a Socialist to boot," Zaritsky said.[90]

A week later in Boston, local AFL leaders organized a picket outside the UK consulate, delivering a statement calling on Britain to recognize Israel and to stop aiding Arab countries, explaining that only then could "the British Labor government expect to retain the firm support and admiration of American Labor."

With the arms embargo still in place, US unions found other ways to support Israel's military. In January 1949, as an armistice was reached in the Arab-Israeli War, the Jewish American-led garment unions donated tens of thousands of caps, shirts, slacks, blouses, and skirts to be used for IDF uniforms.[91]

§

The first elections of the new Israeli Knesset (parliament) were held in early 1949, with a Mapai-led coalition of Labor Zionist parties winning control of the government and Ben-Gurion becoming Israel's first prime minister.

In his memoirs, Dubinsky says he and Ben-Gurion first met around this time when the latter paid a visit to New York. "I told him that, even though I was sympathetic to the creation of Israel, I was not a Zionist," the ILGWU president recalled.

"Why should we fight?" Ben-Gurion replied to Dubinsky. "If I had come to the United States in 1911 when you did and you had come to Palestine in 1906 when I did, today you would be the prime minister and I would be the president of the International Ladies Garment Workers Union."[92]

From there, Dubinsky and Ben-Gurion would become friends, just as the ties between US labor and Israel would only continue to strengthen in the years ahead.

CHAPTER 3

BONDING WITH ISRAEL

By the mid-1940s, the US labor movement had achieved the kind of stature and legitimacy once dreamed of by Samuel Gompers. The unions comprising the American Federation of Labor (AFL) and Congress of Industrial Organizations (CIO) collectively represented around a third of all nonagricultural workers in the United States—a historic high point in US union density. Many top labor officials attributed this success to the federal government's unprecedented intervention in the economy on the side of workers during the New Deal and World War II. They therefore believed that nurturing and consolidating a friendly relationship with Washington was vital to organized labor's continued survival and growth.

At the same time, the brief wartime alliance between the United States and the USSR deteriorated in the immediate postwar years, as both superpowers vied for political, economic, and ideological supremacy first in Europe, then around the world. To wage the resultant global Cold War, Washington looked to various non-government subsidiaries to help bolster anticommunist, pro-US forces abroad while undermining foreign leftist and anti-imperialist movements. Always desperate to showcase their loyalty and patriotism to remain on good terms with the government, and believing the success of a US-dominated international capitalist system would mean plentiful jobs and good wages for their members, American labor officials happily offered their assistance. This felt all the more urgent amid a right-wing crackdown on organized labor fueled by anticommunist hysteria.

The AFL's leadership was made up of veteran anticommunists, who for decades had battled against "reds" for control of US unions and considered themselves the premier experts in thwarting radicals. As World War II ended, high-ranking unionists within the AFL, including David Dubinsky, were already angling to counter communist influence in foreign labor movements. To this end, in late 1944 the AFL founded a new international arm called the Free Trade Union Committee. Initially funded by Dubinsky's International Ladies' Garment Workers' Union (ILGWU), the committee's purpose was to spread anticommunist propaganda to foreign workers—particularly in Western Europe at first—and provide financial support to anticommunist splinter groups within labor movements abroad. By 1949, the Free Trade Union Committee was bankrolled primarily (and covertly) by the recently created Central Intelligence Agency.

For its part, the CIO initially tolerated communist unionists within its ranks and supported amicable relations between Washington and Moscow. But once the Cold War was in full swing, with conservative politicians and corporate employers spreading an anticommunist panic to push through the anti-union Taft-Hartley Act, CIO leaders did an about-face and controversially expelled eleven communist-led unions from their ranks in 1949 and 1950, losing approximately one million members in the process. Now smaller and weaker, the CIO began its rapprochement with the AFL.

In 1955, the two labor federations merged to form the AFL-CIO. Under the presidency of George Meany—a former Bronx plumber, Catholic, and ardent anticommunist—the AFL-CIO essentially became an appendage of the US foreign policy apparatus during the Cold War, routinely working hand in hand with the State Department and CIA to intervene in the affairs of labor movements abroad. However, because they believed themselves to be especially adept at combatting "reds," AFL-CIO officials would sometimes openly criticize US foreign policy when they thought it was failing to wage the Cold War correctly.[1]

Having already established a close relationship with the Histadrut over the preceding decades, US labor officials—both Jews and non-Jews—believed the new State of Israel could serve as a crucial Cold War ally to the United States. In particular, they were convinced that Israel's Labor Zionist government offered a practical example of noncommunist, worker-centered economic development that could be emulated by other countries to prevent them from being pulled into a Soviet orbit. US labor officials also believed that, by publicizing what they viewed as the Histadrut's many successes in building up Israel's economy and positive contributions to Israeli society, they could remind Americans of the importance and necessity of unions at home.

Because their relationship with the US government was more contingent in the 1950s and 1960s than it would become in later years, Israel's first leaders—most of them Histadrut veterans—leaned heavily on their friends in the American labor movement to help them remain on good terms with Washington. This was particularly important because, in these crucial early years of Israel's existence, the AFL-CIO wielded far more political influence than the still small, newly forming pro-Israel lobbying groups like the American Israel Public Affairs Committee (AIPAC). Numbering about fifteen million at the time of the 1955 merger, the AFL-CIO membership "was nearly three times that of the entire Jewish population in the United States and was far more widely spread," writes historian Yoav Fromer, who calls US labor in this period "the 'other' pro-Israel lobby."[2]

An early example of this came in February 1950, when AFL president William Green and CIO president Philip Murray made a rare joint visit to the White House to lobby President Harry Truman on Israel's behalf. The leaders of the nation's two major labor federations asked Truman "to permit the sale of arms to the Israeli government to meet the daily increasing threat to the security of the State of Israel" from neighboring Arab countries, who were being supplied with weapons by the British and French. Further, they called on Truman to increase economic aid to Israel, noting that an initial $100 million US loan had already been spent on trying to absorb the 365,000 Jewish immigrants and refugees who had moved to the new state since its establishment in 1948.

"As unionists and as believers in the continuance of the peace and in democratic opportunity," Green and Murray said in a statement after the White House meeting, "we trust that our government will stand against further aggression directed at the State of Israel and its courageous enlightened people who, like we, are seeking to achieve a decent economy and a full utilization of the resources of nature for the benefit of mankind."[3]

Two months after this visit, ILGWU president Dubinsky and Amalgamated Clothing Workers president Jacob Potofsky—who had succeeded Sidney Hillman upon his untimely death in 1946—wrote a lengthy letter to the State Department asking that arms be sold to Israel in the name of self-defense. They did this at the request of Israeli ambassador Eliahu Eilat, who provided much of the language used in their letter. Eilat had similarly helped Green and Murray prepare for their White House visit by giving them briefing papers, illustrating how US labor leaders were acting as unofficial lobbyists for the Israeli government.[4]

Although such pressure from top union officials, as well as similar advocacy from Jewish American leaders, did not convince Truman to send weapons to Israel, it did compel him to work with the UK and French governments to limit arms sales to Arab states (in addition to Israel) to try preventing another war in the region.[5]

INVESTING IN COLONIZATION

Besides advocating for Israel in Washington, during this period key figures in the US labor movement were also determined to scale up material aid to the new state. In October 1948, Histadrut leaders visited Green to ask for the AFL's support in securing money "to carry on colonization work," as *The New York Times* put it.[6] The following May, a CIO delegation led by Potofsky went to Israel and came home determined to increase donations to the National Labor Committee for Palestine, which was already running a campaign launched in 1945 to raise $3 million from American unions for the Histadrut.[7]

The National Labor Committee for Palestine now changed its name to the National Committee for Labor Israel (NCLI). The name change reflected how, after the establishment of the State of Israel, Zionists and their supporters sought to erase the name and memory of Palestine and its Indigenous people. Palestinian Jews now strictly identified themselves as Israelis, while Palestinian Arabs were referred to as just "Arabs." To combat this attempted erasure of their identity, and to differentiate themselves from other Arab nations, Palestinian Arabs would increasingly call themselves simply Palestinians.

The NCLI's new fundraising drive for the Histadrut was only one example of how US labor was financially supporting the State of Israel in the aftermath of the Nakba. Under Dubinsky's stewardship, the ILGWU led the way. In June 1948, just a month after Israel's founding and amid the unfolding ethnic cleansing of Palestine, the union authorized a $1 million loan to the new state, while also donating $220,000 to the Haganah and Histadrut.[8] A year later, the ILGWU announced it was creating the Amun-Israeli Housing Corporation, with the goal of selling $10 million in bonds for the construction of eight thousand new houses in Israel for Jewish settlers. Dubinsky, Potofsky, Green, and Murray all served on the housing corporation's board. The NCLI and Ambassador Eilat also endorsed the project.

The campaign to sell the housing bonds officially began in April 1950, but, as Dubinsky later complained, "the American Zionists displayed an astonishing lack of interest in our efforts."[9] By 1952, the Amun-Israeli Housing Corporation had sold about $6 million in bonds, falling short of its $10 million goal. Over half of that amount—$3.6 million—was purchased by the ILGWU, its members, and the garment industry employers it bargained with.[10]

Besides the housing bonds, within the first four years of Israel's existence, the ILGWU gave the Zionist state a total of $2.75 million in loans (which were repaid) and over $1 million in donations, the latter going toward a trade school in Haifa, a printing press for the Labor Zionist Mapai, and a cooperative factory. Further, ILGWU Local 10 donated machinery to the Haifa trade school, Local 117 built a rest home for sailors on the Yarkon River, and Local 35 financed worker housing in Holon.[11]

It went completely unacknowledged that these ILGWU-sponsored facilities and homes were being built in places that, for many centuries, had been home to hundreds of thousands of native Palestinians whom Israel had just violently expelled.

Despite championing these efforts, unlike other prominent Jewish American labor leaders, Dubinsky had still never set foot in Palestine and did not seem especially eager to go. "[Y]ou owe Israel a visit—you owe it as a Jewish labour leader as well as an American statesman," Israeli prime minister David Ben-Gurion wrote to Dubinsky in late 1951. "[H]earing is not seeing and you should really see for yourself what is being created here. Do not tell me you are always busy."[12]

The ILGWU president replied that he hoped to visit as part of an AFL delegation at some point in the near future. Perhaps to entice Dubinsky to make the voyage to Israel, in 1953 city officials in Haifa named a new soccer stadium after him, which would be used by schoolchildren for physical education as well as by amateur sports clubs. "In this way, day by day and every hour, your respected and beloved name will be borne on the lips and carried in the hearts of thousands of children, youth and sportsmen," Haifa's mayor wrote to Dubinsky.[13]

Dubinsky finally visited Israel on a nine-day trip in June 1955 hosted by the Histadrut. Upon coming home to New York, the ILGWU president said he was "inspired by everything" he had witnessed in Israel. "I saw the Socialist kibbutzim, the factories, the housing developments under construction, the great industrial developments built by the workers of Israel. Much of it was like a dream—but it was not a dream, it was something I saw and entirely real."[14]

Similar glowing reports were recorded throughout the 1950s by other US union officials, especially leaders of the traditionally more progressive CIO, who seemed to see their ideal vision of a labor-centered society being realized in Israel. Walter Reuther called Israel "the country in the free world nearest to Democratic Socialism," while Transport Workers Union president Mike Quill, after meeting Histadrut leaders in Israel, said, "I wish we in the CIO could boast we had done such a job in the United States." After a 1954 trip to the Zionist state, CIO official Albert Lunceford said the Histadrut "could well serve as an example not only to the Middle East but to American labor as well."[15]

A few months after Dubinsky's 1955 visit to Israel, the ILGWU pledged $1 million for Kupat Holim, the Histadrut's health service, to construct a modern hospital in the ancient city of Beersheba. Located in the Naqab (Negev) desert, Beersheba had been designated part of a future Arab state under the United Nations' partition plan, but was conquered by Israel in the 1948 war. At the time it was a small town of five thousand Palestinian Arabs, defended only by Egyptian volunteers who were quickly defeated. The victorious Haganah soldiers expelled the local inhabitants at gunpoint, engaged in widespread looting, and turned the local mosque into a shop.[16] Over the next decade, with the Histadrut overseeing the construction of housing and infrastructure, Beersheba's population swelled to eighty thousand inhabitants, primarily newly arrived Jewish immigrants.

With the million-dollar donation from the ILGWU, Kupat Holim completed the new hospital in 1959. Dubinsky returned to Israel that October to participate in the hospital's dedication ceremony—which was timed to coincide with the anniversary of Israel's conquest of Beersheba (the ILGWU and Histadrut euphemistically referred to it as the "liberation" of Beersheba). "If Histadrut were in the habit of bestowing medals on its friends abroad, Dubinsky and the I.L.G.W.U. would be the very first recipients," Histadrut general secretary Pinhas Lavon remarked during the visit.[17]

"We of the I.L.G.W.U. and the American labor movement rejoice at the growth and progress of Israel," Dubinsky declared in a speech at the hospital's opening ceremony. "You wrought these miracles out of largely desert land . . . while retaining your respect for individual freedom and the human spirit." Dubinsky made no mention of how Beersheba and much of the rest of Palestine had been violently taken over and ethnically cleansed by Israel eleven years earlier.[18] Now known as the Soroka Medical Center, the hospital in Beersheba built with ILGWU money still stands today.

All of these new facilities were built as the Histadrut experienced exponential growth. Between 1948 and 1958, as Israel's Jewish population rose from around 650,000 to 2,000,000, the Histadrut's membership grew from 170,000 to 620,000.[19] It is important here to recall that the Histadrut was not a trade union federation in the US sense, but rather a Zionist nation-building institution that provided jobs, health care, housing, and other forms of social welfare to its exclusively Jewish members. As labor scholar Jonathan Preminger explains, organized labor in Israel "was not politicized as a grassroots oppositional movement but organized by a national leadership elite for the main national objectives of settlement and immigrant absorption."

The Histadrut, Preminger says, "was not primarily envisioned as a union but founded by socialist-leaning parties to coordinate certain welfare functions by these parties . . . the interests of both labor and capital were presumed to be the same: national (Jewish settlement) interests."[20]

§

In late 1952, AFL president William Green and CIO president Philip Murray died within twelve days of each other. Their respective labor federations created memorial foundations in their honor. The CIO's foundation donated $100,000 to help erect the Philip Murray Memorial Center in the Israeli city of Eilat, on the Red Sea. Opened in 1955, the building would be used as a community center for local Histadrut members, with its own library, theater, and meeting spaces. The AFL's foundation similarly contributed funds to construct the William Green Cultural Center, which opened in 1958 in Haifa to also serve as a place for Histadrut members to gather, relax, and study.[21]

Meanwhile, in the United States, the AFL and CIO's new presidents—George Meany and United Auto Workers (UAW) chief Walter Reuther, respectively—decided to combine their two labor federations to build greater unity and strength. After nearly three years of discussions, in December 1955, the merger was consummated with the founding of the AFL-CIO, with Meany serving as its president. For his part, Reuther remained president of the powerful UAW, the most dynamic and influential union in the newly merged labor federation. In the run-up to the merger, officials from the AFL and CIO together went on joint delegations to Israel, including a visit in the summer of 1955 led by Reuther to attend the opening ceremony of the Murray Memorial Center. A later AFL-CIO delegation in 1958 headed by Jacob Potofsky participated in the dedication ceremony of the Green Cultural Center.[22]

In addition to having their names adorned on new buildings in Israel—which also included a George Meany Stadium in Nazareth and Walter Reuther Youth Center in Holon, both built in the early 1960s—US labor leaders were also recipients of various awards and honors from the Histadrut and the NCLI. Beginning in 1950, the NCLI annually gave out the "Histadrut Humanitarian Award" to recognize high-profile Americans who generated US sympathy for Israel. The yearly award ceremonies were lavish dinners attended by hundreds of VIPs and functioned as fundraisers for the Histadrut. Recipients included Meany in 1956, Reuther in 1958, Dubinsky and Potofsky together in 1959, and United Steelworkers president David McDonald in 1963.[23]

§

Another US unionist who sought to do his part in fostering friendship with Israel was Jimmy Hoffa, controversial leader of the International Brotherhood of Teamsters. During the Arab-Israeli War in 1948, the Teamsters had reputedly helped smuggle guns and explosives from the United States to the Haganah and Irgun in violation of the US/UK arms embargo.

The Teamsters union was heavily influenced by labor racketeers from the world of organized crime, as was the International Longshoremen's Association, the union of East Coast dockworkers. Jewish American mobsters like Meyer Lansky, who had effectively controlled New York City's docks since Prohibition in the 1920s, supported Zionism and coordinated the illegal gun-running operation during the 1948 war. Teamsters members supposedly hid guns inside certain commercial washing machines and transported them to the New York and New Jersey ports, where union longshoremen were told which washing machines were for regular shipments and which were to be diverted to the Zionist militias in Palestine. According to another story, the Teamsters transported small arms hidden inside boxes meant for storing cheese.[24]

Serving as an influential member of the Teamsters general executive board at the time, the Detroit-based, Irish American Hoffa was said to have encouraged the arms smuggling operation due to his sympathy for Jews and, like many other US union officials, his admiration of Labor Zionism. By 1956, Hoffa was a powerful vice president in the union and under intense scrutiny for his mob ties. That April, the Teamsters hosted a gala dinner in Hoffa's honor in Detroit, meant to raise funds to build an orphanage in Israel—but the press noted that the event "also was a vehicle for counteracting bad publicity that has stung Mr. Hoffa and the teamsters in recent months." Held at the Michigan State Fair Coliseum, the dinner was attended by 2,600 guests, including Israeli ambassador Abba Eban and executives of major corporations like General Motors, Ford, Sears, and Montgomery Ward. The event raised approximately $300,000.[25]

Four months later, Hoffa led a delegation to Israel to formally donate the money and attend the cornerstone-laying ceremony for the orphanage. He was joined by other Teamsters officials, corporate executives, and his teenage daughter Barbara Ann. While in the country, the Teamsters vice president met with Ben-Gurion and Foreign Minister Golda Meir. The James R. Hoffa Children's Home broke ground in Ayn Karim, a village southwest of Jerusalem that had served as a base for Arab guerilla fighters in the 1948 war before being captured and ethnically cleansed by Israeli forces. "We hope this children's home will be a center which symbolizes the spirit of Israel," Hoffa said at the cornerstone laying ceremony. "Building this country in a span of a few short years—building its industry, its homes, its schools, its strength—is an undertaking unparalleled in human history. . . . You are a beacon of light in the Middle East."[26]

The following year, Hoffa was elected president of the Teamsters, only for the union to be expelled from the AFL-CIO over its corrupt practices and mob connections.

§

At a September 1950 meeting in Jerusalem attended by fifty American Zionist leaders, Ben-Gurion proposed a new program to allow foreigners—especially in the United States, but also in Canada, Europe, and Latin America—to invest directly in Israeli nation-building. By December of that year, the Development Corporation for Israel (DCI) was founded in New York with the specific purpose of selling State of Israel bonds to institutional investors. The money from the bonds would be used for new, state-led infrastructure projects.

Early on, the Israeli government and American Zionists expected US labor to be a major purchaser of the bonds. Accordingly, Israeli ambassador Abba Eban wrote to ILGWU president David Dubinsky that December asking him to join the new DCI's board of directors. But Dubinsky was not interested in the role, particularly because his union had only recently launched its own private bond drive for the Amun-Israeli Housing Corporation.

In the spring of 1951, Ben-Gurion toured the United States to kick off the DCI's ambitious campaign to sell $500 million in State of Israel bonds. "The success of this bond issue depends upon the support of a great number of people and organizations," the Israeli prime minister wrote to Dubinsky during the trip, "and certainly a major share of that responsibility must fall to the Labour movement which has stood so strongly by our side throughout the years. You, as the heart and soul of the International Ladies' Garment Workers' Union can, and I am sure will, lend all assistance and cooperation to the bond drive. It would mean so much to us to have your promise of support and I know that I will get it."

Dubinsky sent a cordial reply explaining that the ILGWU's own private bond drive for Israeli housing was struggling to reach its $10 million goal and risked "becoming a fiasco" that might damage "not only the prestige of Israel but also of the movement which sponsored the campaign." Therefore, he explained, "We have decided not to undertake or become involved with any endeavor that will interfere with our determination to concentrate on the housing bond drive so that it may be brought to its proper conclusion." In other words, the ILGWU would not be purchasing any State of Israel bonds.[27]

Although the ILGWU did not initially get on board, between 1951 and 1966 alone, US unions at the national, regional, and local level purchased at least $19.8 million in State of Israel bonds. Labor's largest bond purchasers in this period were unions led by non-Jews, including the Teamsters ($3.1 million), the Amalgamated Meat Cutters ($1.9 million), and the UAW ($1 million). The Building Service Employees International Union, Hotel and Restaurant Employees, United Steelworkers, and Retail, Wholesale and Department Store Union each also purchased between $650,000 and $900,000 in bonds during the same period, while dozens of other unions made smaller purchases.[28]

The money came from the unions' general treasuries, strike funds, and health care and pension funds jointly administered with employers. Using these substantial investments from American labor, the Israeli government built ports, roads, pipelines, mines, and factories. Some of the most notable projects financed by the bonds program included the Dead Sea Works for magnesium chloride extraction and the National Water Carrier to irrigate 450,000 acres of agricultural land. The latter project fueled conflict with Syria and Jordan by unilaterally diverting freshwater they used from the Jordan River.

By 1994, the Development Corporation for Israel reported that US labor had purchased over one billion dollars in bonds over the previous four decades.[29] Through the bonds program and various other investments, loans, and donations, it can reasonably be argued that the US labor movement played a significant role in the actual construction of the State of Israel.

ARAB AMERICANS AND PALESTINIAN REFUGEES

While heavily investing in the "colonizing work" of Zionism, US labor leaders demonstrated a notable indifference toward the suffering of the hundreds of thousands of Palestinians whose violent dispossession had made Israel's birth possible. This mirrored how national union officials, almost all white men, also frequently ignored the specific concerns of Black, Latino, Asian, and Native American workers in the United States (including members of their own unions), who tended to be stuck in the lowest paid and least desirable jobs.[30] It was also in part because Palestinians—and Arabs more generally—had virtually no voice in the American labor movement at this time.

The first significant wave of Arab immigration to the United States occurred between the 1880s and 1920s. In this period, over 100,000 Arab immigrants from Syria, Lebanon, Jordan, and Palestine came to live in the Northeast and Midwest. Nearly all Christian, the US government considered them to be white, though in reality they experienced a sort of racial fluidity between white and nonwhite as they simultaneously assimilated into mainstream American society and attempted to hold onto their Arab identity. This group of immigrants often worked as grocers, peddlers, and farmers—but many found employment in the nascent auto factories of Detroit and other cities in the Upper Midwest.[31]

Philip Raymond, a pioneer union organizer in the auto industry in the 1920s and 1930s, was the son of Palestinian and Romanian immigrants. A dedicated communist, Raymond was a leader of the Auto Workers' Union, a precursor to the UAW.[32] George Addes, one of the UAW's cofounders, was a Lebanese American. Addes served as the UAW's secretary-treasurer—its second highest-ranking officer—from 1936 to 1947, when the union experienced its most significant growth by successfully organizing General Motors, Ford, and Chrysler.

Beyond such exceptions, Arab American workers had little to no influence over the US labor movement. But in April 1949, a group of New York ILGWU members—identifying themselves as "a community descendent of Arabic-speaking people"—attempted to make their voices heard by sending a remarkable letter to their union president, David Dubinsky.

In their letter, the group noted (and praised) the ILGWU's fundraising activities for humanitarian purposes around the world, including in Israel and war-ravaged Italy. But explaining that "our union membership is composed of a great number of people descendants [*sic*] of different nationalities," they asked that "such funds might be more widely distributed so that other people who are in dire need of help would not be denied the benefits and blessings of such aid."[33]

"We would like to draw your attention," the letter's signers told Dubinsky, "to the plight of . . . the Arab refugees of Palestine who fled their homes into the desert and neighboring countries. They number around 750,000. They are destitute, homeless suffering human beings threatened by hunger and disease. Their problem is another test for human conscience." They appealed to the ILGWU president as "a man of noble character and high integrity" and "as a leader of our Union" to provide funds to aid Palestinian refugees. "Disregarding the political issues at stake," they wrote, "we are fully aware of the widespread suffering of our people in our homeland, most of whom are innocent bystanders in the present strife."[34]

The twenty-nine signatories included Vickie Karadashly of ILGWU Local 62, who apparently organized the effort, James and Norman Shaleesh of Local 10, Merta Khoury of Local 62, and Amelia Abraham of Local 22. As Karadashly explained in a postscript, though the letter was initially only going to be signed by "people of our [Arab] race," once fellow union members of other ethnicities "heard of our plea," they also "gladly attached their names to our petition"—names like Helen Campanelli and Irma Taverna, both of Local 89, and Jola Springer and Mildred Challenger of Local 22.[35]

Two months later, Dubinsky responded by inviting Karadashly to his office. Although it is unknown what exactly was discussed, a week after they met, Dubinsky announced an ILGWU donation of $5,000 "for the use of Arab-refugee relief" to the American Friends Service Committee (AFSC), the Quaker humanitarian organization providing aid to Palestinian refugees in the Gaza Strip on the UN's behalf. Compared to the millions of dollars the ILGWU was busily giving to the Histadrut and Israeli government, $5,000 was a paltry handout. Nevertheless, both the AFSC and American Middle East Relief, Inc.—an Arab American–led humanitarian organization also fundraising for Palestinian refugees—praised Dubinsky for the contribution, though the latter did not receive a cent from the ILGWU.

In making the donation, the ILGWU president could not help but echo the Zionist narrative that Palestinian suffering was solely to be blamed on reckless and hateful Arab elites. "It is our hope," Dubinsky said in a letter to the AFSC, "that this contribution will in some measure alleviate the plight of many Arab civilians, who have become the innocent victims of a war deliberately provoked by the mufti and other reactionary leaders in opposition to the just and peaceful aspirations of the Jewish people."[36]

There is no official record of how Vickie Karadashly and the other ILGWU members who signed the letter to Dubinsky responded to the $5,000 contribution. But at the union's 1950 convention, a resolution was passed calling on Israel to "make new and extraordinary efforts free from narrow nationalism to eliminate the bitterness and ameliorate the difficulties caused by the acute Arab refugee problem growing out of the war which led to its birth."

The resolution did not specify what Israel should do, like allowing Palestinian refugees the right to return home, but only stressed that "removing this sore spot" would "take from [Israel's] most demagogic enemies a dangerous weapon." Besides this ILGWU resolution, US union conventions generally "side-stepped" any mention of the Palestinian refugees, as an AFL official admitted in a 1955 internal memo.[37]

Although UN General Assembly Resolution 194, passed in December 1948, affirmed the right of Nakba refugees to return home, the Israeli government would continue denying them and their descendants that right. In 1950 and 1952, the Knesset respectively passed the Law of Return and the Nationality Law: two key pieces of legislation that grant Jews from anywhere in the world the right to immigrate to the State of Israel and obtain immediate citizenship—no matter if they, their parents, grandparents, great-grandparents, etc. had ever set foot in historic Palestine. But the laws simultaneously refute any such rights to the Palestinian refugees who, like generations of their ancestors, had continuously lived on the land their entire lives before being forcibly expelled during the Nakba.

Only Palestinians who had managed to resist ethnic cleansing and could prove their uninterrupted residence within the Israeli state's boundaries since before 1948 could be legally eligible for nominal citizenship, though they would still face systemic discrimination.[38]

§

The death, destruction, and displacement of the Nakba nearly destroyed the Palestinian nationalist movement. The notables who had comprised the Arab Higher Committee lost the political influence they had previously held during the Mandate period, though some of them established the short-lived All-Palestine Government, which was dependent on Egypt and dissolved after a few years.

The nascent Palestinian Arab labor movement, which had been centered in Haifa and Jaffa, was shattered by Israel's conquest and ethnic cleansing of those two cities. The Nakba turned thousands of proud trade unionists with the Palestine Arab Workers' Society and Arab Workers' Congress into unemployed, homeless refugees overnight. In the West Bank, which was annexed by Jordan after the Nakba, Palestinian workers gained the rights to organize and strike under a new Jordanian labor law passed in 1953, though in practice these rights would often be restricted. The following year, the General Federation of Jordanian Trade Unions was founded, with veteran organizers from the Mandate-era Palestinian Arab labor movement contributing their experience.[39]

As historian Rashid Khalidi says, there was "thus a sort of political tabula rasa among Palestinians after 1948." The governments of the surrounding Arab states, which had taken in refugees—and, in the case of Jordan and Egypt, had also seized control over the West Bank and Gaza Strip, respectively—now presumed to speak on behalf of the Palestinian people. The leaders of these states violently suppressed Palestinian nationalist activism because it threatened their own power and risked provoking another war with Israel for which they were militarily unprepared. Against the wishes of Arab governments, groups of frustrated Palestinian refugees repeatedly launched spontaneous, uncoordinated raids into Israel, destroying property and often killing civilians. Among Palestinians these fighters were called *fedayeen* ("those who sacrifice themselves").[40]

On October 12, 1953, a fedayeen assault in the Israeli town of Yehud, near the West Bank, killed a Jewish woman and her two children. Jordanian authorities, who patrolled the armistice line and regularly imprisoned suspected fedayeen, denounced the murders and promised Israel their full cooperation in tracking down the assailants. But, ignoring the Jordanian response, on October 14 the Israel Defense Forces (IDF) themselves infiltrated the West Bank and launched a revenge attack on the village of Qibya. The strike was ordered by acting defense minister (and soon-to-be Histadrut leader) Pinhas Lavon and sanctioned by Ben-Gurion. In the dark of night, IDF Special Forces Unit 101, commanded by future Israeli prime minister Ariel Sharon, entered Qibya and proceeded to blow up forty-five homes and murder sixty-nine civilians, two-thirds of whom were women and children.[41]

An early example of what would become Israel's decades-long policy of collective punishment and indiscriminate reprisals, the Qibya massacre instantly earned widespread international condemnation. Ben-Gurion initially tried to deny the Israeli government's involvement, claiming that Jewish settlers, tired of fedayeen raids, had carried out the attack on their own. IDF head Moshe Dayan, who designed Israel's policy of disproportionate retaliation, blamed Jordanian authorities by falsely accusing them of supporting and encouraging the Palestinian fedayeen. When an Israeli intelligence officer privately noted that Dayan's allegation was patently untrue, foreign ministry official Aryeh Eilan replied, "If Jordanian complicity is a lie, we have to keep on lying. If there are no proofs, we have to fabricate them."[42]

The UN Security Council did not believe the Israeli government's lies and, with the support of the US government under Republican President Dwight Eisenhower, passed a resolution denouncing the Qibya massacre. The US State Department issued a press release just days after the incident, expressing "deepest sympathy for the families of those who lost their lives in and near Qibya during the recent attack by Israeli forces" and stating that "those who are responsible should be brought to account."[43]

US labor officials—who thought of themselves as expert cold warriors—quickly came to Israel's defense by strongly criticizing the Eisenhower administration. "For the American government to chime in and line up in the United Nations on the side of Jordan, and issue a condemnation resolution against the people of Israel is something that labor cannot take sitting down," said Transport Workers Union president Mike Quill. Meanwhile, CIO secretary-treasurer James B. Carey pointed to the fedayeen raids that preceded the Qibya massacre and declared there was "a large element of justice missing from the UN's censure of Israel."[44]

By this point outspoken defenders of Zionism, union officials with the Jewish Labor Committee (JLC) issued a statement on the Qibya massacre, explaining that "this tragic event cannot be isolated from everything that preceded it," namely the many "infiltration attacks" waged by fedayeen, which the JLC falsely blamed on the "neighboring states around Israel." The JLC further admonished Eisenhower's State Department for its swift denunciation of the massacre, calling on Washington "to be objective" and "to look at both sides of the issue."[45]

Still, the international fallout after Qibya forced US labor leaders to begin paying more attention to the Arab point of view. For example, in a speech to the JLC's Chicago chapter in early 1955, AFL president George Meany (who would become president of the merged AFL-CIO later that year) expressed his hope that American influence could "see to it that we have real peace based on an equitable adjustment of the troubles between the Arabs and the Jewish people in the old Jewish homeland."[46]

§

After the Nakba, some 150,000 Palestinians remained in areas conquered by Israel, becoming a minority group in their own homeland and receiving special ID cards announcing their non-Jewish identity. Though they were made nominal citizens of Israel and granted voting rights, these so-called Israeli Arabs actually lived under a special military regime until 1966 that systematically stripped them of elemental liberties like freedom of speech and freedom of movement, while allowing the state to expropriate their property and hand it over to Jewish settlers.

This mistreatment stemmed from the fact that Israeli law distinguishes between citizenship and nationality, where the collective rights of Jewish nationals are prioritized above the individual rights of non-Jewish nationals, even though all are nominally citizens.[47] Such discrimination was evident in the fact that Jews from anywhere in the world could easily immigrate to Israel while Palestinian refugees were denied the right of return. Norman Thomas, leader of the Socialist Party of America and an ally to some of US labor's more progressive officials, decried Israeli law as "outright discriminatory" for "creating one set of rules for Jews and another for Arabs."[48] Thomas was not the only prominent Westerner making such criticisms. During a 1955 visit to Jerusalem, renowned German Jewish philosopher Hannah Arendt wrote, "They treat the Arabs, those still here, in a way that in itself would be enough to rally the whole world against Israel."[49]

To shape international public opinion in its favor, the Israeli government spun a narrative that their Palestinian minority population enjoyed full equality and economic prosperity—a tale enthusiastically echoed by successive US labor delegations to the country. One such delegation, in August 1954, cheerily claimed that Palestinian citizens of Israel were "living in peace with their Jewish fellow citizens and well on the road to higher living standards and greater freedom than most of the Arab peoples of the Middle East have ever enjoyed." An AFL-CIO delegation four years later, which paid a visit to the Palestinian-majority city of Nazareth, praised "Israel's fundamental belief" that its Arab inhabitants "should enjoy complete freedom and equality."[50]

The 1954 US labor delegation reported that around twelve thousand Arab workers in Israel were union members. "We were greatly impressed with the Histadrut's success in securing for the Arab workers their rights as workers," said Phil Hannah of the Ohio Federation of Labor, one of the visitors.[51]

What Hannah and the rest of the delegation left out was that the Jewish-only Histadrut was still strictly organizing Palestinians into segregated unions under the auspices of its Palestine Labor League (renamed the Israel Labor League after 1948). Indeed, the delegation's report noted that the Histadrut was having difficulty organizing more Palestinian workers, but blamed this on communists and "Arab reactionary nationalist leaders" instead of on the Histadrut's racially exclusionary policies. It was not until 1959 that the Histadrut began allowing Palestinian citizens of Israel to nominally become members, and not until 1965 that they were granted the ability to have full membership with voting rights.[52]

Whether visiting US labor delegations omitted such details deliberately or out of gross ignorance is not clear. In any case, they appeared to be genuinely impressed and enthused by the Histadrut's central role in Israeli society. Wanting to hold up the Histadrut as a model that labor movements around the world (including in the United States) could aspire to, they sought to present it to US union members and allies in the most favorable light possible.[53]

THE SUEZ WAR

In 1952, Egypt's King Farouk was overthrown in a military coup led by Lieutenant Colonel Gamal Abdel Nasser. After becoming Egypt's president, Nasser prioritized the country's social and economic development. He oversaw agrarian reform, education initiatives, and industrialization projects like construction of the Aswan Dam, which would be used for irrigation and hydroelectricity. In addition, he ended Britain's 72-year military occupation of Egypt. Nasserism—as Nasser's political ideology was called—soon spread to other Arab states, fueling popular movements promoting anti-imperialism, secularism, state-led economic growth, and pan-Arab unity.[54]

Although Nasser had fought against Israel in the 1948 war and supported the Palestinian nationalist cause, he initially sought to avoid a resumption of hostilities with the Zionist state. Accordingly, Egyptian forces in control of the 140-square-mile Gaza Strip—where roughly 300,000 Palestinians were crammed into overcrowded refugee camps—worked to prevent fedayeen raids into Israel, just as Jordanian authorities did in the West Bank.

Fearing Nasser's growing popularity in the Arab world and eager to demonstrate Israel's military superiority, in early 1955 the IDF began carrying out a series of limited attacks on Egyptian armed forces in Gaza as part of its larger strategy of disproportionate reprisals. One such assault in February 1955 saw Israeli paratroopers commanded by Ariel Sharon kill between thirty-seven and thirty-nine Egyptian soldiers, with a loss of eight IDF troops.

That August, another Israeli raid on Gaza, in the town of Khan Younis, killed seventy-two Egyptian soldiers. The same week as this assault, a joint AFL-CIO delegation was visiting Israel, led by UAW president Walter Reuther. "[I]f Israel is invaded, no matter from what side, the people of Israel have the right and the moral obligation to stand up and fight," Reuther said during the trip, confirming US labor's support for the attacks on Egyptian forces.[55]

Not wanting to appear unwilling or unable to stand up to Israeli aggression, and facing mass protests by Gaza's Palestinian refugees, Nasser responded by doing what Israel had been accusing him of all along: having Egyptian intelligence sponsor and coordinate fedayeen raids. He also sought to rebuild Egypt's armed forces, which had been virtually destroyed in the 1948 war. After trying to buy modern weaponry from the United States and Britain to no avail, Nasser turned to the Soviet Union and its satellite countries. Although the Soviet bloc was instrumental in the establishment of the Zionist state in 1948, relations between the USSR and Israel had begun souring in the early 1950s.

By September 1955, Egypt reached a deal with Czechoslovakia—the same Soviet-aligned country that had armed the nascent State of Israel seven years earlier—to purchase tanks, fighter planes, bombers, ships, artillery, and other weapons.[56] With Nasser growing closer to their Soviet adversaries, the US and UK governments backed out of an earlier commitment to help finance construction of the Aswan Dam.

As tensions between Egypt and Israel rose, the UAW's Reuther again publicly weighed in on behalf of US labor. "America must not play footsy with Egypt and the other nations under dictatorships in the Middle East," he declared at the NCLI's annual convention in New York in November 1955. "The dictators are opposed to Israel, not because she occupies physically a land area in the Middle East; they are opposed to Israel for what she stands for morally and politically in that part of the world"—a preposterous statement given that Zionist seizure of land in Palestine was the entire crux of the conflict.[57]

By late 1955, Ben-Gurion was preparing for a full-scale war with Egypt. With President Eisenhower unwilling to stoke conflict by selling weapons to Israel (just as his administration had refrained from selling arms to Nasser), the Israelis turned to France. The French were then waging a bloody counterinsurgency war to maintain colonial control over Algeria. The Algerian nationalists fighting for independence were supported and encouraged by Nasser, so the French government was happy to arm Israel to take on their mutual enemy.

Responding to the US and UK governments withdrawing their planned funding of the Aswan Dam, in July 1956, Nasser nationalized the Suez Canal. Built nearly a century earlier, the canal connected the Mediterranean and Red Seas and thus served as a crucial waterway for world trade. It had been owned by the Suez Canal Company, whose largest shareholders were Britain and France. Nasser now asserted public ownership over the canal and promised to compensate the company's shareholders at prevailing market rates. He aimed to use the canal's toll revenues to finance construction of the Aswan Dam.[58]

The French and UK governments were outraged at losing ownership of the Suez Canal, as they were already in the process of losing many of their long-held colonies across Africa and Asia to national liberation movements. Ben-Gurion saw an opportunity. Israel and France, already growing close over their shared hatred for Nasser, now quietly began formulating a plan to attack Egypt and capture the canal, soon bringing Britain in on the scheme. Together, the three governments hatched a secret plot in which the IDF would invade Egypt and thus give British and French forces a pretext to step in and take over the Suez Canal in the name of protecting the vital commercial waterway from the fighting.

On October 29, 1956, the IDF launched its invasion of Egyptian territory, claiming self-defense in the face of ongoing infiltrations by Palestinian fedayeen. As planned, Britain and France immediately intervened, calling on both Israeli and Egyptian soldiers to keep their distance from the Suez Canal, then bombing Egyptian targets and sending in paratroopers to seize the waterway. In less than a week, Israel occupied the Gaza Strip and Sinai Peninsula after Egyptian forces retreated. Israeli tanks rolled into Palestinian refugee camps in Gaza, where the IDF killed around 450 male civilians.

This apparent victory for the tripartite alliance would be short-lived. The world's two superpowers, the United States and Soviet Union, quickly condemned the attack on Egypt and ordered Israel to immediately withdraw its forces from Sinai and Gaza. Eisenhower was personally furious that his British and French allies had not consulted him before proceeding with this rash act. Washington considered imposing sanctions against Israel, while Moscow threatened to use nuclear weapons on the three aggressor nations. A UN resolution also condemned Israel, France, and Britain and called for a ceasefire.

Facing overwhelming international pressure, Ben-Gurion announced on November 9 that the IDF would indeed withdraw from Sinai and Gaza, while British and French forces similarly withdrew from the canal zone the following month. Despite losing the military battle, Nasser had scored a major geopolitical victory, with Zionism's colonial nature made evident to the whole world.[59]

§

Throughout the Suez Crisis, US labor leaders did not waver in their full-throated support for Israel. On November 5, Dubinsky cabled Histadrut general secretary Pinhas Lavon, the former defense minister who had ordered the deadly assault on Qibya two years earlier.

"While action taken by Israel has been [the] subject of criticism by [the] United Nations, we are keenly aware of [the] grave provocations to which Israel has been subjected by threats and attacks by [the] Egyptian dictator and his allies," Dubinsky told Lavon. "At this most critical moment we wish to assure you of our continuing solidarity and brotherly feelings and express hope that out of [the] travail of [the] present situation will emerge [a] lasting peace."[60]

Later that month, the AFL-CIO Executive Council issued a statement acknowledging that "the invasion of Egypt was in violation of the UN Charter" but added that "it was a direct consequence of years of provocation on the part of Egypt." The Jewish Labor Committee similarly characterized Israel's attack as "a desperate and heroic action of self-defense" while blaming the entire incident on "the provocative actions of Egypt's dictator Nasser." Such statements echoed the talking points used by the Israeli government and Histadrut.[61]

THIRD WORLD CONSIDERATIONS

Czechoslovakia's 1955 arms sale to Egypt was an important milestone in Israel's increasingly fraught relationship with the Soviet Union and Eastern bloc. Despite the communist movement's traditional opposition to Zionism, the USSR and its allied nations—including Czechoslovakia—had crucially supported the creation of Israel in 1948 in the hopes of winning a new ally in the Middle East. Grateful for the help, and eager to retain Moscow's cooperation in allowing Eastern European Jews to emigrate to Israel, the Israeli government and Histadrut initially tried to remain neutral in the budding Cold War—a policy they called "non-identification."

But in 1950, Ben-Gurion symbolically joined with the West in publicly condemning Soviet-backed North Korea's invasion of South Korea. Now that fewer and fewer immigrants were coming from Eastern Europe, the Israeli prime minister was less concerned about alienating Moscow. On the other hand, Ben-Gurion knew he would need Washington's political support in his efforts to get West Germany to pay reparations to Israel for the crimes of the Nazi regime. Soon after staking his position on the Korean War, Ben-Gurion began seeking military cooperation with Western countries.

Israeli-Soviet relations took a further hit in late 1952, when several Jewish leaders of the Communist Party of Czechoslovakia were executed for treason after a show trial in which prosecutors denounced Zionism and Israel. Then, in January 1953, the Politburo accused nine doctors (six of them Jewish) of attempting to poison Soviet leaders. A month later, far-right Zionist terrorists retaliated by bombing the Soviet consulate in Tel Aviv, injuring several people and prompting Moscow to temporarily cut off diplomatic relations with Israel. Although these tensions would be somewhat eased after Stalin's death in March 1953, the Zionist state was now solidly on the side of the West in the Cold War, while the Soviets would increasingly provide military and economic aid to Israel's Arab enemies like Nasser.[62]

§

As the peoples of Africa, Asia, and the Middle East threw off their colonial shackles between the late 1940s and early 1970s, they established newly independent states with hopes of quickly developing their economies to enjoy the fruits of modern industrial life. These countries, together with those of Latin America and the Caribbean, constituted what became known as the "Third World," consciously refusing to align with either superpower in the Cold War contest for geopolitical supremacy. Alongside figures like Indian Prime Minister Jawaharlal Nehru and Indonesian President Sukarno, Nasser was one of the most prominent leaders of this new international bloc.

Despite the Third World's declared neutralism, Washington and Moscow each feared that these newly independent states would align with the rival superpower in the Cold War contest for geopolitical supremacy. By offering economic and military aid, education and training, and scientific and cultural exchanges, the United States and USSR both sought to demonstrate to the nations of Africa, Asia, the Middle East, and Latin America that their respective political and economic systems were the correct path toward development and "modernization."

As ardent cold warriors with close ties to the political establishment, many top US labor officials were themselves eager to show Third World workers that American-style democracy and capitalism would deliver greater material benefits than the "totalitarian" communism of the Soviet Union, People's Republic of China, or Cuba. In trying to make this tough sell to foreign workers, in the 1950s and 1960s, US labor leaders frequently pointed to the example of Labor Zionism in Israel. Various AFL-CIO delegations to Israel in this period publicly lauded the country's achievements in worker-centered nation-building, with a rapidly growing economy and a supposedly flourishing democratic society that they argued other developing countries should aspire to emulate.[63] Holding up Israel as a model for developing countries to follow also served as a rebuke to Israel's main adversary at the time—Nasser—whose influence was expanding from the Middle East into sub-Saharan Africa.

"We in the American labor movement have the same goals as you do . . . the use of democratic methods and modern technology to build a better life for the average people," Amalgamated Clothing Workers president Jacob Potofsky said on a 1958 delegation to Israel. The Zionist state, he insisted, "is truly a laboratory for social and economic development, and American labor is proud that it early recognized the desire of Israel and its people to build a better society and to renew an old civilization from the sands of the desert."[64]

Speaking at a 1961 dinner in Washington hosted by the National Committee for Labor Israel, AFL-CIO president Meany said he could not "repeat too often and too forcefully to the workers, to the people, and to the leaders of all the countries which have recently won or are still fighting to win their national independence: The experience of the trade union movement and democracy in Israel can be of the greatest help to you in building your countries into virile democracies with healthy and vital free trade unions and sound economies."[65]

As dutiful adjuncts to the US empire and ardent anticommunists in their own right, American labor officials sought to transmit their brand of pro-West, nonradical unionism to Third World workers during the Cold War. To accomplish this, they funded and organized numerous educational and training programs for union members around the globe. These specifically included foreign institutes in Latin America, Africa, and Asia that were run by the AFL-CIO but bankrolled by the US Agency for International Development that taught workers how to resist left-wing influence in their unions.

In 1960, the AFL-CIO helped the Histadrut establish the Afro-Asian Institute for Labor Studies and Cooperation. Based in Tel Aviv and offering three- to six-month courses in English and French for both male and female union leaders from Asia, Africa, and the Caribbean, the institute focused on the practical role of workers in economic development. Taught by academics from the Hebrew University of Jerusalem, courses focused on how to manage agricultural cooperatives and administer trade unions.[66]

But like other AFL-CIO-sponsored training programs targeting Third World workers in this period, the institute also functioned as a subtle form of anticommunist propaganda. As one Histadrut official wrote to Meany in 1963: "The Histadrut is especially proud of the fact that it has succeeded in inculcating the students with an awareness of the ascendancy of democratic values and with the faith and consciousness that a country can make a rapid transition into the 20th century through individual freedom of choice in contrast to the dictatorial forced marches of totalitarian regimes."[67]

Within its first four years, the Afro-Asian Institute claimed to have trained 741 students from fifty-seven countries, mostly from Africa. The AFL-CIO and its affiliated unions provided funds for student scholarships, including $120,000 in 1962 alone. The UAW was one of the institute's largest benefactors, donating $150,000 between 1962 and 1969. The institute was formally run by the Histadrut, but Dubinsky, Potofsky, and Reuther served on its board and Meany held the honorary title of cochair.[68] The school would last for fifteen years, ultimately training over 3,700 African, Asian, and Caribbean workers.[69]

THE 1967 WAR

After the 1956 Suez Crisis, an "Arab Cold War" developed in the Middle East and North Africa, pitting radical nationalist movements like Nasserism and Ba'athism against conservative, royalist forces. The former, which were led by countries like Egypt and Syria, increasingly looked to the Soviets for economic and military aid. The latter were tied to the monarchies of Saudi Arabia and Jordan and backed by the United States and Britain.

This rivalry fueled a civil war in North Yemen during the 1960s. Revolutionaries in that country overthrew King Muhammad al-Badr and established a republican government, but armies loyal to the monarchy—and aided by Saudi Arabia and Jordan—fought to put the king back on the throne. As the leader of the wider Arab nationalist movement, Nasser sent sixty thousand Egyptian troops into North Yemen to protect the new republican government.[70]

Attempting to bring about unity amid this unfolding conflict, in early 1964, Nasser hosted a summit of the Arab League in Cairo. There, representatives of the different Arab states found common ground in their shared opposition to Israel, particularly disputes with the Zionist state over control of the waters of the Jordan River. The summit resulted in the founding of the Palestine Liberation Organization (PLO), a nationalist political formation dedicated to establishing an Arab Palestinian state within the boundaries of the old British Mandate, thus doing away with the 16-year-old State of Israel.[71]

Meanwhile, Palestinian nationalists in the post-Nakba diaspora were already organizing around this aim without the formal blessing of Nasser and the Arab League. Dedicated to the belief that Palestinians would have to lead the way to their own liberation, in 1959, a group of young refugees who had grown up in Gaza and Cairo established the underground nationalist organization Fatah (meaning "opening" or "victory"). Looking to Third World liberation movements like those of Algeria, Cuba, and Vietnam for inspiration, Fatah called for direct action to free Palestine from colonial domination.

Unlike the elite notables who had led the Palestinian national movement during the Mandate period, Fatah was composed primarily of refugees who had working-class, lower-middle-class, and rural backgrounds. Despite their mostly humble origins, they had benefited from the educational opportunities that became more universally available to Palestinians after the collapse of the Ottoman Empire, first through the British Mandate authorities and then through the United Nations Relief and Works Agency (the official UN entity providing aid to Palestinian refugees from 1950 onward).[72]

Yasser Arafat, one of the organization's young cofounders, would soon become the most prominent leader in the Palestinian nationalist cause. After UN peacekeepers were deployed to the Sinai Peninsula in the wake of the Suez War, Fatah transferred its base of operations from Egypt to Syria and began preparing guerilla attacks against Israel.

Acting independently of the PLO and Arab League, Fatah moved to take decisive action in the ongoing battle over access to freshwater. On January 1, 1965, Fatah guerillas snuck into Israel and attempted to bomb part of the National Water Carrier, one of the infrastructure projects partly funded through bonds purchased by US labor. Although the bomb failed to explode, the attack served as a symbolic victory for Fatah as it demonstrated the ability of Palestinians to take matters into their own hands without relying solely on the governments of Arab states to act on their behalf.

§

After a radical faction of Ba'athists took power in Syria in 1966, tensions increased between that country and Israel—punctuated by the water conflict and the Syrian government's encouragement of Palestinian guerillas. In April 1967, a border skirmish resulted in Israel's air force shooting down six Soviet-made Syrian MiGs (fighter planes). Soon after this incident, Israeli prime minister Levi Eshkol (who had replaced Ben-Gurion upon his retirement four years earlier) and IDF chief of staff Yitzak Rabin openly threatened to overthrow Syria's government.

Receiving Soviet warnings of Israel's potentially aggressive intentions against his fellow Arab nationalists, Nasser felt compelled to respond. With much of his nation's army bogged down in North Yemen's civil war, the Egyptian president knew he could ill afford another armed conflict with the Zionist state. Nasser correctly surmised that Israel's well-equipped military—which was secretly developing nuclear weapons—was more powerful than all the Arab armies combined. Nevertheless, to safeguard his prestige in the Arab world by showing that he could get tough with Israel, that May Nasser sent troops into the Sinai Peninsula near Egypt's boundary with Israel and blockaded Israeli shipping between the Sinai and Red Sea.

With these actions, Nasser unwittingly gave the Israeli government pretext for a war that would dramatically reshape the contours of the struggle for Palestine to the present day.[73]

§

Immediately after Egypt began its blockade of Israeli ships in May 1967, the US labor movement jumped into action. Thomas "Teddy" Gleason, president of the International Longshoremen's Association, announced that his union's members across the East Coast ports would refuse to load or unload any Egyptian or Syrian vessels until the blockade was lifted. The respective presidents of the National Maritime Union and Seafarers International Union—Joe Curran and Phil Hall—similarly vowed that their members would boycott any Egyptian or allied ships they encountered.

Meanwhile, George Meany had multiple phone conversations with Democratic President Lyndon B. Johnson to make sure he knew of the waterfront unions' protest and to pressure him to stand with Israel. The White House was also flooded with telegrams from the needle trades unions calling on the president to ensure open international waterways for Israeli ships.[74] On May 23, the US president gave a speech expressing dismay over Nasser's actions, stating that "a blockade of Israel['s] shipping is illegal and potentially disastrous to the cause of peace."[75] At the same time, Johnson called for the dispute to be settled diplomatically through the UN.

Three days later, Israeli foreign minister Abba Eban met with Johnson at the White House to warn that an Egyptian attack on Israel was inevitable and to ask how the United States would respond when and if such an attack happened. Johnson urged restraint. He explained that US intelligence agencies were "unanimous" in their assessment that Egypt's recent deployments to Sinai were only defensive, and that Nasser had no intention of striking. Before the meeting with Eban, National Security Advisor Walt Rostow had told the president that the grim picture being presented by the Israelis was not an honest assessment but more likely "a gambit intended to influence the US" to provide

Israel with military aid and approve of Israeli military initiatives. Johnson told Eban that even in the unlikely event the Egyptians did attack, he was confident the far stronger Israeli military would "whip the hell out of them."[76]

Meanwhile, Histadrut general secretary Aharon Becker was sending out messages to labor leaders around the noncommunist world asking them to express their "great friendship and appreciation" for Israel amid the standoff with Nasser. Despite the US intelligence community's confidence that the IDF could easily "whip the hell out of" its Arab neighbors, Becker—like many other Israelis and their foreign allies—dramatically framed the situation as nothing less than an existential crisis for the Jewish people, deliberately weaponizing the memory of the Holocaust to drum up support.

"In this fateful hour to Israel and the Jewish people who suffered so much in the past and gave so many sacrifices during the Nazi regime," Becker wrote to ILGWU president Louis Stulberg, "Histadrut and the whole Israel[i] labour movement stand solidly behind the Israel[i] government[']s determination to secure by all means our national and physical existence [and] the integrity of our borders." Stulberg, who had succeeded David Dubinsky upon the latter's retirement one year earlier, replied, "We wish to express solidarity with you in your present moment of crisis. . . . The unprovoked threat of [Egypt] is not simply an assault on your right to live as a free nation[,] it is also an assault on the world[']s pillar of democracy in the Middle East."[77]

UAW president Walter Reuther, also contacted by Becker, promised that "in this hour of crisis in the Middle East, on behalf of the officers and members of the UAW I send you our pledge of continued friendship and solidarity." Similarly responding to the Histadrut's pleas for international solidarity, the Jewish Labor Committee mobilized union locals across the country to pass pro-Israel resolutions.[78]

On June 1, Meany—ever the cold warrior—issued a statement blaming the entire situation on "Soviet machinations" and arguing that Nasser was merely a puppet of the USSR, which he said aimed to "destroy Israel" to ensure communist domination over the oil-rich Middle East.[79] That same day, Reuther and the other top officers of the UAW also issued a public statement calling for a diplomatic solution to the crisis, which was sent to the White House, State Department, and both chambers of Congress.

"The peoples of the Middle East have been contending and still must contend with grave problems of economic and social underdevelopment," the UAW officials wrote, seeming to lecture Arab governments. "Their prospects for a better life will not be served by political instability and military adventures. A 'holy war' by the Arab states against the people of Israel will, in fact, further disrupt their societies and set back their economic development by many years."[80]

With increasing popular support both at home and in the United States, the Israeli government prepared to launch a first strike against Egypt, Syria, and Jordan (whose king had recently signed a mutual defense pact with Nasser amid the escalating regional tensions). But not wishing to repeat the outcome of the Suez War, they wanted to first get Washington's permission. Though President Johnson had been urging restraint and diplomacy, he was beginning to reconsider.

The US was already losing geopolitical prestige by failing to secure a quick and decisive military victory against communist insurgents in Vietnam. And now the blockade imposed by Nasser—a Soviet ally—was only further damaging US credibility in the Cold War. Seeing the intelligence assessments about the IDF's superior strength, and not wanting to commit US troops to the Middle East amid the unfolding fiasco in Vietnam, Johnson may have believed it was in Washington's best interest to let Israel attack. The steady stream of pro-Israel advocacy coming from

American Zionist groups and Johnson's allies in US labor may have also influenced the president.

On June 1, Major General Meir Amit—the head of Israel's foreign intelligence agency Mossad—held a secret meeting with US Defense Secretary Robert McNamara. In the meeting, Amit indicated that Israel planned to attack first and expressed hope that the United States would provide diplomatic support, as well as any long-term military and economic aid that might become necessary. Crucially, McNamara did not protest. Instead of a "red light," the US government was now giving the Israelis a "yellow light" (as some scholars have called it), which effectively allowed them to launch what history remembers as the Six-Day War.[81]

§

On June 5, the war began when the Israeli air force carried out a surprise attack on Egyptian, Syrian, and Jordanian airfields, destroying four hundred warplanes on the ground in a matter of hours. With their air forces virtually annihilated, the already weaker Arab militaries were now at an even greater disadvantage.[82]

That same evening, approximately 3,500 local trade unionists gathered at the Manhattan Center for a pro-Israel rally hosted by the New York City Central Labor Council. Speakers included Retail, Wholesale and Department Store Union president Max Greenberg; Building Service Employees International Union president David Sullivan; ILGWU vice president Charles Zimmerman; New York City mayor John Lindsay; and Israeli diplomat Michael Comay. Whipped up with war fever and anti-Arab hostility, the crowd loudly booed when Nasser's name was mentioned, with Zimmerman calling the Egyptian president a "little Hitler." At one point, a fistfight broke out in the crowd when it was mistakenly assumed that someone in the audience was opposing calls for financial aid to Israel.[83]

A week earlier, 350 delegates from fourteen US unions had attended the American Trade Union Council for Histadrut's conference in the Pocono Mountains, where they discussed "Arab aggression against the State of Israel." The delegates established a Histadrut Emergency Fund, which immediately received a pledge of $1 million from the ILGWU and Amalgamated Clothing Workers, to help provide humanitarian relief for Histadrut members affected by the war. Once the fighting began on June 5, the Jewish Labor Committee promised "every effort to assist the people of Israel in their struggle for survival, security, and the preservation of their national identity."[84]

§

With Egypt as their main foe, in the first three days of the war, the IDF again captured the Gaza Strip and Sinai Peninsula, just as they had temporarily done during the Suez War eleven years earlier. As Jordan shelled Israeli targets in accordance with its recent security pact with Egypt, the IDF also took the opportunity to conquer East Jerusalem and the entire West Bank by June 7. Then, realizing just how vulnerable enemy forces truly were, the IDF also seized the Golan Heights, a region of Syria near its boundary with Israel, by June 10.

A UN-brokered ceasefire was signed on June 11, bringing hostilities to a halt. After only six days, Israel now occupied all of historic Palestine, as well as parts of Egypt and Syria. Approximately one million Arabs—including hundreds of thousands of Palestinians in the Gaza Strip, West Bank, and East Jerusalem—were now suddenly living under Israeli military rule.[85]

Writing to the Histadrut near the end of the war, Reuther praised the "gallant and successful defense of Israel in the face of overwhelming odds," repeating the false notion that the far stronger Israeli military was the underdog, which he said had "inspired people who love freedom and justice everywhere." The UAW president continued, "We pledge our continued friendship, solidarity and support to the end that a just and enduring peace may be established so that the resources and the spirit of the people of Israel, with the continuing leadership of Histadrut, can be harnessed to the rewarding purposes of peace. Shalom."[86]

§

In the aftermath of the Six-Day War—in which Israel's show of strength put the Arab states and their Soviet patrons to shame—the US government's support for the Zionist state, which had already been strengthening in the preceding years, became more reflexive than contingent. After 1967, the United States overtook France as Israel's number one provider of arms.[87]

Washington's policy on Israel was crystallized in United Nations Security Council Resolution 242 (UNSC 242), approved thanks to US influence in November 1967. The resolution conditionally accepted Israel's territorial conquests in the Six-Day War. Instead of ordering the IDF to immediately withdraw from the West Bank, Gaza, Sinai, and Golan Heights to restore the status quo ante, UNSC 242 said that any withdrawal from the newly occupied territories would have to be conditioned on bilateral peace negotiations with the now weakened neighboring Arab states—a concept popularly known as "land for peace." What's more, by not also calling for Israel's withdrawal from the territory that the UN partition plan had designated for a Palestinian Arab state twenty years earlier, the resolution tacitly recognized the 1949 armistice lines as Israel's permanent international borders.

UNSC 242 failed to make any mention of the Palestinians beyond a quick reference to "the refugee problem." By treating the entire conflict as a matter between Israel and the Arab states, the resolution rendered the stateless Palestinians all but invisible.

When she became Israeli prime minister two years later, veteran Mapai politician Golda Meir felt emboldened in part by the UN's disappearing act to infamously state that "there is no such thing as Palestinians."[88]

A few weeks after UNSC 242 was approved, Histadrut leader Aharon Becker attended the AFL-CIO's annual convention to thank US labor for its support during the war. "I know I am among friends, steadfast over the decades, and proven again in those fateful days we in Israel lived through in May and June of this year," Becker told the delegates. "You stood foursquare with us in our great dangers."[89]

§

For its part, the ILGWU—which, under Dubinsky, had long avoided purchasing State of Israel bonds—announced shortly after the Six-Day War that it would now be buying $1 million in bonds "as a symbol of our fraternity and a mark of our sympathy." The union's new president, Stulberg, also instructed ILGWU officials at the local and regional levels to strongly encourage rank-and-file members to make personal donations to the recently created Histadrut Emergency Fund.[90]

This latter move provoked the ire of the New York–based Action Committee on American-Arab Relations and its founder, Dr. Mohammad T. Mehdi. An Iraqi immigrant and staunch advocate for the Palestinian cause, Mehdi took inspiration from the Arab nationalist movements sweeping the Middle East as well as the emerging Black Power movement in the United States. He and his relatively small Action Committee represented a new assertiveness among Arab Americans beginning to take root in the late 1960s, particularly when it came to the issue of Palestine. As historian Pamela Pennock explains, Mehdi's committee organized pickets outside events where State of Israel bonds were sold, filed antidiscrimination lawsuits, and demanded US media outlets give equal time to Palestinian perspectives.[91]

In a cable to the ILGWU president sent on June 19, 1967, Mehdi said his Action Committee had "received hundreds of complaints that you have been forcing members of your union to contribute one day's pay to [the] Israeli drive. Many women complainants were forced to contribute as a result of threats that they would lose their jobs if they did not. This action of yours represents not labor unionism but labor dictatorship." After advising the union to return the funds to the members who had allegedly been intimidated into donating, Mehdi concluded, "Your failure to respect rights of non-Zionists and anti-Zionists [*sic*] union members will bring our retaliation."[92]

It is unclear whether the ILGWU responded, or if any "retaliation" ever occurred—but the complaint signaled how, in a fast-changing social and political environment, US union officials would no longer be able to wholeheartedly advocate and fundraise for Israel without receiving pushback from Arab Americans and Palestine solidarity activists.

CHAPTER 4

STRAINED FRIENDSHIP

The brutality and deceit that defined the US government's war on Vietnam, waged from the mid-1960s to early 1970s in the name of "containing" communism, led many Americans to see Washington's foreign policy as imperialistic rather than altruistic. Overlapping with contemporaneous movements for racial justice, women's equality, gay and lesbian rights, and environmental protection, the antiwar movement in this period served as a sharp rebuke to the social and political status quo of Cold War America.

It was during this swell of radicalism that the Six-Day War occurred, after which Israel imposed a military occupation over the nearly one million Arabs living in the West Bank, Gaza Strip, East Jerusalem, Sinai Peninsula, and Golan Heights. Just as they were already organizing to oppose American racism and imperialism, many young US leftists started openly denouncing Israel as a violent colonial state. This was especially true of activists associated with the growing call for Black Power.

While the mainstream movement for African American civil rights sought racial integration through nonviolence and legal changes, Black Power took a more revolutionary and militant stance against white supremacy, capitalism, and imperialism. Inspired by earlier expressions of Black nationalism and by

Third World liberation struggles, the Black Power movement took off in the late 1960s, in the context of the Vietnam War. Its emergence signified a rift among those involved in the wider struggle for African American freedom. This divide took various forms, including conflicting views of Zionism.

As historian Robin D. G. Kelley has noted, between the 1940s and 1960s, Black American intellectuals, activists, and political leaders overwhelmingly sympathized with Zionism because they identified with Jews suffering persecution. This included A. Philip Randolph, president of the Brotherhood of Sleeping Car Porters and the most prominent Black labor leader in the United States. Like his white counterparts in union officialdom, in early 1948, Randolph came out in support of the establishment of Israel. "Because Negroes are themselves a victim of hate and persecution, oppression and outrage," he said at the time, "they should be the first to be willing to stand up and be counted on the side of the struggle of the Jew to achieve partition of Palestine and . . . to set up a commonwealth in Palestine."[1]

Nineteen years later, when the Six-Day War began, a now 78-year-old Randolph was the most high-profile speaker at the pro-Israel union rally in the Manhattan Center hosted by the New York City Central Labor Council. There, he promised that "22 million black Americans of the United States" would fully support Israel in its efforts to defeat its Arab enemies. As noted in the Histadrut newspaper *Davar*, Randolph's message stood in contrast to the political orientation of younger, more radical African American activists who considered Egyptian president Nasser to be an anticolonial hero.[2]

Indeed, groups associated with the Black Power movement, including the Black Panther Party and Student Nonviolent Coordinating Committee, responded to the 1967 war by condemning Israel's new territorial conquests and expressing solidarity with Palestinians.[3] As Black Power gained popularity among

African American union members, particularly in the auto industry, it would help inspire rank-and-file challenges to labor officialdom's ironclad support for Zionism.

§

Just as a younger generation of US radicals were beginning to voice opposition to Israel, and as public opinion became more critical of Cold War foreign policy, the power of the American labor movement coincidentally started to erode. From the late 1960s onward, US industrial corporations increasingly used speedups, automation, outsourcing, and offshoring to keep profits up in response to slowing growth rates and increasing foreign competition. The resultant factory shutdowns and mass layoffs, combined with intensifying anti-union attacks by corporations and right-wing politicians, meant US union density went into a decline that has continued to the present day.

Faced with these challenges, in the 1970s and 1980s the American Federation of Labor and Congress of Industrial Organizations (AFL-CIO)'s anticommunist officials clung ever tighter to their Cold War ideology and, relatedly, to their relationships with Labor Zionist leaders in Israel. Having benefited from the US-dominated international capitalist system since the 1940s, they seemed to believe that if only the American empire could be rejuvenated after suffering a humiliating blow in Vietnam, US labor might have a chance at hanging onto its fleeting influence. Seeing Israel as an essential Cold War ally amid the rise of revolutionary anti-imperialist movements around the world, US union officials would remain staunchly committed to Zionism in this period—even as social and political developments in the United States and Middle East made it increasingly difficult to do so.

LOCAL 1707

Between Israel's founding and 1973, US unions donated some $17.6 million to the Histadrut, the nation-building Labor Zionist institution that doubled as a labor federation. In 1975, AFL-CIO president George Meany called Israel "the only nation I know of that is the creation of a free trade union—the Histadrut," and one observer noted that if "the State of Israel was a creation of Histadrut . . . then American labor had much to do with the creation of Histadrut."[4]

Various public facilities continued being built in Israel with US union money throughout the 1960s and 1970s, including the George Meany Sports Stadium in Nazareth, the Walter Reuther Children's Home in Holon, the Service Employees International Union's medical clinic in the village of Isfiya, the Ed Miller Youth Center in Tel Aviv (named after the president of the Hotel Employees and Restaurant Employees union), a rest home built by the International Union of Painters in Kfar Blum Kibbutz (which had begun as the Léon Blum Colony decades earlier with help from US labor fundraising), a cold storage plant built by the Amalgamated Meat Cutters in Kiryat Shmona, and the five-story Potofsky Health Clinic built by the Amalgamated Clothing Workers in Bnei Brak.

Although US labor faced numerous political and generational splits during the era of the Vietnam War, in 1972 Meany proudly declared that "there is no disagreement within the American labor movement when it comes to the State of Israel."[5] But despite this confident assertion, the friendship between the US labor movement and Israel was not entirely harmonious. One of the first serious tests to the relationship involved American workers employed by the Development Corporation for Israel (DCI), the entity that sold Israeli bonds in the United States.

The DCI's approximately five hundred professional and clerical employees—who worked at the organization's New York headquarters and sixty branch offices across the country—were represented by Local 1707 of the AFL-CIO-affiliated American Federation of State, County, and Municipal Employees (AFSCME). Between 1961 and 1971 alone, AFSCME Local 1707 went on strike against the DCI four times to secure new collective bargaining agreements after negotiations broke down. The 1961 work stoppage only lasted a few days, as did a strike in 1967, which occurred only days prior to the Six-Day War. Both ended with the union and DCI agreeing to new two-year contracts with decent raises.[6]

When the latter contract expired in May 1969, DCI workers with Local 1707 again went on strike across the country, this time during a national Israeli bonds drive. The strike made headlines in Philadelphia when workers picketed outside the luxurious Bellevue Stratford Hotel, where an Israel-sponsored gala dinner honoring former US vice president (and failed 1968 Democratic presidential candidate) Hubert Humphrey was being held. The pro-union Humphrey refused to cross the picket line, which threatened to derail the evening's festivities. But at 7:15 p.m., an emergency court injunction was served declaring the picket to be an "unlawful secondary boycott," since the hotel itself was not being struck. With the picketers leaving upon being told of the injunction, Humphrey arrived an hour later alongside Mayor James H. J. Tate and the dinner went ahead.[7]

Soon after the incident with Humphrey, Local 1707's strike ended when another two-year contract agreement was reached. But when that contract expired in May 1971, the DCI's five hundred professional and clerical employees walked off the job yet again to demand a successor agreement with good pay and benefits. This work stoppage would last five weeks and become the most contentious episode between Israel and American labor up to that point.

Twenty days into the 1971 strike, with no signs of progress at the bargaining table, several US unions and central labor councils began pulling back from their commitments to purchase bonds in the hopes of pressuring the DCI into reaching a deal with Local 1707. Several union locals and central labor councils across the country canceled planned events promoting the sale of Israeli bonds. Emil Mazey, secretary-treasurer of the UAW, sent a letter to the DCI warning that his influential union would not purchase bonds until the strike was settled.

Meanwhile, a committee representing US-based Labor Zionist groups put out a statement calling for a swift settlement of the work stoppage, saying, "We cannot look upon this as an ordinary labor-management dispute since the vital interests of Israel are involved"—a reference to the importance of US labor's continued investment in the Zionist state. But the strike dragged on, with management claiming they already offered a generous compensation package and that Local 1707 was being unreasonable.

On June 16, 1971, thirty-one days into the stoppage, the New York City Central Labor Council formally called on its affiliated unions and 1.2 million members to stop purchasing Israeli bonds and to refrain from participating in all bonds functions until the strike was resolved. This was the first time the US labor movement explicitly used its substantial financial investments in Israel as leverage against an arm of the Zionist state. Importantly, it was only for the sake of resolving a labor dispute inside the United States and had nothing to do with supporting the Palestinian people. Indeed, Local 1707 members and their labor allies made sure to clarify that they were still strongly pro-Israel and that they were only critical of the DCI management's bargaining position. On the picket lines, strikers carried signs reading, "Israel Needs Us."[8]

Only four days after the New York City Central Labor Council's statement, a tentative agreement was reached between the DCI and Local 1707, granting the pay increases the union had been seeking.[9]

THE OCTOBER 1973 WAR

Tensions between Israel and the neighboring Arab states—especially Egypt—continued in the years following the Six-Day War of 1967. Wanting to recover the territory lost to Israel in that conflict, Nasser eventually rejected the UN-brokered ceasefire in 1969 and ordered artillery shelling, air raids, and hit-and-run attacks in the Israeli-occupied Sinai Peninsula. Under the leadership of Prime Minister Golda Meir, Israel responded in early 1970 by bombing Egypt's interior, which in turn prompted the Soviet Union to provide Egypt with a hefty supply of surface-to-air missiles, anti-aircraft guns, radar systems, and MiG fighter planes. This conflict became known as "the war of attrition."

Nasser died of a heart attack in late 1970 and was succeeded by his deputy, Anwar al-Sadat. The two countries remained at a stalemate into 1973, with no diplomatic activity over the future of the territories occupied by Israel since the Six-Day War. Maintaining the post-1967 status quo was favorable to Meir as it kept Israel in a stronger political and military position. Further, it emboldened Zionist expansionists to build settlements in the newly occupied territories to literally lay the groundwork for eventual annexation. Despite settlement of occupied territory blatantly violating international law, Israel's Labor Zionist government encouraged it.

The maintenance of the status quo between Israel and Egypt was preferred not only by Meir, but also by the administration of US President Richard Nixon at the urging of National Security Advisor (and soon-to-be Secretary of State) Henry Kissinger. By the early 1970s, Washington had come to see Israel as a vital US ally in the oil-rich region for maintaining geopolitical "stability" and warding off Soviet influence. Kissinger, who viewed the Middle East through a Cold War lens, believed that a lack of diplomatic progress would discourage the Arab states and thus alienate them from their Soviet patrons for not being able to deliver results.[10]

To break the ongoing deadlock, on October 6, 1973, Sadat and Syria's Ba'athist president Hafez al-Assad launched a surprise attack on the areas under Israeli occupation. Meir and other Israeli officials were taken by surprise, not only because October 6 was Yom Kippur—the holiest day on the Jewish calendar—but also because they had become militarily overconfident in the previous years. Neither Sadat nor Assad believed their armies could defeat the far better trained and equipped Israel Defense Forces (IDF). Their objective was only to retake some territory in the Sinai and Golan Heights, respectively, to change the realities on the ground and therefore alter the diplomatic picture. After quickly regrouping from the initial attacks, the IDF regained the initiative and sent Egyptian and Syrian forces into retreat.[11]

Meanwhile, Nixon and the US Congress stepped in by authorizing $2.2 billion in emergency military aid to Israel. As a form of political retaliation, Saudi Arabia and other Arab members of the Organization of Petroleum Exporting Countries imposed an oil embargo on the United States and allied nations, causing energy prices to skyrocket. Gasoline for cars had to be rationed, national speed limits were established, and other measures were taken to conserve petroleum.

The fighting stopped on October 25, through another UN-brokered ceasefire. The October War, or Yom Kippur War as it is called by Israelis, gave the governments and populations of the Arab states a renewed sense of confidence. It also forced Washington to recognize the urgency of reestablishing diplomacy between Israel and its neighbors, with Kissinger shuttling back and forth between Jerusalem, Cairo, and Damascus in early 1974 to negotiate disengagement agreements.[12]

§

As in other armed conflicts between Israel and its neighbors, US labor officials fiercely supported the Zionist state during the October War. In the days after the war broke out, the American Trade Union Council for Histadrut instructed affiliated unions to send messages to Congress and the White House demanding emergency US military and economic aid be given to Israel.

The AFL-CIO held its biennial convention in Bal Harbour, Florida, between October 18 and 23 as the fighting in the Middle East raged. In addition to calling on Nixon to resign amid the unfolding Watergate scandal, the delegates unanimously approved a resolution to "stand with Israel," "indict" the USSR for "equipping, training, and encouraging the armed forces of the Arabs" in their "war of aggression," and urge the US government to resupply Israel through a "massive airlift."[13] Observers noted labor's apparent unity on Israel, which stood in contrast to the sharp disagreements over the Vietnam War that had partly led to the UAW's withdrawal from the federation a few years earlier (the auto workers' union would later rejoin the AFL-CIO in 1981). In the middle of the convention, Golda Meir personally telephoned AFL-CIO president George Meany to thank American labor for its support.

Immediately after the convention, as news broke of the ceasefire in the Middle East, the AFL-CIO Executive Council established a war relief fund for Israel to assist Histadrut members affected by the fighting. While the AFL-CIO itself put up an initial $50,000, Meany called on the top officers of affiliated unions to take up collections among their members. The International Ladies' Garment Workers' Union (ILGWU) raised $300,000 within days. At the same time, the heads of the AFL-CIO's maritime unions, including the Seafarers International Union and International Longshoremen's Association, threatened to boycott all ships carrying cargo to or from the Soviet Union if the ceasefire broke down.[14]

Also shortly after the Bal Harbour convention, the ILG-WU's general secretary-treasurer, Sol Chick Chaikin, flew to Israel to assess the scene. Landing at Lod Airport in Tel Aviv, Chaikin observed a hangar where several large US C-5A transport planes were delivering military equipment. Over the course of about a week, Chaikin visited the front lines in the Golan Heights and Sinai Peninsula and made a stop in Jerusalem, meeting with Israeli government officials to discuss the military and diplomatic situation. Chaikin was back in New York by early November, where he spoke at the fiftieth anniversary dinner of the National Committee for Labor Israel and described the battlefields he had just witnessed, praising the US labor movement for aiding the Zionist state.[15]

During the first week of November, the New York City Central Labor Council hosted a gathering of one thousand local unionists at the Manhattan Center to rally support and raise funds for Israel. Only two years earlier, the same labor council had urged its members not to purchase Israeli bonds during AFSCME Local 1707's monthlong strike, but that had only been a tactic to pressure the Development Corporation for Israel at the bargaining table. Now, at the November 1973 rally, a telegram from Meany was read aloud to the audience. "Israel bears a union label," the AFL-CIO president said, referring to the strength and influence of the Histadrut. "There can be no greater threat to Israel today than an ambiguous or indecisive American stand. Your actions can help communicate to the entire world the determination of [the] American people that Israel shall survive and prosper."[16]

The following January, a five-man AFL-CIO delegation visited Israel on the Histadrut's invitation. Led by AFL-CIO secretary-treasurer Lane Kirkland, International Longshoremen's Association president Teddy Gleason, and Amalgamated Clothing Workers president Murray Finley, the visitors issued a joint statement with the Histadrut condemning Arab and Soviet "aggression," while also vowing to use US labor's influence in Congress to lobby for increased military assistance to Israel.[17]

Unlike previous wars involving Israel, American labor officialdom's response to the October War prompted a notable rank-and-file rebellion, specifically within the United Auto Workers. Although several grassroots union reform movements sprung up in the 1970s targeting entrenched bureaucracies in the UAW, United Mine Workers, United Steelworkers, and Teamsters, this one would be unique in that its chief complaint was US labor's unflinching support for Zionism.

PALESTINIAN NATIONALISM AND ARAB AMERICAN AUTO WORKERS

Following the Six-Day War of 1967, Palestinian nationalism experienced a political and cultural renaissance. Palestinian intellectuals like writer Ghassan Kanafani and poet Mahmoud Darwish articulated a national identity based on a shared sense of dispossession and alienation. In addition to the Yasser Arafat–led Fatah, several other militant nationalist groups gained prominence, including the Popular Front for the Liberation of Palestine (PFLP), a secular Marxist-Leninist organization that became especially known in the West for hijacking commercial airplanes in the late 1960s and early 1970s.

Despite ideological and strategic differences, what the various national resistance groups had in common was a belief that the Palestinian cause could no longer depend solely on the beneficence of the Arab states, which had been resoundingly defeated by Israel in the 1967 war. After that war, groups like Fatah and the PFLP took control of the Palestine Liberation Organization (PLO). The PLO had originally been created by the Arab League in 1964 to try channeling and containing Palestinian resistance efforts against Israel, but, from the late 1960s on, Palestinians themselves would run the organization as an independent entity. As head of Fatah, the largest of the nationalist groups, Yasser Arafat became chair of the PLO Executive Committee.[18]

The PLO's founding charter, drafted at the Arab League summit in 1964, had called for making all of historic Palestine into an Arab state—effectively doing away with the State of Israel. But by the late 1960s, the PLO was beginning to moderate its position by calling for the establishment of a single, secular state for both Arabs and Jews. Although still rejecting Zionism, this reformulated vision recognized the right of Jews to remain in Palestine as equal citizens in a future, democratic state.[19] Not surprisingly, this proposal was a complete nonstarter for Zionists in both Israel and the West since such a state would, by definition, mean the end of a Jewish ethno-state.

For its part, the Palestinian labor movement also began experiencing a nationalist revival in this period. Thanks to pressure from its Palestinian members, the General Federation of Jordanian Trade Unions opened branch offices in the West Bank in 1965, two years before the fateful Six-Day War. (Because of this, the present-day Palestinian General Federation of Trade Unions lists its founding date as 1965.) In 1972, these West Bank trade union branches—now trying to operate under the jackboot of Israeli military rule—broke from the Jordanian union federation and instead became the independent General Federation of Trade Unions in the West Bank, headquartered in Nablus.

"In this way, the Palestinian labor movement declared its independence and adherence to Palestinian nationalism," a report by the Arab World for Research and Development would later explain.[20] Despite facing constant repression by the Israeli occupation forces, including deportation of their leaders, Palestinian trade unions aligned themselves with the PLO in the national liberation struggle. They organized to oppose Israeli efforts to confiscate more land and advocated for the growing number of Palestinian day laborers from the occupied territories whom Israel's booming economy would increasingly rely upon as an easily exploitable workforce.[21]

§

With numerous armed conflicts and political upheavals rocking the Middle East in the 1960s and 1970s, and with the US government simultaneously loosening immigration restrictions through the 1965 Immigration and Nationality Act, tens of thousands of Arabs—particularly from Palestine, Yemen, and Lebanon—migrated to the United States. Many moved to Metro Detroit, which was already home to a small population of mostly Christian Arabs, especially Lebanese. The new arrivals, who included many more Muslims, did not as easily pass as white as the earlier wave of Arab immigrants.

By the early 1970s, approximately eighty-five thousand Arab Americans lived in the Detroit area. They were concentrated in Dearborn and Hamtramck, respectively home to the Ford River Rouge complex and the Dodge Main Assembly plant. In Dearborn, they faced routine harassment from the city's notoriously racist mayor.

Around the same time, the Black Power movement was sweeping the auto factories. African American workers at Dodge Main formed the Dodge Revolutionary Union Movement (DRUM) in 1968 and protested racial discrimination on the job, mistreatment by management, and an unresponsive UAW bureaucracy. DRUM led a series of wildcat strikes and inspired the creation of additional revolutionary Black caucuses at other nearby plants, which eventually united into the League of Revolutionary Black Workers.

Alarmed by this militancy, the auto companies turned to hiring large numbers of recently arrived Arab immigrants, believing they would be more docile and give them less trouble than African American workers. By 1973, some fifteen thousand Arabs toiled in the Detroit auto plants. Though they were UAW members, they were routinely placed into the most physically demanding and lowest-paid jobs, with little to no objections from the mostly white union leadership. They faced linguistic and cultural barriers and encountered racism from shop foremen, union representatives, and public officials.[22]

Though some Arab workers joined the Black-led wildcats and the League of Revolutionary Black Workers and its allies publicly voiced support for Palestinian liberation, contact between the two groups was minimal at first thanks to management's intentional separation of them on the shop floor.

Energized by the growing Palestinian nationalism of this period and inspired by the Black Power movement, Arab Americans in Metro Detroit started forming community organizations to fight back against housing discrimination and other forms of racism. As historian Pamela Pennock explains, these local groups coalesced into the American Arab Coordinating Committee.[23] In August 1973, the committee organized a march in Dearborn to protest the police murder of Nagi Daifullah, a 24-year-old Yemeni immigrant in California. Daifullah had been an organizer with Cesar Chavez's United Farm Workers and was brutally beaten to death that month by a Kern County sheriff's deputy.

Upon the outbreak of the October War in 1973, Detroit Arabs were shocked to learn that UAW Local 600, which represented workers at the Ford River Rouge complex, had purchased over $300,000 in State of Israel bonds with their union dues money six years earlier. They further became aware that, as part of its pension portfolio, the national UAW at that time held $785,000 in Israeli bonds. These bond purchases were brought to light by Alan Amen, a Lebanese American community activist and Wayne State University student whose grandfather and father worked at Ford.

On October 13, around three thousand Arab workers marched in Dearborn to the Local 600 office, demanding the bonds be liquidated. Soon after, they formed an Arab Workers Caucus within the UAW, forging alliances with the League of Revolutionary Black Workers and with other leftist groups like the Spartacist League and Revolutionary Union.[24]

The Arab Workers Caucus learned that on November 28, UAW president Leonard Woodcock would be honored by B'nai B'rith International, a Zionist charitable organization, with its Humanitarian of the Year Award at a gala dinner in downtown Detroit. At the start of the October War, Woodcock had issued a public statement "unreservedly" condemning "the unprovoked Egyptian-Syrian military attack" and expressing "our solidarity and support with the State of Israel, the Histadrut, and all Israeli workers." Woodcock also called for peace "along lines that reflect both justice and the realities of the power positions of the contenders"—a blatantly paradoxical statement.[25]

The workers used Woodcock's B'nai B'rith dinner as an opportunity to demand the union divest from Israel. As explained at the time by Ismael Ahmed, a community organizer and future head of the Michigan Department of Human Services, the "newly formed caucus wanted to point out the hypocrisy of this leader who would force his constituency to finance the murder of their brothers and sisters back home with their union dues."[26]

The caucus circulated seventy thousand flyers in Arabic and English calling on Arab auto workers to join in a wildcat strike on the day of Woodcock's award ceremony. In an advertisement published in the Detroit Free Press, the American Arab Coordinating Committee questioned whether the UAW leadership was acting in members' best interests by spending "over ¾ million dollars" on "non-economical, low-interest, foreign bonds." The ad further noted that the UAW had an estimated fifteen thousand Arab members, and that "tens of thousands of Arab Palestinian workers in Israel from Arab territories militarily occupied by Israel in 1967 are not protected by even minimal labor union guarantee."[27]

At Dodge Main in Hamtramck, where Arab immigrants comprised upward of 25 percent of the workforce, two thousand workers heeded the call for the November 28 wildcat strike and production was shut down for the day. Other plants in the area experienced slowdowns.

That evening, about a thousand people protested outside Cobo Hall, where Woodcock was being honored at the $100-a-plate dinner attended by the mayor of Detroit and chair of General Motors. Holding signs that read "Dispose of the Bonds" and "Jewish People Yes, Zionism No," the Arab protesters chanted "don't abuse workers' dues" and "no more bombs, no more bonds." Woodcock snuck into the venue through a back door to avoid the protesters.[28]

§

In the aftermath of this extraordinary rebuke to the UAW leadership, Local 600 president Walter Dorosh met with members of the Arab Workers Caucus and promised to help liquidate the Israeli bonds, but demanded no further public protests against union officials.

For his part, UAW secretary-treasurer Emil Mazey issued a condescending statement a few weeks after the wildcat action. "I am told that a number of UAW members of Arab descent were persuaded to leave their jobs at a Detroit Chrysler plant and join the people who were picketing Woodcock. It was, of course, their right to picket. But a worker in any of the Arab countries who would do likewise would soon find himself in jail," Mazey said. "American workers of Arab descent ought to expend their energies helping their compatriots get rid of the feudal and totalitarian overlords who are ruling those lands with an iron fist."

Mazey also alleged that "members of the US Communist Party" were "agitating" Arab union members to sow divisions, which he attributed to their "slavish" devotion to Soviet policy. Furthermore, he defended the UAW's purchase of Israeli bonds, saying they had "a very good rate of return" at 5.5 percent, and claiming that the money was not used for military purposes, but only for infrastructure and development projects.

"We are proud of our record at home and abroad, and no amount of distortion or outright lies will be able to tarnish it," Mazey concluded. "These totally unwarranted attacks on the UAW are the work of unscrupulous propagandists who have their own axe to grind."[29]

Undeterred, the Arab Workers Caucus continued organizing, comparing UAW officers who had "sold out" to corporate capital with Arab political leaders who had acquiesced to US imperialism. The caucus sent delegates to the 1974 UAW constitutional convention in California, who put forward a program calling not only for disposal of the bonds, but also for more workplace rights, the hiring of language interpreters at the auto plants, and the dismissal of any union officers or staff found guilty of racial or ethnic discrimination. Additionally, the Arab workers' program demanded "the DIRECT ELECTION by the entire UAW membership of their leadership,"[30] a goal that would eventually be attained in 2022, though the caucus went further by also seeking full minority representation among union leadership.

"UAW should stand firmly in support of all workers and people struggling in Africa, Asia and Latin America," the caucus's program read. "In the Middle East, UAW should support the principle of establishing a secular, non-theocratic, democratic state in Palestine for all people, Jews and Arabs, and stand against any outside intervention."[31]

The convention's resolutions committee, chaired by Dorosh, ignored all of these demands. Nevertheless, by organizing among the rank-and-file over several months, the Arab Workers Caucus convinced multiple UAW locals to dispose of their own Israeli investments, resulting in the liquidation of $48,000 in bonds by 1975.[32]

DOUBLING DOWN ON ISRAEL

While the UAW Arab Workers Caucus was making some headway within its union, key figures in the reawakened Palestinian nationalist movement were being assassinated by Mossad, including intellectuals like Ghassan Kanafani, a prominent PFLP member. As Egypt and Syria entered into peace talks with Israel following the October War, some in the PLO were recalculating their long-term objectives. In June 1974, the PLO leadership adopted a program that called for a national authority to be established over "any part" of Palestinian territory that might become liberated from Israeli rule. This left open the possibility of a future Palestinian state existing alongside Israel, instead of fully replacing Israel—an idea that would eventually come to be known as the "two-state solution."

This significant shift toward diplomacy and compromise angered some Palestinian militants, who consequently broke away from the PLO and formed their own rival factions. The most notorious of these was the Abu Nidal Organization, which assassinated several PLO leaders and indiscriminately murdered Jewish civilians with the backing of Iraq's Ba'athist government.

In the autumn of 1974, the PLO was granted observer status at the United Nations and Arafat addressed the UN General Assembly in New York, demonstrating how the mainstream of the Palestinian nationalist movement was gaining legitimacy on the world stage. A year later, the UN General Assembly passed a resolution condemning Zionism as "a form of racism and racial discrimination"[33] with the support of African, Middle Eastern, and communist-led countries, as well as Mexico (the measure would later be revoked by the General Assembly in late 1991).

Around the same time, US Secretary of State Henry Kissinger was trying to broker an interim peace deal between Israeli prime minister Yitzhak Rabin and Egyptian president Anwar al-Sadat. As scholar Seth Anziska writes, "Kissinger's approach was a means of conflict management: by removing Egypt as a strategic and diplomatic threat, Israel's position would be secured and American dominance in the region would be preserved."[34]

But the talks fell through in March 1975. Kissinger attributed this result to Israeli intransigence, prompting President Gerald Ford to announce a "reassessment" of the US-Israel relationship. For several months in the middle of 1975, the Ford administration refused any new arms deals with Israel. In response, seventy-six US senators signed a letter of protest to the president demanding he remain "responsive" to Israel's needs. The letter was written by the American Israel Public Affairs Committee (AIPAC), a pro-Israel lobbying group founded in the 1960s that would become increasingly influential on Capitol Hill over the next several decades.[35]

AIPAC and other pro-Israel groups, particularly the Anti-Defamation League, were explicitly smearing the emerging Palestine solidarity movement in the United States as antisemitic. In 1974, Arnold Forster and Benjamin Epstein of the Anti-Defamation League published *The New Anti-Semitism*, a book arguing that criticisms of Israel—especially from leftist Black and Arab Americans—constituted a novel form of anti-Jewish hate. Over the next few decades, Zionist groups and their allies would continuously, and ever more recklessly, push the narrative that any sympathy for Palestinian liberation was inherently antisemitic.[36]

Ford and Kissinger's pause on new arms deals with Israel outraged AFL-CIO president George Meany, who blamed the stalled negotiations on Egypt's unwillingness to recognize the Zionist state. "We in the labor movement know something about bargaining," Meany said that April. "We, too, become 'inflexible' if we are called upon to place in serious jeopardy the life and existence of our trade union, which is what enables us to bargain in the first place." Egypt and other Arab nations, he insisted, were determined to "bring about the extermination of the Israelis." Meany was also greatly displeased with the UN's decision a few months earlier to recognize the PLO, which he denigrated as "an organization without a territorial or representative mandate of any kind; an organization openly espousing violence and murder."[37]

At the same time that Meany and the AFL-CIO were devoting their energies to delegitimizing the Palestinian nationalist movement (just as it was finally gaining international attention and sympathy), US unions in the 1970s were in crisis.

To hang onto their profits amid slowing economic growth and increased foreign competition, American industrial employers were cutting labor costs by introducing automation and speedups while moving production to nonunion states in the South and Southwest. US union density was rapidly declining, and labor leaders like Meany often seemed more focused on waging the Cold War overseas than organizing the unorganized at home.[38] The traditionally Jewish-led needle trades unions were especially suffering as apparel companies began moving production overseas to cheaper labor markets in Latin America and the Caribbean.

§

Despite the protests of Arab American auto workers in Detroit, US labor kept purchasing State of Israel bonds throughout the

1970s, even as the size and strength of American unions continued declining amid corporate machinations. By the middle of the decade, organized labor had purchased hundreds of millions of dollars' worth of the bonds (reportedly anywhere from $100 million to $800 million)—with the mob-linked International Brotherhood of Teamsters leading the way.[39]

Already by December 1972, when Teamsters president Frank Fitzsimmons visited Israel and met with Prime Minister Golda Meir, the truckers' union had bought $15 million in Israeli bonds over the previous twenty years. One of the only union leaders to endorse Republican President Richard Nixon in his successful reelection bid the month before, Fitzsimmons had close ties with the administration, and promised Israeli officials during his visit that he would use his influence to oppose "the Arabists in the State Department" who wanted to pressure Israel into giving up the post-1967 occupied territories.[40]

The following spring, the Teamsters organized a massive, $11 million bonds drive that brought the union's total Israeli bonds purchases up to $26 million. The campaign culminated that May in a $100-a-plate testimonial dinner for Fitzsimmons at the Washington Hilton. The Teamsters president was honored with the Israel Silver Anniversary Award "for service in the cause of Israel's development," handed to him by Israeli ambassador Simcha Dinitz. Writing about the evening's festivities, attended by 2,500 Teamsters from around the United States, *Washington Post* reporter Donnie Radcliff wryly noted how "the crowd clapped to such good old Jewish favorites as 'McNamara's Band,' 'Danny Boy,' and 'When Irish Eyes Are Smiling.'"

Demonstrating Fitzsimmons's warm relationship with the administration, several members of Nixon's Cabinet came to the dinner and quietly discussed the unfolding Watergate scandal. Fitzsimmons also received congratulatory telegrams from Nixon himself and from Golda Meir.[41]

A few weeks later, as allegations surfaced that Nixon's Department of Justice was looking the other way on Teamsters corruption in exchange for the union's support, the Development Corporation for Israel (DCI) distanced itself from the testimonial dinner. "It was Teamsters business. It was all their baby," DCI executive Borah Schneider said of the event. "Fitzsimmons was picked because of the tremendous amount of money the Teamsters have spent on bonds. But we had nothing to do with the dinner."[42] It was a curious statement considering that multiple Israeli government officials had participated in the event.

Throughout the decade, the Teamsters held numerous testimonial dinners for its leaders to raise money for Israeli bonds, including for the mob-linked Jackie Presser.[43]

In October 1976, New Jersey Teamsters official Joseph Pecora, secretary-treasurer of Local 863, was honored by the local chapter of the DCI with a gala dinner that reportedly raised another $3.5 million in bond purchases. The event was denounced by the Professional Drivers Council (known as PROD), a rank-and-file Teamsters reform caucus that fought against corruption in the union. PROD argued it was entirely inappropriate to honor Pecora since he was a reputed Newark gangster who had been charged six years earlier with embezzling $6,000 in union funds for private trips to Atlantic City and Florida. Not only that, but Pecora had also faced accusations of using his position in the Teamsters to strong-arm local A&P grocery stores into selling a brand of laundry detergent manufactured by a company tied to the mob. When questioned by the Senate Commerce Committee about this in October 1971, Pecora refused to answer any questions, invoking the Fifth Amendment fifty-four times.[44]

Journalist Steven Brill noted that the intense amount of Teamsters' bond buying in the mid-1970s raised eyebrows in law enforcement circles, but they apparently found nothing suspicious. Asked why the truckers' union was so interested in investing in Israel, DCI spokesperson Meyer Steinglass told Brill that the bonds had "great PR value," especially for Teamsters officials "looking for respectability." Steinglass continued, "[I]n this union the guys at the top can make the locals buy the bonds. I mean, you know what they say, 'You can find yourself under a truck if you don't obey.'"[45]

§

One US labor official who boasted of having "been to more Israel Bonds dinners than anyone else walking around the [United] States"[46] was Lane Kirkland, who served as the AFL-CIO's secretary-treasurer in the 1970s.

A Protestant from South Carolina, Kirkland was arguably the most passionate advocate for Zionism within US labor officialdom. Like George Meany, he was also a virulent anticommunist who believed that the AFL-CIO's power and influence was inextricably linked to the continued strength of the US empire.

In 1973, Kirkland married Irena Neumann, a Czech-born Jew who survived Auschwitz and briefly lived in Israel after its founding and whose twin sister was an Israeli citizen. The couple frequently hosted both Israeli visitors and Russian dissidents at their home in Washington, DC, which was sprinkled with archaeological artifacts from the Middle East, including a figure of Horace given to Kirkland by the mayor of Jerusalem and a 4,000-year-old pot from Jericho.[47]

In the 1976 presidential election, Republican Gerald Ford was defeated by Democrat Jimmy Carter, who sought to counter Soviet influence in the Middle East by having the United States secure a comprehensive peace in the region. Weeks after taking office, Carter publicly called on Israel to withdraw from the territories it had occupied since the 1967 war and became the first US president to speak of "a homeland provided for the

Palestinian refugees who have suffered for many, many years."[48] This signaled the possibility of a major change in US policy on the Palestine question, no doubt brought about by the PLO's increasing legitimacy on the world stage.

Two months after Carter made these comments, in May 1977, Israel experienced its biggest political shake-up to date when the Labor Zionist parties lost Knesset elections for the first time. The right-wing Likud Party—the ideological heir to Ze'ev Jabotinsky's Revisionist Zionists—won a plurality of seats and formed a government led by new Prime Minister Menachem Begin, who had headed the terrorist group Irgun in the 1940s.[49]

Responding to all these developments, Kirkland declared that when it came to US labor's support for Israel, "We won't shift with the public opinion polls or modify our support depending on which party is in power." He did not seem to recognize that Carter's comments on Palestine were part of a nuanced approach to achieving US geopolitical supremacy in the Middle East through peacemaking and, like other top labor officials, believed he knew better than Washington how to best wage the Cold War. Speaking on behalf of the AFL-CIO, Kirkland continued, "We have been appalled at the short-sighted views of some American policy makers who have chosen to demonstrate their evenhandedness by strengthening the hand of Israel's enemies and by demanding concessions on the part of Israel that increase, rather than lessen, the dangers of another Holocaust."[50]

When Meany retired in November 1979 at the age of eighty-five, Kirkland succeeded him as AFL-CIO president. Two months later, in what was billed as his first public remarks after assuming the labor federation's top job, Kirkland vowed that the AFL-CIO would do "all in its power to prevent any erosion of support" for Israel. He was speaking at yet another gala dinner, accepting an award from the National Jewish Community Relations Council of Greater Philadelphia. During his speech, the new AFL-CIO head revealed the full extent of his anti-Palestinian sentiments. As the ostensible leader and spokesperson of the US labor movement, Kirkland denounced the idea of opening formal diplomatic relations between the United States and the PLO to work toward the creation of a Palestinian state.

"A Palestinian state would . . . be a terrorist state that employs assassins, kidnappers and bomb-throwers as a matter of official policy," Kirkland said. "How can it be in the interest of the United States to facilitate the creation of such a state, even if Israel did not exist?" Attempting to whip up a Cold War panic, he further argued that a Palestinian state would be firmly in the communist camp due to the Soviet Union's frequent backing of Arab nationalist governments and growing support for the PLO. "Unless suicide has become our foreign policy, the United States must not let this happen. Our country should be utterly intransigent in opposing the emplacement of such a knife at the throat of human decency."[51]

A few months later, Kirkland spoke at a fundraiser for Israeli bonds in Washington, also attended by Carter, and called on the US government to issue an "unequivocal declaration that America stands against the creation of a Palestinian state dedicated to Israel's destruction." He accused those in Washington who favored talks with the PLO of only trying to placate Arab countries "whose hands are on the oil spigot," and said a future Palestinian state "would injure and endanger the economic, political and strategic interests of the United States and the entire Western alliance."[52]

As Kirkland's remarks demonstrate, as union density continued falling amid the breakdown of the postwar economic order, top officials in the US labor movement appeared determined to use their diminishing political influence to keep Palestinians stateless and politically marginalized. As committed cold warriors wedded to US global dominance, Kirkland and other hawkish laborites were frightened by recent international events, including the Islamic revolution in Iran and the Soviet invasion of Afghanistan. President Carter hoped to counter such trends by fostering peace between Israel and its Arab enemies and integrating a more stable Middle East into the US sphere of influence. Although anticommunist union officials like Kirkland were open to the idea of diplomacy between Israel and the neighboring Arab states, they were convinced Carter was going too far in even entertaining the thought of a Palestinian state, as they believed the establishment of such a state would only further embolden America's enemies and thus further marginalize the AFL-CIO.

In 1979, the Jewish Labor Committee (JLC) similarly criticized Austrian chancellor Bruno Kreisky and West Germany's former chancellor Willy Brandt for holding a high-profile meeting and press conference with Yasser Arafat in Vienna, after which the two European leaders expressed "extreme concern" over Israel's "settlement activities in the occupied territories."

"The history of the PLO has been characterized by terrorism as a primary method of operation," said Jacob "Jack" Sheinkman, president of the JLC and secretary-treasurer of the Amalgamated Clothing and Textile Workers Union. "The holding of several days of publicized meetings followed by a press conference, gives the P.L.O. a legitimacy among democratic, liberal, and labor forces unwarranted by its history, its deeds, and its public declarations."[53] In 1980, the ILGWU's Chick Chaikin—who by now was the union's president—also publicly questioned "the morality of terrorism, the morality of the means which the PLO has been anxious to apply" as a way to delegitimize the Palestinian cause.[54]

Like some of their conservative counterparts in the US government, these labor officials refused to recognize that the PLO was a broad umbrella organization comprising not only armed fighters, but also politicians, diplomats, and civil society groups.

Further, they deliberately blurred any distinction between the PLO and its extremist rivals like the Abu Nidal Organization.[55]

And, of course, Zionist militias in the 1940s had themselves used terrorism to pursue their own political goals, including the Irgun's deadly bombing of the King David Hotel. The Irgun's leader, Menachem Begin, had never faced justice for that terrorist attack and was serving as Israel's prime minister at the same time US labor leaders were denouncing the PLO for terrorism. Yitzhak Shamir, Begin's fellow Likud politician, was another right-wing terrorist in the 1940s. Shamir had ordered the assassination of UN diplomat Folke Bernadotte in 1948, was never held accountable, and would succeed Begin as Israel's prime minister in 1983.[56]

Beyond this, Zionist militias had committed numerous massacres during the Nakba to terrorize Palestinians into fleeing their lands to make room for the State of Israel.

US labor officials apparently saw nothing hypocritical in strongly supporting and praising a state that was founded and maintained through brutal violence and terrorism while simultaneously demonizing Palestinians for sometimes using violent tactics (along with many nonviolent forms of resistance) to secure self-determination in the face of a heavily militarized settler-colonial state.

FROM CAMP DAVID TO BEIRUT

The right-wing Likud Party, which won control of the Israeli government in 1977, was determined not only to bring free market reforms to the country's economy, but also to one day annex the occupied West Bank, East Jerusalem, and Gaza Strip. Though Prime Minister Begin understood that annexation was politically out of the question in the short term, he and the other Revisionist Zionists of the Likud believed (and still believe) that all of historic Palestine—and perhaps even land beyond that—should belong to "Greater Israel."

To further this goal, and to try assuaging US fears that his election might exacerbate geopolitical tensions in the Middle East, Begin came into office signaling his willingness to make peace with the Arab states neighboring Israel. By neutralizing the ongoing threat of war through permanent peace treaties, the new prime minister hoped to further isolate the PLO and thus make it easier for Israel to continue building settlements in the West Bank and Gaza without international pushback, until eventually annexation would become a fait accompli.

Ready to pull away from the Soviet orbit to gain Western economic and military aid, and hoping to build on the diplomacy that had followed the October 1973 war, Egyptian president Sadat was by this point interested in pursuing peace negotiations with Israel. That November, he sent shock waves throughout the region by going on an official state visit to Jerusalem. With Egypt having been Israel's mortal enemy for the previous thirty years, it was an historic trip with a profound psychological effect on the Israeli population, which Sadat hoped would open them up to the serious possibility of peace. Speaking before the Knesset, the Egyptian president called for Israel's withdrawal to its pre-1967 boundaries and asserted the right of the Palestinians to self-determination, but also acknowledged Israel's right to be recognized and to have security. He returned to Cairo having laid the groundwork for further discussions.[57]

A few weeks later, the AFL-CIO held its biennial convention in Los Angeles. Like other Zionist Americans, the labor federation's leaders had been both surprised and moved by the Egyptian president's trip to Jerusalem. Understanding that a bilateral agreement between Israel and Egypt would not only bring Cairo into the Western camp in the Cold War, but would also marginalize the PLO, AFL-CIO leaders wanted to encourage the peace process to continue. For the first time, a representative of Egypt's labor movement was invited to attend the AFL-CIO convention—a courtesy that had long been accorded to Histadrut officials. At the gathering in LA, Histadrut general secretary Yeruham Meshel and Egyptian Trade Union Federation president Saad Muhammad Ahmed were welcomed together onto the stage, where they shook hands, then raised their clasped hands in the air.

Describing the moment, veteran labor journalist Albert K. Herling wrote in the *New York Jewish Week*: "There was a silence of about five seconds—a silence of disbelief, and then a roar of cheers and pounding applause as more than 2,000 delegates and guests jumped to their feet." Herling continued, "Never in the decades that this reporter has been attending conventions of the American Federation of Labor, Congress of Industrial Organizations and then those of the merged organization, has there been such an emotionally charged atmosphere."[58]

Calling Sadat "an honest man who wants peace," Meshel expressed hope for continued dialogue and noted that "in Israel, only Governments talked together; here it is not Governments but trade unions who have to meet and have to help hammer out a lasting peace." Ahmad, who also served as Egypt's Minister of Labor, said he was especially interested in "the establishment of brotherly relations between the Egyptian and American labor movements."[59]

Along the latter lines, immediately after the convention, the ILGWU's Chaikin went to Cairo with his wife, Rosalind, and AFL-CIO international affairs director Ernest Lee (Meany's son-in-law), where they were "welcomed very warmly and very hospitably." During their four-day visit, Chaikin and Lee held several meetings with Ahmad and other Egyptian officials, asserting that "no lasting relationship with the AFL-CIO could ever evolve" without the establishment of cordial ties between Egypt's trade unions and the Zionist Histadrut. Reporting on the trip later, the ILGWU president condescendingly accused his hosts of having "an almost child-like understanding" of the peace process because they wanted Israel to "give back everything and do everything that Sadat requests."

Believing that Arabs alone were responsible for the decades-long conflict, and that Israel had no need to compromise, Chaikin said he lectured the Egyptians about how "they had to learn the meaning of negotiation" and that peace would only "come to the Middle East when the leaders of the Arab nations, the dictators, the sheiks, the autocrats, the generals, begin to respond to the needs of their own people, begin to think in terms of the humanity which they represent."[60]

The ILGWU president further criticized Egypt for lacking "free" trade unions, noting that, like Ahmad, many Egyptian union leaders also served as government officials, particularly as members of the National Assembly. This was an awkward point considering that, for most of Israel's brief history, several Histadrut officials had also served in the government—including as prime ministers—and yet American unionists like Chaikin constantly praised Israel for having a "free" labor movement. Indeed, Meshel, the Histadrut's general secretary at the time, was then simultaneously serving as a member of the Knesset.

Throughout 1978, bilateral talks continued between Egypt and Israel, urged along by the Carter administration. Finally, that September, Carter convened a 13-day summit at the presidential retreat of Camp David in Maryland, bringing Sadat and Begin together to come to a final agreement. The result of the summit was the Camp David Accords, which consisted of two "frameworks" for peace. One of them outlined details for a treaty involving complete Israeli withdrawal from the Sinai Peninsula in exchange for full normalization of relations between the two countries. This eventually led to an actual treaty in March 1979, with Egypt becoming the first Arab state to recognize Israel.

The other framework reached at Camp David was a vague plan for a regional peace, calling for multilateral talks between Israel, Egypt, and Jordan and "representatives of the Palestinian people." It did not name the PLO—the internationally recognized representative of the Palestinian people—but instead recommended the election of a "self-governing authority" for the Palestinians. Begin and the Israeli government would only consider granting "autonomy" to Palestinians living in the occupied territories, but not ending Israel's occupation and settlement activity, and certainly not allowing for the establishment of a sovereign Palestinian state.[61]

PLO leaders felt betrayed. Not only by Egypt, but also by the United States after secret US-PLO talks in Lebanon had apparently gone nowhere. Although the Camp David framework vaguely called for eventual Israeli withdrawal from the West Bank and Gaza Strip, Begin was quick to announce that the building of illegal settlements would continue and that there would never be a Palestinian state. Meanwhile, Sadat moved forward on normalizing relations with Israel and was rewarded with generous US economic and military aid. As historian Seth Anziska contends, for the Israeli government, "the pursuit of a peace deal with Egypt had also become a means to avoid peace with the Palestinians."[62]

Visiting Cairo and Jerusalem in April 1981, AFL-CIO president Kirkland emphasized how the Israeli-Egyptian peace did nothing to advance the Palestinian nationalist cause. Encouraging continued cooperation between the Histadrut and Egyptian Trade Union Federation, Kirkland simultaneously went out of his way to reaffirm his total hostility to the PLO, telling a group of Histadrut officials, "Even if you Israelis should start to deal with them we still will reject them."[63]

While Sadat and Begin jointly won the Nobel Peace Prize, Egypt was suspended from the Arab League for making a deal with the enemy without consulting with the League's other members. It appeared to the other Arab states and the PLO that Sadat had sold them out to get the Sinai Peninsula back and endear himself to the Americans.

Especially outraged were the Middle East's growing Islamic revolutionary movements, which had become a potent political force in the 1970s after twenty years of secular nationalism and attempts at Western-style modernization had failed to deliver economic prosperity and geopolitical independence. The ascendance of these movements was particularly evident after the 1979 revolution in Iran brought Shia Muslim clerics into power, who proceeded to institute an Islamic republic.

In October 1981, members of Egyptian Islamic Jihad assassinated Sadat in retaliation for the Camp David Accords.

§

Around the same time as Sadat's murder, the Israeli government was drawing up plans for an invasion of neighboring Lebanon, which had served as the PLO's military and political stronghold since its expulsion from Jordan in 1971. Home to various ethno-religious groups—including Sunni and Shia Muslims, Maronite Christians, and Druze—Lebanon had also become an indefinite shelter for hundreds of thousands of Palestinian refugee families dating back to the Nakba. During the 1970s, the PLO established a kind of "state within a state" inside southern Lebanon, administered by its own quasi-government based in Beirut. Segments of the Lebanese population resented the fact that armed Palestinian fighters controlled parts of their country.

Starting in 1975, Lebanon was convulsed by a highly complex, fifteen-year civil war pitting the PLO and allied Lebanese leftists against multiple right-wing Maronite Christian militias, among numerous other factions fighting each other. The largest of the Maronite militias was the Phalange, an extreme right-wing paramilitary founded in the 1930s and modeled after the Hitler Youth and Italian Fascist Party. As the war began, the Phalange—which received weapons and training from Israel because of its opposition to the PLO—carried out massacres and forced expulsions at Palestinian refugee camps. Some Palestinian factions retaliated with massacres of Maronite communities.[64] The war only escalated in 1976 when Syria invaded Lebanon to extend its own regional influence and suppress the growing power of the independent PLO.

After making peace with Egypt and annexing the Golan Heights, by the end of 1981, Menachem Begin wanted to directly intervene in the ongoing Lebanese civil war. His main goals were destroying the PLO and installing a puppet regime in the country under Israeli ally Bashir Gemayel, leader of the right-wing Phalange. Begin and his Cabinet believed these moves would make it far easier for Israel to annex the West Bank and Gaza, allowing the realization of their "Greater Israel" vision.

For years, Palestinian militants had launched cross-border attacks on Israel from their bases in southern Lebanon, often targeting civilians, which Begin used to justify the need for an Israeli incursion into the country. In the early months of 1982, war plans were secretly drawn up by Minister of Defense Ariel Sharon—the same military commander who, as a young man nearly thirty years earlier, had overseen the notorious Qibya Massacre.

In June 1982, the Israeli invasion of Lebanon began with an initial air force bombing of ostensible PLO targets in Beirut, followed by 120,000 IDF soldiers entering the country. Though Begin publicly promised that Israeli troops would march only forty kilometers into Lebanon to push Palestinian fighters a safe distance from the border, his and Sharon's bolder objectives soon became clear. After brief battles with Syrian forces in the country, which were halted by a ceasefire, the IDF quickly marched all the way north to Beirut. Israeli tanks surrounded the capital city and demanded the surrender of PLO leadership.

Over the next two months, the Israelis laid siege to Beirut, terrorizing the population through constant bombardment from land, air, and sea, and at times cutting off the city's power and water supply. Thousands of civilians were killed and entire residential areas were obliterated. With journalists from around the world reporting on the horror from inside the besieged city, Israel faced widespread international criticism. Whatever international goodwill had been engendered through the peace treaty with Egypt was rapidly being lost.

Although Washington had provided Israel with billions of dollars in weapons systems and munitions and US Secretary of State Alexander Haig had given his approval for the invasion, by early August 1982, President Ronald Reagan's administration was calling for an end to the shelling of Beirut. A defiant Begin argued that the siege was necessary to prevent another Holocaust, an argument even some of his fellow Israelis said was over the top. As US diplomat Philip Habib was trying to broker an agreement for the PLO to leave Lebanon, Sharon ordered a saturation bombing of Beirut that killed between three hundred and five hundred civilians in a single day. Furious, Reagan warned Begin that the future of the US-Israeli relationship was in jeopardy. Meanwhile, polls showed the American public was becoming more critical of Israel.[65]

In the midst of all this, on August 15, US labor officials put out a full-page advertisement in *The New York Times* with the all-caps headline: "THE AFL-CIO IS NOT NEUTRAL. WE SUPPORT ISRAEL." The ad contained a statement that had been approved by the AFL-CIO Executive Council ten days earlier. "The AFL-CIO Executive Council considers the Israeli invasion of Lebanon entirely justified on security grounds," the statement read. "To protect its security, Israel was justified not only in altering its stated objective of removing the immediate threat but in attacking its source—the command structure of the PLO itself," a reference to the siege of Beirut.[66]

The AFL-CIO leadership blamed the heavy civilian casualties not on the Israeli bombardment, but on the "PLO's tactic of deliberately locating its forces in residential areas and storing its ammunition in schools, hospitals and other public facilities"—an excuse all too commonly used to justify Israel's indiscriminate slaughter of noncombatants. The statement concluded by urging "the U.S. government to continue withholding recognition from the PLO . . . it is a terrorist organization. To reward it with recognition is to encourage terrorism as a political tactic around the world."[67]

According to William Winpisinger, then the president of the International Association of Machinists and a member of the AFL-CIO Executive Council, the statement was largely the handiwork of the labor federation's president, Lane Kirkland. Years later, Winpisinger said that the statement had only been approved after a contentious meeting in which Kirkland would not brook any dissent. "In exasperation I said 'Can't we at least condemn the killing?' and Lane jumped all over me and said 'Israel is catching enough hell around the world, and one of their best friends isn't going to turn on them now,'" Winpisinger recalled.[68]

At the end of August, through a US-sponsored agreement, Yasser Arafat and some fifteen thousand PLO officials and fighters evacuated Beirut and the rest of Lebanon and were scattered across the Middle East and North Africa. PLO leaders had asked for assurances that the civilian Palestinian refugees they were leaving behind would live in peace and security, and although US and Lebanese officials agreed, the Israelis refused to make any such guarantees.

The same week as the mass PLO evacuation, the Lebanese parliament elected Israel's client—Phalange leader Bashir Gemayel—to the country's presidency. Only three weeks after his election, Gemayel was killed by a Syrian-backed assassin. In response, Sharon ordered the IDF to invade west Beirut (which Israel had promised Washington it would not do), supposedly to secure that part of the city from terrorists. But PLO fighters had already evacuated, so by "terrorists" Sharon simply meant the Palestinian civilians left behind.

On September 16, IDF commanders in west Beirut knowingly allowed Phalange militiamen to enter the now defenseless Palestinian refugee camp of Shatila and adjacent neighborhood of Sabra to murder and rape women, children, and elderly men. The slaughter continued for the next two days, leaving anywhere from eight hundred to three thousand civilians dead. Fully aware of what was happening, the IDF did nothing except fire flares into the night sky to illuminate the camps for the murderous Phalange fighters. Sharon told the Israeli Cabinet the "results will speak for themselves . . . let us have the number of days necessary for destroying the terrorists."[69]

News of the Sabra and Shatila massacre made international headlines immediately, with grisly images of the victims' bodies broadcast on television screens around the world, sparking worldwide condemnation of Israel. Begin complained, "Goyim [non-Jews] kill goyim, and they come to hang the Jews." Later investigations, including one overseen by an Israeli Supreme Court justice, held the Israeli government responsible for the atrocity due to the IDF's intentional inaction.[70]

In Tel Aviv on September 26, upward of 350,000 people marched in protest, calling on Begin and Sharon to resign. One protester, who had been born in Poland and immigrated to Mandatory Palestine in the 1930s, explained that "I'm ashamed to now be a Jew. I came to Israel and worked for it to be a sign for the whole world. Now I'm ashamed for what we've done."[71]

The international labor movement also protested. On September 23, the left-wing dockworkers union in the Italian port of Livorno refused to load or unload two Israeli cargo ships. Meanwhile, the Geneva-based International Metalworkers Federation—which was composed of various manufacturing unions around the world, including the UAW—put forward a statement on the Sabra and Shatila massacre, calling Israel and the United States "contributory factors to this latest outrage." Issued by Herman Rebhan, the former UAW international affairs director now serving as general secretary of the International Metalworkers Federation, the statement called on Begin and his Cabinet to "resign and make way for an Israeli government committed to a peaceful solution."[72]

Despite all this, Kirkland still stubbornly refused to criticize Israel. "The worldwide revulsion it has evoked," he said, referencing the Sabra and Shatila massacre, "must be turned against the vicious terrorism that has been the special hallmark of the conflict in the Middle East and that has been openly espoused as an appropriate tactic by the PLO and its supporters."[73]

In early 1983, Sharon was removed from his post as Israel's minister of defense over the Sabra and Shatila massacre. That summer, as Israel agreed to start a gradual withdrawal from Lebanon (which was only completed in the year 2000), Begin resigned in disgrace.

THE EL AL STRIKE

The close-knit relationship between US labor and Israel would face one of its greatest tests in the mid-1980s. But it would not be over Israel's human rights abuses and war crimes, but rather over a protracted strike of American workers at El Al, Israel's state-owned airline. With 40 percent of its flights going between New York City and Tel Aviv, El Al maintained a presence at John F. Kennedy International Airport and a regional office in Manhattan. The airline had about three hundred US employees in New York, around 220 of whom were unionized through the International Association of Machinists (IAM). They included mechanics, reservation clerks, storekeepers, commissary agents, flight dispatchers, and passenger service agents.

Thanks to a combination of mismanagement and decreasing tourism, El Al fell into financial hard times in the 1970s. And, in the ten years between 1972 and 1982, its Histadrut-affiliated workers in Israel staged nearly seventy wildcat strikes to demand improved compensation and working conditions, causing frequent disruptions in service that only further hurt the airline's bottom line. Finally, in September 1982, El Al was put into receivership by Israel's bankruptcy court and was shut down for four months to undergo restructuring. When the airline reopened the following January, still under receivership, the new management implemented harsh austerity measures to try making the state-owned company profitable again. These included laying off 20 percent of its Israeli workforce (about one thousand employees), freezing wages, and doing away with many work rules.

Around the same time, in March 1983, El Al's collective bargaining agreement with the 220 IAM members in New York expired, prompting negotiations for a successor agreement. Management came to the bargaining table determined to force the same austerity on its American workers as they had already imposed on their Israeli employees. The airline's proposals included a three-year wage freeze, a reduction in vacation days, the right to contract nonunion workers to perform duties normally performed by IAM members, and a weakening of job classifications to allow the cross-utilization of employees (i.e., having workers perform duties that fell outside their job description).

After a year of negotiations, El Al refused to budge on its concessionary demands. Management argued that because the airline's Israeli workforce had already made economic sacrifices for the sake of the company, US employees now had to do the same. By March 1984, the IAM bargaining team signaled its willingness to accept a two-year wage freeze, followed by modest 3 to 4 percent raises in the third year, but held out against El Al's proposals around contracting outside employees and cross-utilizing workers. "It's not a question of money," said reservation agent and IAM member Lisa Blazer, "it's basic job security."[74]

Management still did not move, and so on March 16, 1984, the workers went on strike. Little did they know the work stoppage would drag on for over two years and prompt the personal intervention of top officials from the Israeli government and AFL-CIO.

§

The IAM members employed by El Al were proudly pro-Israel. As Blazer told a reporter, "It's not Israel we're against, it's the management of the company."[75] They considered themselves loyal employees, having never before gone on strike, while their Israeli counterparts had been on strike almost constantly in the previous decade. In a message sent to the union members a few days before the strike began, IAM District 100 chief negotiator Gene Hoffman highlighted their unusual degree of dedication:

> Working for El Al is an experience that will not be easily understood by other workers in the U.S.A., as to work for El Al, is not just being another airline employee, but is to be a part of the Israeli government. The State of Israel has been involved in many confrontations with their neighbors and we too as employees were also involved in the many confrontations and in a most willing and positive manner. I personally do not know of any employee who ever complained of their assignments

> during these trying times. During those times, we have loaded ammunition, war supplies and traveled to many Air Force bases through out [*sic*] the U.S.A. We also ran fund raising [*sic*] drives and collected large sums of money from our own staff. This is not what the average airline employee is expected to do, but we did it and are proud that it was done.[76]

But as the workers soon discovered, their record of loyalty meant nothing to El Al management.

Immediately after the work stoppage began, El Al imported approximately ninety Israeli strikebreakers who held dual US citizenship, putting them up at a hotel in Midtown Manhattan and bringing them to JFK Airport in an armored limousine. The airline also hired private security guards to intimidate picketers. After the IAM and AFL-CIO raised alarms about the use of Israeli scabs, Histadrut general secretary Yerucham Meshel condemned El Al "in the strongest possible terms." The strikebreakers were soon recalled to Israel, but the airline only replaced them with American scab workers. Due to such hardline tactics, within the strike's first three weeks, about eighty IAM members crossed the picket line and returned to work, fearful of losing their jobs.[77]

Most offensive to the IAM strikers were allegations of antisemitism leveled at the union by David Schneider, El Al's general manager for North America. Schneider told Israeli newspapers that union officials were making antisemitic and anti-Israel remarks at the bargaining table and that picketers were calling him "things like fucking Jewish bastard, etc." and asking him, "How many children did you kill in Lebanon today?" He claimed that by going on strike at El Al as opposed to any other foreign airline, the IAM was discriminating against Israel.[78]

Outraged, the striking union members—at least half of whom were Jewish and had often worked unpaid overtime and donated entire paychecks to support Israel during times of war and crisis—passed a resolution decrying "El Al Israel Airlines for lying to the Israeli media by labeling our Union and it's [*sic*] leadership as anti-semetic [*sic*]." Their statement called management's allegations a "despicable tactic . . . to try and justify their union busting actions."[79]

§

By the summer of 1984, the El Al dispute had no end in sight. Using scab labor, the airline reported that its operations in New York were unhindered by the ongoing strike. Union leaders needed to find other ways to exert pressure on the company.

When a $1 million State of Israel bond held by the IAM matured that June, the union opted not to renew it. Then in July, at IAM president William Winpisinger's urging, Kirkland and the AFL-CIO Executive Council formally called for a boycott of El Al, instructing US union members not to patronize the Israeli airline until the strike was resolved. It was the first and only time the AFL-CIO's national leadership endorsed any kind of anti-Israel boycott. Kirkland and Winpisinger hoped the move would force Israeli prime minister Yitzhak Shamir, the Likud politician who succeeded Begin, to step in and settle the dispute.[80]

Meanwhile, despite sympathizing with the IAM, the Jewish Labor Committee became worried the strike was undermining US union support for Israel. "This dispute is receiving increased attention and wider publicity. The fact that El Al is state run is being noted," JLC director Martin Lipan wrote in a letter to two hundred Jewish American leaders. "The longer this dispute is permitted to fester, the more attention it will receive, and the greater damage it will do to Israel's interests."[81] Other JLC leaders similarly warned that "if the state-run airline persists in its recalcitrant attitude," it would make it "more difficult to elicit the kind of enthusiastic and almost universal support" for Israel among the union rank and file.[82]

In response, several pro-Zionist Jewish American organizations called on Israeli government officials to resolve the strike, but their pleas appeared to fall on deaf ears from the Shamir government.

Following Israeli elections that put the country's Labor Party back in power, JLC president Herb Magidson wrote to all Knesset members urging them to take note of the El Al strike and "to recognize the danger of the situation and insist on a speedy and fair resolution of the issues." Shimon Peres, the new prime minister, visited the United States in October 1984 and made time to meet with both Kirkland and the JLC's Lipan, promising both men that he would look into the labor dispute.[83]

In February 1985, the work stoppage was nearing its one-year mark. Both sides had agreed to settle the major contract issues through arbitration, but the IAM was also pushing for a "return to work" agreement to allow the approximately ninety union members who remained on strike to get their jobs back. El Al had replaced them all with scab employees and was unwilling to take back all the strikers, claiming about twenty of them had engaged in "misconduct" on the picket lines and that they would create "an unhealthy atmosphere" at work if they were brought back.[84]

That same month, the AFL-CIO's Union Label and Service Trades Department—the unit in charge of enforcing boycotts of struck companies—sent a resolution to the Federation's Executive Council that, if approved, threatened to drastically cut US labor's long-standing ties to Israel. Noting El Al management's refusal to bargain in good faith and its attempts to bust the union, the resolution vowed that until the Israeli government forced the state-owned airline to finally settle the dispute, all AFL-CIO affiliates and departments would do the following:

1. Call in their Israeli bonds immediately or at maturity,

2. Announce their refusal to purchase Israeli bonds, or attend Bond dinners and functions, and

3. Urge that union members and officers refuse to visit Israel until a contract is ratified.[85]

In short, the proposed resolution called for the US labor movement's divestment from the State of Israel and a boycott of the country itself.

This extraordinary measure would never be voted on. Kirkland recommended that "rather than adopt a statement committing the AFL-CIO to a boycott against a friendly democratic country, which could have many additional consequences," the Executive Council should hold off on a vote pending developments in the negotiations. Kirkland argued that the mere threat of the resolution would convince Peres to intervene in the strike, adding that "the anti-union campaign by El Al at Kennedy Airport in New York was a holdover from the policies of Israel's Likkud [*sic*] government which is now out of office."[86]

By that spring, the Israeli prime minister sent a representative to settle the strike on his behalf.[87] But no settlement on the return-to-work issue was reached all through the summer of 1985. That fall, Kirkland—who normally was loath to criticize Israel—wrote to Peres expressing his "deep disappointment" and "sense of outrage" that the dispute remained unresolved.[88] Still, Kirkland and the AFL-CIO Executive Council did not take a vote on the divestment and boycott resolution introduced earlier that year. Instead, at the labor federation's convention held in October, a more symbolic resolution was passed condemning El Al's anti-union tactics and saying the airline "projects an unfair image of the nation of Israel."[89]

The acrimony and the negotiations continued for several more months, until a tentative agreement was finally reached in late May 1986 and ratified the following month. The deal allowed all ninety remaining strikers to get their jobs back within sixty days, with the replacement workers being laid off, as well as pension and health care improvements. The IAM's strike finally ended and the AFL-CIO's boycott of the airline was lifted, but the long-standing friendship between US labor and the Israeli state was left badly bruised.[90]

CHAPTER 5

INTIFADA

Between deindustrialization, corporate union busting, and relentless right-wing attacks, the US labor movement suffered a massive drop in size, strength, and influence during the 1980s. As this happened, and as many union officials accepted concessions at the bargaining table in the hopes of staving off more factory shutdowns and job losses, rank-and-file union members continuously lost faith in the established labor leadership.

A younger generation of progressive, militant unionists argued that in a rapidly globalizing economy, international labor solidarity was necessary to safeguard workers' rights both at home and abroad. To that end, throughout the 1980s they called on their unions to reject US imperialism and to support worker struggles in places like El Salvador, the Philippines, and South Africa. As the Cold War came to an end by the start of the 1990s, the American Federation of Labor and Congress of Industrial Organizations (AFL-CIO)'s traditional anticommunist obsession appeared increasingly outdated and meaningless to many in the labor movement who were more concerned about reversing union decline, confronting multinational corporations, and protecting workers' rights.

During this period, a historic uprising known as the Intifada broke out in Palestine. Braving violent repression at the hands of Israeli soldiers, hundreds of thousands of mostly young, working-class Palestinians organized persistent protests and economic disruptions to demand an end to decades of oppression. This popular rebellion became the most significant challenge the Zionist project had faced since the Great Arab Revolt of the 1930s. As the American labor movement was simultaneously grappling with its future and rethinking its role in the world, some US unions began openly expressing solidarity with the Palestinian people for the first time ever—cracking open the door to further US labor activism around Palestine in the decades to come.

THE UPRISING

The year 1987 marked the twentieth anniversary of the Six-Day War. For two decades, Israel had occupied the West Bank, Gaza Strip, and East Jerusalem, which now had a combined population of 1.5 million Palestinians. With 541,000 people crowded into a 140-square-mile area, Gaza had become one of the most densely populated places in the world. In the post-1967 occupied territories, Palestinians lived under the daily oppression of Israeli military rule, where they were restricted from so much as displaying the Palestinian flag, and experienced the ongoing humiliation of being pushed off their lands to make room for ever more illegal Zionist settlements.

In addition, Palestinians experienced grinding poverty and lack of opportunity due to Israel's restrictions on economic development in the territories. This deliberate underdevelopment served to create a steady supply of desperate and exploitable workers for Israel's own ever-growing economy. As the Israeli economy modernized and the Likud Party became more popular, old Labor Zionist notions like "Hebrew Labor"—which had reflected the commitment of newly arriving Jewish settlers to perform manual labor at the expense of Arab workers—were gradually abandoned.

By the 1980s, every day, some 100,000 Palestinians from the West Bank and Gaza passed through security checkpoints to enter Israel's pre-1967 boundaries and work low-wage, menial jobs at construction sites, factories, farms, restaurants, and municipal sanitation departments before crossing back after their shifts.[1] Because they worked inside Israel "proper," part of their wages—totaling millions of dollars per year—were automatically deducted by the Israeli Labor Ministry as contributions to social welfare programs such as health care, sick pay, unemployment insurance, pensions, and disability insurance. But, as noncitizens, they were not eligible to receive these benefits that they were paying for.

On top of that, because they often worked at nominally union workplaces with collective bargaining agreements, Palestinian day laborers also had 1 percent of their wages deducted as fees to the Histadrut. But Histadrut leaders refused to represent these workers, claiming that doing so would give the impression that they favored annexation of the Gaza Strip and West Bank. As a result, Israeli employers were free to violate union contracts and discriminate against Palestinian workers by paying them lower wages than they paid Jewish employees.

Inside the West Bank and Gaza, Palestinian trade unions were fractured throughout the 1980s due to their respective affiliations with the competing parties within the Palestine Liberation Organization (PLO)—including Fatah, the Popular Front for the Liberation of Palestine, the Democratic Front for the Liberation of Palestine, and the Palestine Communist Party (which was reestablished in 1982, joined the PLO five years later, and was eventually renamed the Palestinian People's Party). In some respects, the Palestinian unions of this period were only paper organizations functioning as appendages of the political parties, but this was partly due to the systematic repression they faced from Israeli occupation forces whenever they attempted to advocate for workers.[2]

For example, in July 1987, Feisal Hindi, a trade union official in the West Bank city of Qalqilya, was arrested because his General Institutions Workers Union issued a guidebook for Palestinian workers that explained their workplace rights under Israeli law. This supposedly violated an Israeli military censorship law imposed on the occupied territories. "Most of the workers in Qalqilya work in Israel," Hindi said later. "They pay taxes which help pay for the Israeli occupation and they pay dues to the Histadrut and get no representation. When our union tries to do something for these workers they come and arrest us and say we are terrorists."[3]

That same month, Israeli authorities again invoked the censorship law to forcibly shutter a cooperative print shop run by the Jerusalem Printers Union, which had been set up two years earlier to provide work for unemployed members. "They gave us no warning at all," explained the union's leader, Majed al-Labadi. "They never came and said 'you shouldn't be printing this' or 'that publication is illegal.' They just came in and closed us down."[4] The occupation forces also did not tolerate union democracy. In early 1987, three legally registered unions in Gaza each had their headquarters raided and officials arrested after they held leadership elections without first getting permission from the Israeli authorities.[5]

The Israeli government justified such repressive measures to the International Labor Organization by claiming that Palestinian trade unions were not genuine unions, but merely fronts for terrorism because of their affiliation with the PLO. Such claims were echoed by the Histadrut, which also exhibited racist attitudes toward Palestinians, as it had since its founding six decades earlier. For example, when employees at a textile factory in the Israeli city of Dimona were facing layoffs in

1984, the Histadrut workers' council at the plant reportedly demanded that Palestinian workers be terminated before any Jews. In 1987, when a Gaza businessman tried purchasing a construction materials factory in the Israeli town of Kiryat Gat, the town's Histadrut Labor Council threatened a general strike. "We will not allow a Jewish factory to come under ownership of an Arab merchant from the Territories," one of the local Histadrut leaders said.[6]

§

In December 1987, after an Israeli military vehicle killed four Palestinians in a Gaza traffic collision, a wave of mass demonstrations broke out in the post-1967 occupied territories that would continue for the next five years. Hundreds of thousands of men, women, and children took to the streets to denounce the occupation and demand freedom while defiantly displaying the Palestinian flag. It was the largest, most sustained mass protest movement in Palestine since the Great Arab Revolt of 1936–1939.

The uprising—or Intifada, as it would be known (from the Arabic word meaning "awakening" or "shaking off")—was the response to decades of pent-up frustrations over the daily indignities of military rule. It took the Israeli government by surprise, as it did the PLO's top leaders, who had been chased away to distant Tunisia following Israel's invasion of Lebanon five years before.

Though the Intifada began spontaneously, it was fueled by grassroots organizing within the cities, towns, and refugee camps of the West Bank and Gaza Strip. Local organizers coalesced into the Unified National Leadership of the Uprising, which sympathized with the PLO and was quickly forced underground amid mounting Israeli repression. Yitzhak Rabin, Israel's former prime minister now serving as defense minister in the Labor Party government, ordered soldiers to use "might, force and beatings" against the protesters, including breaking their arms and legs. Occupation forces carried out mass arrests and deportations, detained thousands without due process, instituted strict curfews, and shut down schools and universities. Troops used clubs, teargas, rubber-coated bullets, and live rounds against unarmed Palestinian demonstrators. But the uprising continued.

"We are walking now with our chests bared," an unnamed 22-year-old bicycle mechanic from Gaza's Bureij refugee camp told reporters. "We don't care anymore. Our life is not worth it. If we get killed, maybe it can produce a better life for our people."[7]

Images of Israeli soldiers viciously beating young protesters were beamed out across the international media. Although Western news reports played up sporadic incidents of Palestinians attempting to fight back with rocks or Molotov cocktails, global audiences nevertheless could see that the violence was overwhelmingly one-sided. Indeed, the most forceful tactics Palestinians used in the Intifada were entirely nonviolent, such as boycotts, withholding taxes, and strikes.

Echoing the 1936 general strike that kicked off the Great Revolt, several mass work stoppages were held throughout the Intifada, usually lasting one to two days each. The general strikes were called by the Unified National Leadership, which issued communiqués and circulated leaflets exhorting Palestinians to stay off the job on specified days and join demonstrations. Some of the work stoppages were organized separately by Hamas, a newly formed Islamic resistance organization at odds with the PLO's secular vision and covertly encouraged by Israeli authorities in the hopes of further dividing the Palestinian nationalist movement.[8]

On designated strike days, tens of thousands of Palestinian day laborers would refuse to cross into Israel's pre-1967 boundaries for work, forcing construction sites, restaurants, textile mills, and other businesses to shut down for the day. At the same time, shopkeepers in the West Bank and Gaza closed their stores, meaning no sales of Israeli-made products exported into the territories. The strikes cost Israel's economy an estimated $6 million per day.[9] Besides arresting organizers, Rabin temporarily banned the shipment of food aid into Gaza refugee camps and cut off fuel supplies in an attempt to pressure Palestinians to get back to work and reopen their shops, but the sporadic strikes rolled on. The Blacksmiths Union offered free repairs of the metal shutters on shops that Israeli soldiers broke while trying to force them to reopen.

The earliest general strike was observed in Gaza, the West Bank, and East Jerusalem on December 15–16, 1987, about one week into the Intifada. On December 21, another strike was held across the occupied territories, only this one was also observed by at least 250,000 Palestinian citizens of Israel living inside the country's pre-1967 boundaries. It was the first time since Israel's founding that its Palestinian citizens—who, despite their nominal citizenship, had long suffered systematic discrimination—joined in unified action with their fellow Palestinians in Gaza and the West Bank. They demanded an end to the occupation and the creation of a Palestinian state. The December 21 strike reportedly cost the Israeli economy $7.65 million.[10]

Many other general strikes were held in the West Bank and Gaza as the Intifada continued over the next few years. Some were timed to coincide with particular events, including US Secretary of State George Shultz's visit to Israel in February 1988 and the fortieth anniversary of the Nakba that May.[11]

SOUTH AFRICA COMPARISONS AND US LABOR

As with Israel's siege of Beirut a few years earlier, the violent attempts to suppress the Intifada shocked and disturbed many Americans, challenging their manufactured perception of Israel as a righteous nation of underdogs. In the United States and much of the rest of the world, it was difficult not to see parallels between Palestine and South Africa.

Since 1948—the same year as Israel's founding—South Africa's minority white settler population of Afrikaners had imposed a brutal system of racial segregation and subjugation on the Indigenous Black majority called apartheid. Throughout that entire time, Black South Africans had resisted and organized for their liberation, and the white apartheid regime used systematic repression to stay in power. All the while, Washington maintained friendly relations with South Africa's white rulers because they were reliably anticommunist allies in the Cold War. By the 1970s and 1980s, as Black South Africans escalated their popular resistance efforts through general strikes and mass demonstrations, African Americans and progressives in the United States—many of them veterans of the civil rights and anti-Vietnam War movements—became fed up with their government's acceptance of the racist apartheid regime.

Anti-apartheid activism in the US intensified through the Free South Africa Movement, which swept the country in the mid-1980s. Starting in November 1984, tens of thousands of protesters consistently held nonviolent, civil disobedience actions at the South African Embassy in Washington and at consulates across the country—with over two thousand people arrested over the next six months alone. At the same time, college students held large rallies and organized encampments on their campuses to demand that their universities financially divest from the apartheid state.

Importantly, the US labor movement backed these efforts, with Black unionists taking the lead. West Coast dockworkers with the traditionally left-wing International Longshore and Warehouse Union (ILWU)—who had long supported the anti-apartheid movement—refused to unload South African cargo, and major AFL-CIO-affiliated unions like the American Federation of State, County, and Municipal Employees (AFSCME), United Auto Workers (UAW), and United Mine Workers (whose memberships all included large numbers of African American workers) stepped up the boycott and divestment activities they had begun organizing in previous years.

Although the AFL-CIO's top leadership publicly condemned apartheid, the federation's president, Lane Kirkland, was initially reluctant to support the boycott and divestment strategy due to fears that a sudden collapse of the apartheid regime—as opposed to a planned, orderly transition—might lead to left-wing, Soviet-friendly forces coming to power in South Africa. Instead, Kirkland tended to follow US President Ronald Reagan's policy of "constructive engagement," which favored a softer approach of dialogue with South Africa's white rulers in the hopes of incentivizing them to give up apartheid voluntarily and gradually, rather than be forced to do so immediately through outside pressure.

"Constructive engagement" was a calculation by US cold warriors who feared the spread of communism in southern Africa and knew that the apartheid regime could be counted on to remain firmly anticommunist. It was also unsurprisingly the tack preferred by US multinational corporations with heavy investments in South Africa like General Motors and Mobil. Only after being pushed by African American trade unionists, several union presidents, and the broader labor movement did Kirkland finally endorse boycotting and divesting from South Africa in 1986.[12]

Comparisons between Israel and South Africa had been made since at least the early 1960s. Speaking before the UN General Assembly in 1961, South Africa's far-right prime minister and apartheid architect Hendrik Verwoerd argued that "[Israelis] took Israel from the Arabs after they had lived there for a thousand years. In that I agree with them. Israel, like South

Africa, is an apartheid state."[13] Palestinians themselves long likened the oppression they faced at the hands of Israel to South Africa's apartheid system. In 1965, for example, Fayez Sayegh—a scholar, diplomat, and founder of the Beirut-based Palestine Research Center—wrote that "whereas the Afrikaner apostles of apartheid in South Africa . . . brazenly proclaim their sin, the Zionist practitioners of apartheid in Palestine beguilingly protest their innocence!"[14]

After Israel began its military occupation over the Palestinians living in the West Bank and Gaza in 1967, the similarities became even more blatant. In November 1973, when Arab American auto workers in Detroit were preparing to go on their historic wildcat strike to protest the UAW's investments in Israeli state bonds, their local community allies from the American Arab Coordinating Committee explained in a newspaper advertisement that "purchase of Israeli bonds is regarded by these workers similarly as would a UAW investment in racist South Africa would be regarded by black workers."[15]

There were also direct ties between the two states. From the early 1970s onward, the Israeli government maintained a secret military alliance with apartheid South Africa. Israel exported its high-tech weaponry to South Africa—which was used by the racist white regime to violently control the Indigenous Black population—while South Africa provided Israel with the uranium and other raw materials needed to expand its covert nuclear arsenal.[16]

In the 1980s, as the growth of the Free South Africa Movement coincided with the Intifada in Palestine, it became increasingly common for activists and commentators around the world to draw parallels between the two struggles.[17]

Three months into the Intifada, in March 1988, a California-based group of left-wing activists called the Campaign to End All Aid to Israel/For a Democratic and Secular Palestine took out a full-page advertisement in *The New York Times* with a statement comparing Israel to South Africa and demanding the US government suspend all military and economic assistance to the Zionist state. "Were we subjected to a brutal occupation, daily humiliation, military rule, mass imprisonment and institutionalized torture, we too would rise up in revolt. . . . Israel is an apartheid state, founded on pillage and predicated on exclusivity. Rights flow from ethnic and religious identity," the statement declared.

Instead of seeking a two-state solution, the statement called for a single, democratic, racially pluralistic state—the same demand made in South Africa by the anti-apartheid movement. "In Israel, no less than in South Africa, minimum justice requires dismantling the apartheid state and replacing it with a democratic secular Palestine, where Jews and Arabs, Christians and Moslems, live together with equal rights and opportunities," it read.

Over three hundred prominent individuals put their names on the statement, including academics, artists, clergy, and attorneys—as well as over a dozen local union officials and staffers from around the country. The most well-known unionist to sign on was Jim Guyette, former president of Local P-9 of the United Food and Commercial Workers. Between 1985 and 1986, Guyette had led a high-profile, but ultimately failed, strike at the Hormel plant in Austin, Minnesota.[18]

Responding to rising pro-Palestinian sentiment in the United States, including among union members, Kirkland and the AFL-CIO Executive Council issued a statement of their own in early 1988. They acknowledged that "in their effort to maintain order" amid the uprising, Israeli troops "have on occasion resorted to unnecessary force." While not condoning violence against civilians, the Executive Council generously attributed it to the "inexperience" and "frustrations" of Israeli soldiers.

Further, the AFL-CIO leaders dismissed attempts to liken Israel to South Africa, calling any such comparison "a calumny we categorically reject and resent." The Executive Council pointed to Israel's Palestinian citizens, claiming they enjoyed equal rights and full democracy and saying that "to compare such a society with South Africa . . . is not only to slander but to rob democracy of its defining characteristics and thus to subvert the very idea of democracy."[19] In declaring this, the AFL-CIO Executive Council not only ignored the systemic discrimination and oppression of Palestinian citizens of Israel—hundreds of thousands of whom had recently gone on a general strike to protest what they themselves called Israel's "apartheid policies"[20]—but also totally sidestepped the plight of the 1.5 million Palestinians living under Israeli military rule in the West Bank and Gaza.

The council's statement mentioned that the frustrations of Palestinians in the post-1967 occupied territories were "understandable," but attributed all their suffering to the PLO. "The real tragedy of the Palestinians of the West Bank and Gaza Strip is that they have failed to develop leaders willing and able to negotiate with Israel," the AFL-CIO officials said. This effectively absolved the occupying force of any responsibility and disregarded how the PLO had made sincere attempts to engage in diplomacy over the years only to be rebuked, demonized, and delegitimized not just by the Israeli and US governments, but by AFL-CIO leaders themselves.[21]

It was obviously far easier for top US labor officials to denounce the oppression of Black South Africans than to criticize Israel's similar oppression of Palestinians because they were not financially and ideologically invested in South African apartheid.

LABOR COMMITTEE ON THE MIDDLE EAST

Despite the AFL-CIO Executive Council's staunchly pro-Israel position, many US unions demonstrated unprecedented solidarity with Palestinians during the Intifada. This was thanks to a newer generation of unionists who had first been politicized through the social movements of the 1960s and early 1970s, including struggles opposing racism and imperialism. What's more, thanks to the civil rights reforms and rank-and-file rebellions of the previous two decades—which included the UAW's Arab American members asserting their dignity—organized labor in the 1980s was more racially and culturally diverse than ever before. This allowed for a broader range of perspectives on various social and political issues, including the question of Palestine.

Four months before the outbreak of the Intifada, a group of around ten progressive trade unionists in the Bay Area, California, launched the Labor Committee on the Middle East (LCOME) with the goal of educating American union members about "the key role played by U.S. labor 'leaders' in maintaining domestic and international support for Israel's continued occupation and repression of 1.5 million Palestinians in the Israeli-occupied West Bank and Gaza," as well as building "conscious support within the labor movement for our Palestinian sisters and brothers in their struggle to rid themselves of more than two decades of Israeli occupation and forty years of dispossession."[22]

LCOME was cofounded by Steve Zeltzer, a stationary engineer for the City of San Francisco and shop steward with the International Union of Operating Engineers Local 39, and Jeffrey Blankfort, a veteran reporter and member of the Newspaper Guild. Zeltzer had participated in the anti–Vietnam War movement and Blankfort had covered the war in Lebanon as a photojournalist. Both advocated for the Bay Area labor movement to take a strong stand against US imperialism and militarism in the Middle East, but were met with hostility by union officials and even some fellow activists when it came to criticizing Israel, prompting them to start LCOME with the goal of educating US unionists.

With many US unions becoming more active in the Free South Africa Movement at the time, Zeltzer and Blankfort especially aimed to shine a light on the connections between Israel and apartheid South Africa. As its first public action, LCOME picketed a Histadrut fundraiser at San Francisco's Fairmont Hotel on October 15, 1987, to protest how the Israeli labor organization's largest corporate subsidiary, Koor Industries, operated a joint venture with the state-owned South African Steel Corporation called Iskoor Steel. Among the attendees at the fundraiser dinner were members of the California state legislature and top officials of the California Federation of Labor and San Francisco Labor Council.[23]

As a nominally Israeli company, the Histadrut-controlled Iskoor not only allowed South Africa to export steel to the United States and Europe in defiance of sanctions and economic boycotts, it also manufactured tank armor and other equipment for the South African military despite a UN arms embargo. "It was a logical direct connection," Zeltzer explained decades later. "While we were fighting for the AFL-CIO and US unions to support the anti-apartheid struggle, we said 'how can we ignore the fact that Israel is actually supporting the apartheid regime as well, economically and militarily?'"[24]

Following the start of the Palestinian uprising, LCOME launched a quarterly newsletter in summer 1988 entitled *Middle East Labor Bulletin*. Edited by Blankfort and coordinated by Zeltzer, the *Bulletin* was distributed at national union conventions and financially supported by at least fifty other trade unionists around the country. Over the next seven years, until it was discontinued in 1995, it would publish informative articles about workers' struggles in the occupied Palestinian territories and elsewhere in the Middle East, as well as updates about efforts within US unions to offer support for Palestinian workers amid the violent crackdown on the Intifada.

With organizing and encouragement from LCOME supporters within their ranks, several unions soon passed resolutions criticizing Israel and expressing solidarity with Palestinians, something that had never happened before. In early 1988, for example, AFSCME Council 10—representing twenty-seven thousand staff at the University of California system—passed a measure urging the AFL-CIO to dump its estimated $300 million in Israeli bonds and break ties with the Histadrut over its discriminatory treatment of Palestinian workers. The Alameda Central Labor Council in Oakland also passed a resolution calling on the US government to use "its massive economic and military aid to Israel as leverage" to stop the violent attacks on Palestinian protesters.[25]

In Lorain, Ohio, workers at the town's steel mill with United Steelworkers Local 1104 in January 1988 voted in favor of a measure demanding that Washington cut off aid to Israel over its "suppression and treatment of peoples living in the occupied territories of the Gaza strip and West Bank." The next year, members of United Steelworkers Local 8751 in Boston also passed a resolution calling for an end to US aid to Israel and for unions to divest from Israeli bonds.[26]

The ILWU—the progressive union of West Coast dockworkers—approved a measure at its national convention in April 1988 comparing Israel to apartheid South Africa, criticizing the Histadrut's discriminatory practices, and urging the US government to pressure Israel to stop the violence, end the occupation, and support an international peace process to secure a Palestinian state. At its own national convention that same year, the similarly left-wing United Electrical Workers (UE) passed a resolution calling for recognition of the PLO as the "authentic representative of the Palestinian people" and for the creation of a Palestinian state alongside Israel. "The U.S. Government has contributed to the continued conflict by its one-sided support for Israel and its failure to take into account the legitimate aspirations of the Palestinian people," the UE resolution stated.[27]

AFSCME, the Service Employees International Union (SEIU), and the Newspaper Guild also condemned Israeli repression at their own national conventions in 1988. The Newspaper Guild particularly criticized Israel for shutting down the Palestinian Press Service and arresting at least thirty Palestinian journalists since the start of the uprising. "In muffling the voice of Arab opposition on the one hand and blindfolding the eyes of Israeli and foreign correspondents on the other, Israel is emulating the press policy of another government under siege, South Africa," the Guild's resolution said. "Its proponents have offered a chillingly parallel rationale: that without journalists to witness it, there would be no rebellion."[28]

At its 1989 national convention, the UAW broke from its history of unswerving support for the Zionist state to denounce the "extreme and unacceptable" use of "violence inflicted on Palestinians in the West Bank and Gaza, particularly by the Israeli Defense Forces." The auto workers' union further called for an international peace conference that would include the PLO to end the occupation and recognize Palestinian self-determination.[29]

Though only statements, these various resolutions highlighted how the US labor movement's positions on Palestine were dramatically evolving in response to the Intifada and its similarities to the South African anti-apartheid struggle. This was also demonstrated at the April 1989 Labor Notes conference, a gathering in Detroit of one thousand rank-and-file union activists from around the country determined to inject some much-needed strategy and militancy into the labor movement. On a panel about international solidarity, the conference attendees heard from Tamer Isawi, president of the faculty union at Birzeit University in the occupied West Bank. Isawi, who had been brought to the conference by the Labor Committee on the

Middle East, spoke of the repression faced by Palestinian workers and received a standing ovation from the crowd.

"This was the first time that a Palestinian trade unionist had addressed an American labor audience of this, or any significant size," a report in LCOME's *Middle East Labor Bulletin* explained. "It signaled the long-delayed passage of the Palestinian workers' struggle across the threshold of the U.S. international labor solidarity movement, which has consistently been opposed by the leadership of the AFL-CIO."[30]

Indeed, at the AFL-CIO's own convention later that same year, the Executive Council excluded a proposed resolution submitted by the central labor council of Madison, Wisconsin, that condemned Israel for unlawfully deporting a handful of Palestinian union leaders. Instead, the delegates were given (and approved) an omnibus resolution on a host of international issues, which included a statement that praised the Histadrut while only tepidly criticizing the Israel Defense Forces for occasionally using "unnecessary force," blaming the "unfortunate climate of tension" on "the PLO-inspired intifada [which] is not conducive to negotiations."[31]

§

Some US unionists also assisted the American-Arab Anti-Discrimination Committee (ADC)—the largest Arab American civil rights organization—in its attempt to hold Israel accountable for denying labor rights to workers in the West Bank and Gaza Strip.

In 1988, the ADC filed a petition with the Office of the US Trade Representative requesting that Israel be removed from the Generalized System of Preferences (GSP). The GSP allowed developing countries to export products to the United States duty free. Israel had sent $500 million worth of products under the program the previous year. But US law mandated that any country enjoying GSP privileges had to follow internationally recognized labor standards, including freedom of association, the right to collective bargaining, minimum wage laws, and safe working conditions. The US Trade Representative had removed Chile, Nicaragua, Paraguay, and Romania from the GSP program in 1987 after the AFL-CIO alleged labor violations in those nations.[32]

The ADC complaint accused Israel of denying Palestinian workers in Gaza and the West Bank the right to organize and administer unions, especially by shutting down union offices, banning union meetings, and arbitrarily detaining or deporting union leaders. It further alleged that the 100,000 Palestinian workers from the occupied territories who daily crossed into Israel for work were being systematically denied the same social security measures as Israeli workers, such as workers' compensation, old-age benefits, and maternity leave.

In October 1988, a month before the Office of the US Trade Representative was to hold a hearing on the ADC's petition, four American local union leaders traveled to the occupied West Bank and spent eight days meeting with Palestinian workers, as well as some Israeli legal advocates. Brought together by the ADC, the delegation consisted of Gene Bruskin, organizing director for the Laundry and Dry Cleaning International Union Local 66 in Massachusetts; Walter "Jeff" Washington, a Ford worker and president of UAW Local 900 in Detroit; Jeff Perry, treasurer of the National Postal Mail Handlers Union Local 300 in New York City; and William Rayson, a steward with Local 1071 of the National Association of Letter Carriers in Miami, Florida. They were hosted by Marty Rosenbluth, a Jewish American and former UAW organizer who was then living in the West Bank and working as a researcher for Al-Haq, a Ramallah-based human rights organization.[33]

It was the first time that a delegation of US unionists had traveled to Palestine and not been hosted by the Histadrut or any other Zionist institution, but instead had gone with the specific intention of listening to Palestinians. Rosenbluth took the visitors to several West Bank towns and introduced them to Palestinian workers and union activists who told of the routine repression they suffered at the hands of Israeli occupation forces. The delegation also learned how Palestinian unions endeavored to achieve "better wages, medical insurance, worker education, legal aid, and safer working conditions."[34]

Years later, Bruskin recalled that it was "heartbreaking and outrageous as a Jew" to see how Israel maintained "complete and unremitting control" over the daily lives of Palestinian workers. He also noted that witnessing Rosenbluth's warm relationship with many West Bank residents challenged "the myth that [Palestinians] were somehow against Jews," explaining that "they knew he was Jewish . . . [and] they were hugging him."[35]

At the end of the trip, as the US visitors were about to board their flight back home, an Israeli security guard pulled Bruskin into a closet-sized room at the airport. Holding the Jewish American unionist at gunpoint, the guard ordered him to divulge the names of every Palestinian he and the other delegates had met with in the West Bank, warning that failure to cooperate would result in missing the flight and being "stuck" in Israel. "I knew if I gave their names, [the Israelis] would put them in prison," Bruskin later explained. "So I said, 'I don't know. I'm not going to do it. You'll have to shoot me.' Probably was a stupid thing to say." But he was soon released and able to board the plane after ADC representatives called the US consulate, which in turn called the Israeli authorities at the airport and apparently pressured them to let Bruskin go.[36]

After returning to the United States, the delegates went to Washington, DC, to testify at the US Trade Representative hearing in support of the ADC's complaint—but they were only allowed to submit written statements into the record. Pro-Israel representatives of the AFL-CIO and Jewish Labor Committee spoke at the hearing about how Arab workers in Israel enjoyed full equality and labor rights because it was the only democracy in the Middle East, and how Palestinian unions only faced restrictions because they were fronts for PLO terrorism. "The irony was striking," Bruskin wrote soon after. "There we were, U.S. trade unionists, sitting in the hearing room and listening to officials from the AFL-CIO testify who had probably never sat down with Palestinian trade unionists or visited a West Bank village."[37]

Still, the US Trade Representative heard testimony from Rosenbluth and Mohammad Rashid al-Reshiq, secretary general of the Drivers and Mechanics Union in East Jerusalem. They meticulously verified the ADC's allegations, with al-Reshiq testifying that Israeli authorities restricted his union's ability to communicate with members and frequently harassed union officials at their office.

A few months later, the US Trade Representative rejected the ADC's petition and recommended keeping Israel in the GSP program. The decision was based on President George H. W. Bush's convoluted argument that if the United States recognized Israel's legal responsibilities to workers in the post-1967 occupied territories, it would be tantamount to legitimizing the occupation. But this was ludicrous because, under international law, recognizing the responsibilities of an occupying power does not imply that the occupation in question is itself acceptable.[38]

§

In May 1990, LCOME helped organize a small conference in Philadelphia attended by thirty-five unionists from seventeen unions across the United States and Canada to form the Palestine Labor Action Network (PLAN). The network's mission was to "distribute information on Palestinian workers and unions, [and] defend arrested Palestinian workers." Bob McCloskey, business agent with SEIU Local 660 in Los Angeles, and Jaime Veve, a member of Transport Workers Union Local 100 in New York, were elected to respectively serve as PLAN's West Coast and East Coast coordinators.[39]

PLAN's most visible campaign was advocating for the release of detained trade unionist Hani Beydoun. A leader of the Jerusalem Hotel Workers' Union, Beydoun was arrested without cause by Israeli occupation forces in March 1990, one of scores of Palestinian union organizers detained amid the uprising. What made him different was that he was known personally by many North American union members and leaders.

Before his imprisonment, in the summer of 1989, Beydoun had been invited to participate at the UN's Non-Governmental Organizations Symposium on the Question of Palestine in New York, where he spoke on a panel about the denial of workers' rights in the occupied territories. After this, he toured eighteen US and Canadian cities, meeting with trade unionists, Congress members, the directors of Amnesty International, and former presidential candidate and civil rights leader Jesse Jackson. It was not long after returning home to the West Bank that Beydoun was arrested by Israeli soldiers, held in a Ramallah prison, and denied legal representation. No reason was provided for his imprisonment until July, when he was charged only with being the leader of a union affiliated with the PLO.

During Beydoun's detainment, PLAN helped mobilize two thousand letters and telegrams from US and Canadian union members to the Israeli government demanding his immediate release. A May 1990 resolution adopted by AFSCME Social Service Local 1108 in Los Angeles noted that "it appears that the brutal detention of Brother Beydoun is in retaliation for his testimony" at the UN symposium, where he provided "direct evidence of the barbarous denial of human and labor rights of Palestinian workers in Israel and the occupied territories."[40] SEIU's Western Conference passed a similar resolution, and figures like Canadian Labour Congress president Shirley Carr and Alameda Central Labor Council executive secretary-treasurer Owen Marron also sent letters to Israeli authorities.[41]

PLAN tried to get the AFL-CIO to back the demand for Beydoun's release, but it is unclear whether the federation took any position on the matter.[42] An August 1990 letter by an official from the AFL-CIO's international affairs department noted that Beydoun had been arrested for his PLO affiliation and not for any trade union activity—implying that his detention was therefore not really a labor issue—and said nothing about his treatment or his rights.[43]

THE OSLO ACCORDS

The Camp David Accords and expulsion from Lebanon in the early 1980s had served to weaken the PLO's political and military strength. Now, amid a surge of pro-Palestinian sentiment around the world thanks to the Intifada, the PLO's leaders decided it was an advantageous moment to sue for a permanent peace with Israel. To be welcomed to the negotiating table by the US government, in late 1988, Yasser Arafat formally accepted the two-state solution, recognized the State of Israel, and renounced armed resistance. Despite these major, unilateral concessions, the Israeli government still refused to negotiate with him.

In October 1991, the United States and USSR convened a Middle East peace conference in Madrid, Spain, bringing together representatives from Israel, Jordan, Syria, and Lebanon. Because the Soviet Union was then in the process of disintegration—leading to the end of the Cold War by December of that year—it ultimately played no real role in the conference. US Secretary of State James Baker took the lead and allowed a delegation of Palestinian lawyers and academics from the occupied territories to participate despite Israel's initial refusal to talk directly with them. Though the Palestinian delegation did not formally represent the PLO, they were in constant phone communication with Arafat during the talks.[44]

Over the previous year, the PLO had politically isolated itself by refusing to join the rest of the Arab world in denouncing Iraqi president Saddam Hussein's invasion of Kuwait and supporting the US-led military intervention to drive his army back into Iraq. This served to alienate many of the Arab governments the PLO traditionally relied upon for diplomatic support. Now more alone than ever, Arafat and other PLO leaders holed up in Tunisia were especially eager, perhaps even desperate, to reach a peace deal with Israel.

The US-sponsored talks between Israel and the Palestinian delegates continued for two years with no tangible progress. Finally, in mid-1993, Yitzhak Rabin—now Israel's prime minister again—decided to enter into direct negotiations with the PLO, opening a secret channel with the help of Norwegian diplomats in Oslo. Within a couple of months, Israel's foreign minister Shimon Peres and the PLO's Mahmoud Abbas agreed to a declaration of principles, which set up a plan for limited self-rule by Palestinians in the occupied territories.

Under the plan, Israel would still maintain control over the land, water, and borders of the West Bank and Gaza Strip, but civil administration and security in some parts of the territories would be overseen by a new Palestinian National Authority. The Oslo agreement said nothing about the illegal Israeli settlements in the occupied territories, the precise geographic boundaries of a future Palestinian state, or the right of Palestinian refugees to return home.

"The AFL-CIO applauds the recent Peace Accord between the state of Israel and the Palestine Liberation Organization," read a resolution passed at the labor federation's October 1993 convention. Before the signing of the Oslo agreement, the AFL-CIO Executive Council had initially planned to put forward a measure blaming "Arab dictators" for obstructing the "peace process [that] has floundered for decades," but was forced to change course given the fast-moving developments. The new resolution called on the US government to provide "development and democratization assistance to the people of the West Bank and Gaza" and reiterated the AFL-CIO's "strong support for Histadrut."[45]

The following year, Arafat and other PLO leaders returned to live in the post-1967 occupied territories, while Jordan and Israel signed a formal peace agreement recognizing each other's borders and establishing full diplomatic relations. The Oslo agreement—which did nothing to guarantee Palestinian sovereignty—was hailed in the West as a historic breakthrough. Accordingly, Arafat, Rabin, and Peres were awarded the Nobel Peace Prize.

In 1995, a second Oslo accord was reached between Israel and the PLO, which carved the West Bank and Gaza into three separate administrative areas. In Area A, which comprised 18 percent of the territory and the largest Palestinian population centers, the newly created Palestinian Authority (PA) would be given civilian administration and security control. In Area B, which was 22 percent of the territory and included sparsely populated Palestinian villages, the PA was put in charge of administration, but Israel controlled security. The other 60 percent of the territory was in Area C, which included Zionist settlements, and would remain under complete Israeli control. Most PLO fighters returned to the occupied territories to serve in the PA's new security forces.[46]

§

Meanwhile, the divided Palestinian trade unions—which were each tied to rival factions within the PLO and often competed for jurisdiction within the same economic sectors—began a series of negotiations with each other in 1990 with the goal of unifying into a single labor federation.

The unification process was undertaken in response to the Intifada-inspired militancy among rank-and-file Palestinian workers, who were busily organizing heretofore nonunion workplaces in the occupied territories like an RC Cola plant in Ramallah. Although the rank and file wished to see more union democracy and better union administration come out of the unification, the negotiations were dominated by top officials from the different political factions, each vying to secure more influence in the future labor federation.[47]

Finally, by 1994, some 187 different unions in the West Bank and Gaza had been consolidated into only twelve unions under the banner of the Palestinian General Federation of Trade Unions (PGFTU). Unionists aligned with Fatah maintained majority control over the PGFTU's leadership structure, with Arafat ally Shaher Sa'ed serving as the federation's general secretary. As part of the Oslo talks, Palestinian and Israeli unionists brokered a deal in which the Histadrut agreed to transfer some of the funds it deducted from Palestinian day laborers' paychecks over to the PGFTU.[48]

But the PGFTU's leadership soon came under criticism from some rank-and-file Palestinian unionists who accused it of being an unelected clique that was more an arm of the PA than an authentic voice for the working class. The tension between labor officials and grassroots workers was on full display in early 1997, when West Bank schoolteachers staged a wildcat strike. Believing their interests were not represented by the PGFTU-affiliated General Union of Palestinian Teachers, rank-and-file educators democratically elected a Teachers Coordinating Committee of twenty-five of their peers—none of whom were members of Fatah or any other party—to demand that the PA authorize a 200 percent increase to their $300-per-month salaries.

The strike began that February after the PA's Ministry of Education offered only a 10 percent raise. By April, the work stoppage had reportedly spread to a majority of the West Bank's twelve thousand teachers at nearly seventeen hundred public schools. The PGFTU's Sa'ed tried convincing the Teachers Coordinating Committee to give up the strike, as did Arafat. When they refused, Arafat had at least fifteen members of the committee jailed and interrogated for six days until they agreed to call off the strike. The educators returned to work having won no concessions. "The teachers were doomed to fail," said Basim Makhoul, an economics professor at al-Najah University in Nablus. "They were unaffiliated. If they had been in Fatah, they would have been protected. But then if they had been in Fatah, they wouldn't have gone on strike."[49]

§

Aside from breaking public sector strikes, the PA had no real authority in the Palestinian territories beyond what was expressly granted by Israel. Instead of moving toward greater sovereignty after the Oslo deal, the West Bank, East Jerusalem, and Gaza were increasingly cut off from each other by a new system of barriers, walls, fences, and security checkpoints built and overseen by the Israeli military.

Despite all this, the Likud Party and other right-wing Zionists were outraged by the Oslo Accords because they stood in the way of Israel annexing the West Bank and Gaza Strip. In February 1994, a US-born Jewish extremist—who lived in an illegal settlement near the West Bank city of Hebron—used an assault rifle to murder twenty-nine Palestinians and wound over a hundred others during prayers at the Ibrahimi Mosque. On November 4, 1995, another Israeli right-winger assassinated Prime Minister Rabin as revenge for having negotiated the Oslo Accords.

NEW LEADERSHIP OF THE AFL-CIO

By the time of the Oslo Accords, the US labor movement was well over a decade into a sharp decline brought about by deindustrialization, globalization, corporate attacks, and union officials' complacency. In the early 1990s, many unionists were growing frustrated with the leadership of AFL-CIO president Lane Kirkland, who often seemed more interested in waging the Cold War abroad than in organizing nonunion workers in the United States.

Though Kirkland took a victory lap after the fall of the Berlin Wall and dissolution of the Soviet Union, he and the AFL-CIO were unable to stop passage of the North American Free Trade Agreement in 1993—a procorporate deal that ensured more US manufacturing jobs would be moved to Mexico, where workers could be paid far less. After this defeat, a group of fed-up union presidents effectively pushed Kirkland out of the AFL-CIO presidency, in what some described as a palace coup.[50]

At the labor federation's 1995 convention, the delegates elected John Sweeney to be the AFL-CIO's new president. Over the previous fifteen years, Sweeney had served as president of the Service Employees International Union, one of the few US unions to actually see membership growth in these years thanks to ambitious and strategic organizing campaigns among janitors and health care workers.

Unlike Kirkland, Meany, and many other labor officials who preceded him, Sweeney was not an ardent cold warrior. Instead, he was squarely focused on domestic issues impacting US workers. Under his leadership, the AFL-CIO finally shut down its anticommunist, government-funded overseas institutes that had been created at the height of the Cold War and consolidated them into a single entity called the Solidarity Center. Though still funded almost exclusively by the federal government—and therefore still generally in line with Washington's foreign policy agenda—the Solidarity Center appeared to be different from its predecessor institutes in that its activities tended to prioritize raising labor standards in poorer countries over weakening leftist forces around the world.[51]

Nevertheless, Sweeney emulated his predecessors by maintaining strong ties between US labor and Israel, particularly by encouraging unions to invest their pension funds in State of Israel bonds. In 1998, to commemorate the fiftieth anniversary of the Zionist state, the Development Corporation for Israel honored Sweeney with a "Labor Achievement Award." The following year, Sweeney ally and AFL-CIO secretary-treasurer Richard Trumka—the former president of the United Mine Workers—told unions they should "invest in the bonds that are such a tangible link between our movement and the continuing struggle to nurture and protect the State of Israel."[52]

Meanwhile, the Histadrut also experienced a decline in influence and membership during the 1980s and 1990s thanks in part to the rise of free market economic policies. In 1995, Israel's new National Health Insurance Law separated the Histadrut from the Kupat Holim health care network it had long controlled, meaning patients no longer needed to be Histadrut members to receive care. Also in this period, the Histadrut-owned Bank Hapoalim and industrial conglomerate Koor were sold off. All of this resulted in a dramatic membership drop for the Histadrut, with Israel's overall union density plummeting from 80 percent in 1981 to 43 percent in 2000.[53]

During the Intifada, the Histadrut offered qualified support for negotiations with Palestinians. At its 1990 convention, delegates called for "a just solution to the Palestinian problem" and backed the US-sponsored peace talks that formally excluded the PLO, similarly expressing "readiness to enter into dialogue with any trade union in the West Bank and Gaza that does not engage in subversive, terrorist activities"—which seemed to be code for any union not affiliated with the PLO. At the same time, possibly reacting to the many resolutions criticizing Israel passed by US unions during the uprising, the Histadrut expressed concern over "the relentless attempts by Israel's enemies to distort its national image and the nature of Zionism" and vowed "to explain the true meaning of Zionism as the national liberation movement of the Jewish people and the progressive character of the State of Israel."[54]

Back in the United States, the National Committee for Labor Israel (NCLI)—the organization that had been channeling American union donations to the Histadrut since the 1920s—was struggling to stay financially afloat due to the declining fortunes of organized labor in both countries. Although the NCLI continued fundraising for the Histadrut's various educational and social welfare programs, by the early 1990s the contributions it brought in could not keep up with its operational costs. As a result, NCLI president Jay Mazur—who also served as president of the International Ladies' Garment Workers' Union—oversaw the organization's repeated restructuring and downsizing until it was finally shut down in 2006.[55]

In 2000, Mazur accompanied AFL-CIO president Sweeney and Communications Workers of America president Morton Bahr on a delegation to Israel. In a sign of how US labor officialdom's positions had changed after the ascension of new leadership at the AFL-CIO—and particularly in light of the Oslo Accords—the delegation also visited the occupied West Bank. "We met with workers from both sides, who expressed a real desire and commitment to work for peace," Sweeney explained two years later. "At that time, a secure and lasting peace seemed within reach, a peace grounded in security for Israel and hope for a prosperous future and fulfillment of the aspirations of the Palestinian people."[56] But that "hope"—if it was ever real—would soon be shattered.

CHAPTER 6

LABOR FOR PALESTINE

Throughout the twentieth century, the US labor movement's formal positions on Palestine were shaped almost exclusively by high-ranking union officials—mostly white men committed to American empire and Labor Zionism—with little to no input from rank-and-file members. But in the wake of the Intifada and Oslo Accords, and in the context of the end of the Cold War and the declining power of unions, this began to change. Instead of being free to unilaterally implement an aggressively pro-Israel agenda, top union officials in the early twenty-first century increasingly found themselves having to react to a more assertive and racially diverse rank and file demanding that US labor stand in solidarity with Palestinians.

Though the Cold War was now over, removing a key justification for US imperialism and militarism, it was soon replaced with the "Global War on Terrorism" targeting anti-Western political forces around the world, especially in the Middle East and Central Asia. As a heavily armed Western outpost in that region, Israel would be a crucial US ally in this new crusade, much as it had been in the previous global crusade against world communism—only this time with no rival superpower to keep US-sponsored violence in check.

Although the American Federation of Labor and Congress of Industrial Organizations (AFL-CIO)'s new leaders did not share the rabid anticommunism of their predecessors, they did share their ardent political and ideological support for the Histadrut and Labor Zionism. Like earlier generations of union officials, they were also eager to demonstrate US labor's loyalty and patriotism in the wake of the devasting attack of September 11, 2001. They therefore mostly went along with Washington's new "war on terrorism," which also meant continuing to champion Israel.

At the same time, rank-and-file workers in the United States participated in the antiwar movement that arose following 9/11 and in the closely connected international Palestine solidarity movement that blossomed amid the fraught outcome of the Oslo process. Sickened by the escalating violence and oppression around the world—especially in occupied Palestine—pockets of local US unionists in a variety of sectors and industries built a sustained protest movement calling on national labor officials to end their complicity with Zionism in particular and with American empire more generally. Despite the best efforts of top labor leaders, this grassroots challenge would not go away—indeed, it would only grow as Israel's brutality toward the Palestinian people became ever more severe and grotesque in the first decades of the century.

THE SECOND INTIFADA AND "WAR ON TERRORISM"

Gaza, the West Bank, and East Jerusalem became increasingly cut off from one another and internally fractured in the immediate aftermath of the Oslo Accords. A growing system of permits, security checkpoints, walls, and fences severely constrained Palestinians' freedom of movement. Between 1993 and 2000, Israel confiscated more than 40,000 acres of Palestinian land, built 250 miles of bypass and security roads, and added 100,000 illegal settlers to the West Bank and Gaza Strip, effectively doubling the settler population.[1]

Much of this was overseen by Israeli prime minister Benjamin Netanyahu, who was narrowly elected in 1996 only months after Rabin's assassination and was completely opposed to the creation of a Palestinian state.

The son of an aide to Ze'ev Jabotinsky (the right-wing originator of Revisionist Zionism), Netanyahu was born in Tel Aviv one year after Israel's founding but spent much of his youth in suburban Philadelphia, where his father worked as a college professor. Netanyahu returned to Israel after high school to serve in an elite unit of the Israel Defense Forces (IDF) before coming back to the United States to study at the Massachusetts Institute of Technology. In the early 1980s, he served as Israel's deputy ambassador to the United States, and in 1988 was elected to the Knesset as a member of the Likud Party.

More adept at public relations than policymaking, Netanyahu fashioned himself an expert on antiterrorism and was a skilled spokesperson for Likud's vision of permanently subjugating the Palestinians in the name of national security, becoming the party's leader in 1993. He would eventually become the longest-serving prime minister in Israeli history and the country's most consequential leader after David Ben-Gurion. As prime minister in the late 1990s, Netanyahu was determined to undermine the spirit of the Oslo Accords by allowing the expansion of illegal Israeli settlements in the West Bank.[2]

The Islamic resistance organization Hamas, which had relentlessly criticized the Palestine Liberation Organization (PLO) for collaborating with Israel in the Oslo process, now became more popular among an increasingly impoverished and hopeless Palestinian population in the occupied territories—just as Islamic political movements were in ascendance across the

Middle East in response to the perceived failures of secular nationalism. Hamas articulated the sense of betrayal that the Oslo Accords inspired in many Palestinians, as well as their desire to continue struggling for liberation. With this in mind, and in direct response to violent settler attacks—like the Ibrahimi Mosque massacre—that were killing scores of Palestinian civilians, Hamas began carrying out suicide bombings inside Israel's pre-1967 boundaries.[3]

In 1999, Netanyahu was defeated in his bid for reelection, replaced as prime minister by Labor Party leader Ehud Barak. Because the Oslo Accords had stipulated that the final status of the post-1967 occupied territories would be determined within five years of their signing—and so far, no progress had been made—Barak and Arafat held a last-minute summit in July 2000 hosted by US President Bill Clinton at Camp David.

At the summit, Barak proposed that Israel be allowed to permanently annex parts of the West Bank and thus divide it into isolated chunks. He also sought continued Israeli control over the borders, airspace, and freshwater sources of a future Palestinian state and demanded that such a state be banned from ever establishing its own army. "It is hard to imagine any leader accepting these terms," write US political scientists John Mearsheimer and Stephen Walt. "Certainly no other state in the world has such curtailed sovereignty, or faces so many obstacles to building a workable economy and society."[4]

While the Israeli proposals were unlikely to garner agreement from Arafat, whose credibility among Palestinians had already suffered due to the Oslo Accords, the negotiations especially broke down over the question of the final status of East Jerusalem, with both sides wanting complete sovereignty of the area—particularly of the Haram al-Sharif, or Temple Mount. Considered a holy site to Jews, Christians, and Muslims, the Haram is located on a hill in East Jerusalem's Old City and is home to the Western Wall (constructed in antiquity), the al-Aqsa Mosque, and the Dome of the Rock. Neither Arafat nor Barak would budge on who would get control over the Haram, contributing to the Camp David summit ending without an agreement.

Meanwhile, Ariel Sharon—the longtime IDF officer and former defense minister who had personally carried out the 1953 Qibya massacre and directed the 1982 siege of Beirut (which included the Sabra and Shatila massacre)—became the Likud Party's new leader. Campaigning against Barak and seeking to inflame public discontent over the failed peace talks, Sharon made a confrontational visit to the Haram on September 28, 2000, just two months after the Camp David summit ended without a deal. Accompanied by hundreds of Israeli police officers in riot gear, he stood on the steps to the Dome of the Rock—the third holiest site in Islam—and provocatively declared that the Haram would forever remain in Israel's possession.

Sharon quickly fled the scene as a crowd of Palestinian protesters gathered. Some of the protesters threw stones at the riot police, only to be shot with rubber-coated bullets and live ammunition, with hundreds injured and at least four killed. The Second Intifada had begun.[5]

§

Lasting until 2005, the Second Intifada would be far bloodier than the first. Disgusted that a decade-long "peace" process had brought only more occupation, settlements, and poverty, Palestinians again took to the streets en masse to protest. The Israeli government—under the leadership of Sharon once he was elected prime minister in early 2001—aimed to quickly militarize the conflict to avoid another protracted, grassroots social movement as with the First Intifada. In the first few days of the new uprising, IDF soldiers fired around 1.3 million rounds of ammunition.[6]

Hamas and Palestinian Islamic Jihad retaliated by organizing a wave of deadly suicide bombings inside Israel's pre-1967 boundaries, targeting civilians on buses, in cafes, and at shopping centers. Former PLO fighters, now part of the Palestinian Authority (PA) security forces, abandoned their earlier renunciation of force and took up arms against the Israelis. Fatah, the largest faction within the PLO, began carrying out suicide bombings of its own in competition with Hamas. With ground troops and US-supplied warplanes, helicopters, and tanks, the Israeli military violently reoccupied portions of the West Bank and Gaza that it had withdrawn from after the Oslo Accords.[7]

As the bloodshed escalated, the United States was itself rocked by the infamous terrorist attack of September 11, 2001. The attack was organized by Islamic fundamentalists formerly backed by Washington to oppose the Soviet invasion of Afghanistan in the 1980s, but now affiliated with al-Qaeda, a militant network funded and led by Saudi multimillionaire Osama bin Laden. Within weeks, the US government declared a "Global War on Terrorism," passed draconian new national security laws, and invaded Afghanistan (al-Qaeda's home base). Further, in a cynical bid to exploit the 9/11 attacks to remake the geopolitical map of the Middle East, the administration of Republican President George W. Bush prepared to implement preexisting neoconservative plans to invade Iraq and install a pro-US government.

In New York City, where thousands had been killed on 9/11 with the shocking destruction of the World Trade Center towers, a group of local union officers and rank-and-file activists issued a statement on September 27, under the banner of New York City Labor Against the War (NYCLAW), which expressed opposition to Bush's war agenda by demanding justice rather than vengeance. "No one should suffer what we experienced on September 11," the statement said. "Yet war will inevitably harm countless innocent civilians, strengthen American alliances with brutal dictatorships, and deepen global poverty," as well as "generate further terror in this country against Arabs, Muslims, South Asians, people of color and immigrants, and erode our civil liberties."[8] The statement, which also referenced Israeli occupation, was circulated widely across the labor movement over the next several weeks, with nearly eight hundred local unionists and hundreds more across the United States and around the world signing on.

NYCLAW, the first post-9/11 antiwar labor organization, was a grassroots group coconvened by several local union leaders, including Michael Letwin, president of the Association of Legal Aid Attorneys, United Auto Workers (UAW) Local 2325; Larry Adams, president of National Postal Mail Handlers Union Local 300; and Brenda Stokely, president of American Federation of State, County, and Municipal Employees (AFSCME) Local 215. NYCLAW and its statement were also endorsed by sixteen New York City principal union officers, including Arthur Cheliotes, president of Communications Workers of America Local 1180; Barbara Bowen, president of the Professional Staff Congress (American Federation of Teachers Local 2334) at the City University of New York; and Jonathan Tasini, president of the National Writers Union.[9]

§

NYCLAW was part of a nascent antiwar movement in the United States that drew connections between Bush's newly declared war on terror and Israel's ongoing assault on Palestinians amid the Second Intifada. Both used "national security" as justification for conquest and occupation, both targeted Muslim and Arab populations, and both were being funded by US taxpayers, with Washington giving Israel over $3 billion per year in military aid.

In February 2002, after Israeli fighter jets bombed the Nablus offices of the Palestinian General Federation of Trade Unions (PGFTU)—a move condemned by unions around the world—delegates of the seventy-five thousand–member San Francisco Labor Council (the local arm of the AFL-CIO) narrowly passed a resolution condemning Israel for the "bombing of civilian and political targets" and for "oppressing and dividing the Jewish and Arab worker for the benefit of national and international capital."[10]

Submitted by Charles Minster, a landscape gardener at the Presidio and delegate to the labor council for Local 1141 of the Laborers' International Union of North America (LIUNA), the resolution also declared that "the U.S. proves to be the main culprit in this struggle by supplying the Israeli State billions of dollars in arms to suppress the Palestinian struggle for Statehood and ancestral lands."[11]

Minster told reporters that there was "not a ghetto in this country that can compare with Palestinian refugee areas as far as the horrors those people have to live through." He accused the US and UK governments of stoking the violence by continuing "to supply arms to a buffer state in the Mideast. That's what [Israel] was created for in the first place. Britain and the U.S. could [not] care less about Jewish rights and privileges. They wanted a buffer state among the oil-rich Arab countries."[12]

But within a month, the resolution was rescinded after the San Francisco Labor Council faced intense backlash from pro-Israel organizations in the Bay Area with ties to the Democratic Party, including the Jewish Community Relations Council, whose executive director called the measure "shockingly one-sided and mean-spirited."[13]

For their part, national labor leaders like AFL-CIO president John Sweeney generally went along with Bush's foreign policy agenda in the name of patriotism and national unity following

9/11 (though the AFL-CIO would eventually, in 2005, come out against the US occupation of Iraq, thanks to the efforts of US Labor Against the War, a network of antiwar unionists). Still, in early April, the AFL-CIO Executive Council issued a statement that demonstrated how US labor officialdom was trying to appear more evenhanded with regard to Palestine in the years since Kirkland's forced retirement. "Israel cannot achieve security with military force. The Palestinians will not achieve statehood with terrorist bombings," the Executive Council's statement read. "Palestinian statehood requires that Israel be made secure; Israel[i] security requires that Palestinians be freed of occupation. The only solution in the Middle East is a peace process that ends in a political settlement."[14]

But only ten days after this statement, Sweeney spoke at the National Rally for Israel—a mass gathering of an estimated 100,000 people in Washington, DC, meant to showcase popular American support for Israel's assault on the West Bank and Gaza. Standing on the steps of the US Capitol alongside the likes of Benjamin Netanyahu, former New York mayor Rudy Giuliani, and Deputy Secretary of Defense Paul Wolfowitz, Sweeney said, "On behalf of the thirteen million working women and men of the AFL-CIO, I stand with you to express our support for the people of Israel in this darkest of hours." He promised the labor federation would "continue to defend Israel's right to exist and the right of its people to live in peace" and made no mention of Israel's bombing of the PGFTU headquarters two months earlier.[15] Illustrating the overall tenor of the rally, Wolfowitz—a leading neoconservative and architect of the soon-to-come invasion of Iraq—was literally booed off the stage for merely saying, "Innocent Palestinians are suffering and dying as well."[16]

Angered by the AFL-CIO president's participation in the event, antiwar unionists affiliated with the Bay Area Labor Committee for Peace and Justice and other groups circulated a petition directed at Sweeney, criticizing him for associating "U.S. labor's name with support for the Israeli invasion of the West Bank, which has resulted in the widespread death and destruction of the Palestinian people and property." The petitioners argued it would be "more appropriate for the highest official in U.S. labor to be meeting with peace groups" and calling for "teach-ins in every U.S. Labor Council so that workers could learn and debate the complexities of the Mid-east crisis."[17]

In the wake of Sweeney's appearance at the pro-Israel rally, antiwar union members became increasingly vocal about US labor officialdom's long-standing ties to the Zionist state—especially as the violent efforts to crush the Second Intifada continued. That May, NYCLAW organized a picket outside the New York Sheraton during a cocktail reception with AFL-CIO leaders and Israeli consul general Alon Pinkas. Coming just weeks after a brutal IDF assault on the West Bank refugee camp of Jenin, the event was hosted by the Development Corporation for Israel, with Pinkas on hand to personally thank US labor officials for their impressive track record of purchasing State of Israel bonds. More labor-sponsored Israeli bonds fundraisers were held throughout 2002, including a testimonial dinner for LIUNA president Terence O'Sullivan and a tribute to the AFL-CIO-affiliated A. Philip Randolph Institute.

These fundraisers caught the attention of antiwar unionists, as did a March news article in the *Forward* quoting the director of the NCLI estimating that "the American labor community holds $5 billion in Israel bonds."[18] As Letwin, one of the coconveners of NYCLAW, said at the time, "It's bad enough that our tax dollars are going to fund Israel, but our union dues—that's intolerable."[19]

At the end of the year, NYCLAW cosponsored a US tour for two Palestinian trade unionists from the PGFTU: executive committee member Mohammed Saleh Aruri from Ramallah in the West Bank and Hekmat al-Serraj from the PGFTU's Women's

Affairs Department in Gaza. At least one other PGFTU representative had planned to join the tour, but was not granted a travel visa by the Israeli authorities.

From November to December, Aruri and al-Serraj visited twenty cities in twelve states and the District of Columbia. Speaking to audiences of union members and peace activists, the two described the impact of Israeli-imposed travel restrictions on Palestinian workers. "I had to come to the U.S. to meet Mohammed, who lives only a few miles from my home," al-Serraj explained. "All because he lives in the West Bank, and I live in Gaza."[20] They explained how, since the start of the Second Intifada, 130,000 Palestinians had lost their jobs inside Israel due to their physical inability to get to work because of road closures. Workers who tried to go to work anyway, they said, were often killed by the IDF. As a result, there was now a 50 percent unemployment rate in the occupied territories, with 65 percent of Palestinians living below the poverty line.

Besides NYCLAW, other cosponsors of the tour included the Bay Area Labor Committee for Peace and Justice, the King County Labor Council in Seattle, AFL-CIO staffers in Washington, DC, and the Arab American–led organization Al-Awda: The Palestine Right to Return Coalition. During their stop in New York City, Aruri and al-Serraj spoke in several venues, including at a large event at the AFSCME District Council 1707 hall hosted by NYCLAW. Interestingly, they also met with members of the pro-Israel Jewish Labor Committee, but there does not appear to be a public record of what was discussed in that meeting.[21]

A NEW ERA

The outburst of Palestine solidarity organizing by US unionists in the year 2002—occurring in the midst of both the Second

Intifada and the start of the "Global War on Terrorism"—marked the beginning of a new era in the history of the American labor movement's involvement in Palestine. From that year onward, growing numbers of rank-and-file union members would consistently exert pressure on labor leaders to reconsider their relationship with Israel.

Perhaps in response to this pressure, in 2003 the AFL-CIO's government-funded Solidarity Center launched a formal partnership with the PGFTU. By distributing grants and providing technical expertise, the Solidarity Center's stated mission in the West Bank and Gaza would be to "support the PGFTU to build national unions, organize workers into trade unions, and help assist in the creation of a democratic and transparent union structure," as well as to advocate "for the creation of sustainable jobs and the enforcement of labor laws."[22]

But this new program had more to do with Washington's foreign policy priorities than the AFL-CIO's commitment to helping Palestinian workers. As the United States launched its criminal invasion of Iraq in March 2003, the National Endowment for Democracy—the government entity that provides most of the Solidarity Center's funding—significantly scaled up its programming in the Middle East to help bolster popular support in the region for Bush's "regime change" agenda. Accordingly, the Solidarity Center received nearly $1.5 million that year alone to help build new, pro-US labor unions in occupied Iraq, as well as a nearly $600,000 regional grant "to strengthen democratic trade unionism in the Middle East"—including in Gaza and the West Bank.[23]

Meanwhile, the emerging network of antiwar, pro-Palestine labor activists in the United States directed most of its attention in 2003 to protesting the invasion of Iraq. But at the national convention of Al-Awda in April 2004, the delegates adopted a proposal from NYCLAW to begin a campaign protesting

US labor's ties with Israel. With that in mind, six months later, Al-Awda and NYCLAW jointly formed Labor for Palestine: a new network of unions and community groups to serve as a locus of organizing and political education.

In its founding statement, Labor for Palestine noted that "international solidarity, the right of national self-determination, and social justice are among the most basic trade union principles" and called for an end to "the complicity of the U.S. government and labor with Israeli apartheid." Specifically, the statement urged US unionists and labor bodies to: (1) fully support Palestinian national, democratic and labor rights throughout historic Palestine, including the right of all Palestinian refugees to return to their homes and land; (2) demand an end to US military and economic support for Israeli apartheid; (3) divest all labor investments in Israeli apartheid; and (4) affiliate with Labor for Palestine.[24]

In the years after its 2004 founding, Labor for Palestine issued numerous statements and petitions expressing solidarity with the Palestinian liberation movement (signed onto by thousands of union members and allies), issued briefing papers and pamphlets to educate US unionists about labor's complicity with Zionism, organized pickets outside pro-Israel public events attended by labor officials, and encouraged and defended local unions and labor councils that took pro-Palestine stances.[25]

§

In November 2004, Yasser Arafat died at the age of 75 after suffering what doctors said was a hemorrhagic stroke. During the final two years of his life, while the Second Intifada raged, the longtime PLO leader had been confined to his Ramallah headquarters by the IDF on the orders of Ariel Sharon's government. Arafat was succeeded by Mahmoud Abbas, a veteran Fatah official whose main qualification was that he had managed to survive over the previous thirty years while so many of his comrades were assassinated. Abbas was elected to serve a four-year term as president of the Palestinian Authority in 2005. He has remained in the position ever since, despite never being reelected.

For his part, Sharon sought to end the Second Intifada—and, with it, the prospects for a future Palestinian state as envisioned by the Oslo Accords—by taking two drastic, unilateral measures: constructing a massive barrier wall to seal off Palestinian areas of the West Bank and withdrawing Israeli settlements from the Gaza Strip. The West Bank wall was primarily built on Palestinian land starting in 2002, with entire communities bulldozed to make room for it.[26] In 2004, the International Court of Justice advised that the wall was illegal, but this made no difference to Israel or its primary backer, the United States. In August 2005, the IDF forced over nine thousand Jewish settlers to immediately leave the Gaza Strip, razing their illegal settlements to the ground. A few weeks later, the Israeli military itself pulled out of Gaza but continued controlling all outside access to the strip by air, land, and sea.

Sharon took these actions with Bush's approval, but without bothering to negotiate with the Palestinian Authority. The newly built wall, a massive addition to the broader system of barriers and fences, would further divide the West Bank into a series of isolated cantons with the intention of allowing Israel to eventually annex major blocs of Jewish-only settlements. In the year after the unilateral withdrawal from Gaza, another twelve thousand Israelis settled in the West Bank. "Withdrawal from Gaza was thus not a prelude to a peace deal with the Palestinian Authority but a prelude to further Zionist expansion on the West Bank," writes historian Avi Shlaim. And with Gaza now free of any Jewish settlements, Shlaim says, the Israeli military would have "unrestricted freedom to drop bombs" indiscriminately and terrorize the population of the coastal enclave.[27]

§

Still aspiring to one day annex Gaza, many in Sharon's Likud Party, including Benjamin Netanyahu, loudly protested the prime minister's decision to withdraw. Faced with this internal opposition, Sharon broke from Likud and formed his own political party, only to suffer a stroke in December 2005 and end up in a coma for the remaining nine years of his life.

A month after Sharon's stroke, parliamentary elections were held in the Palestinian territories. Hamas had boycotted the previous year's presidential election, officially refusing to recognize the legitimacy of the PA and Oslo framework. But the organization now did a complete reversal by running candidates for the Palestinian Legislative Council. In the run-up to the election, Hamas downplayed its conservative Islamic views and muted its calls for armed resistance, instead promising Palestinian voters political reforms and economic prosperity.[28]

For most Palestinians who had continued suffering privation and subjugation under Fatah's leadership, Hamas's moderate message of change was an appealing one, so much so that it won a majority of seats in the legislature, even winning in some Palestinian Christian neighborhoods.[29]

The same international actors who had been promoting electoral democracy in the Palestinian territories via the Oslo framework, including the US government and European Union, scorned Hamas's democratic election victory because of its ongoing refusal to formally recognize Israel. Attempts by Fatah and Hamas to form a unity government were stymied by Israel, the United States, and other foreign powers, who suspended economic aid to the PA—leading only to a further increase in Palestinian poverty.

Rather than build unity, Fatah and Hamas were increasingly at odds, partly because of this international meddling, leading to an outright military conflict between the two parties that saw Hamas take exclusive control over the Gaza Strip in 2007 and establish its own, separate authority there. After this, Israel intensified its total land, air, and sea blockade over Gaza, effectively imprisoning its entire population, which by then had grown to 1.4 million people. "What had begun with international refusal to recognize Hamas's election victory," writes historian Rashid Khalidi, "had led to a disastrous Palestinian rupture and the blockade of Gaza."[30]

The PGFTU had used the presidential and parliamentary elections to advocate for economic development, social welfare, and job creation in the Palestinian territories, receiving support in its voter education efforts from the AFL-CIO's Solidarity Center. Between 2006 and 2007, as the conflict between Fatah and Hamas escalated, the PGFTU's offices were raided by armed fighters on multiple occasions and its leaders endured several assassination attempts and kidnappings. These attacks were blamed on Hamas, which in turn accused the PGFTU of being merely an extension of Fatah—though at least one kidnapping was carried out by Fatah "by mistake," according to a Fatah politician.[31]

AFL-CIO president Sweeney sent four letters to Mahmoud Abbas between November 2006 and July 2007 expressing outrage over these incidents targeting the PGFTU, demanding the Palestinian Authority conduct full investigations and do more to protect Palestinian trade unionists. This was in stark contrast to the AFL-CIO's noticeable silence over the years whenever Israeli forces had detained Palestinian unionists or bombed their offices. Sweeney's letters to Abbas could thus be construed as part of the international effort to further drive a wedge between Fatah and Hamas.[32]

BOYCOTT, DIVESTMENT, SANCTIONS

Frustrated by the failed Oslo process—which only ever offered Palestinians a geographically fractured pseudo-state with no sovereignty—in 2005 a coalition of over 170 Palestinian civil society groups formally called on allies and sympathizers around the world to boycott, divest from, and sanction the State of Israel. The coalition included refugee rights groups, networks of nongovernmental organizations, student associations, cultural and religious institutions, women's groups, grassroots community organizations, and trade unions—including the PGFTU.

Inspired by the global movement that had successfully pressured South Africa to end apartheid over a decade earlier, the coalition specifically called on "international civil society organizations and people of conscience all over the world to impose broad boycotts and implement divestment initiatives against Israel similar to those applied to South Africa in the apartheid era" and appealed to such organizations to pressure their "respective states to impose embargoes and sanctions against Israel." These nonviolent tactics of boycotts, divestment, and sanctions—or BDS—would, it was hoped, force Israel to "recognize the Palestinian people's inalienable right to self-determination" and fully comply with international law.

The BDS call listed three baseline demands on Israel that all Palestinian civil society groups in the coalition agreed upon: (1) end the occupation and colonization of all Arab lands occupied since 1967; (2) recognize the fundamental rights of Palestinian citizens of Israel and give them full equality; and (3) respect, protect, and promote the right of Palestinian refugees to return to their homes as stipulated in UN General Assembly Resolution 194.[33]

In the 1980s and early 1990s, several major US unions had supported and helped organize similar international boycott and divestment campaigns targeting apartheid South Africa. For example, AFSCME pressured state pension funds to divest $20 billion from South Africa, and the United Mine Workers organized a boycott of Shell Oil because it did business in the country and exploited Black South African workers. These campaigns later led anti-apartheid leader Nelson Mandela to praise the US labor movement for its critical role in bringing apartheid to an end.[34]

But attempts to use the exact same nonviolent tactics on Israel for the cause of Palestinian freedom would prove to be far more controversial for US unions—with the pro-Israel Jewish Labor Committee (JLC) repeatedly intervening to shut down any and all union support for the BDS movement.

§

Even before the formal BDS call in 2005, local unions in the United States were trying to organize boycott and divestment activities against Israel over human rights violations, including by targeting the construction equipment manufacturer Caterpillar, Inc. The American corporation sold its CAT D9 bulldozers to the Israeli military, which frequently used them in the occupied territories to destroy Palestinian homes and vegetation.

On March 16, 2003, 23-year-old US peace activist Rachel Corrie was killed by an Israeli-operated CAT D9 while visiting Gaza as a volunteer with the International Solidarity Movement—a Palestinian-led organization inviting foreigners to participate in nonviolent protests and document human rights violations in the post-1967 occupied territories. Corrie had attempted to prevent the demolition of a Palestinian family's home in Rafah by standing in front of an incoming bulldozer, literally putting her body on the line. Although witnesses said that she was clearly visible to the Israeli soldier operating the CAT D9, the soldier kept advancing anyway, intentionally running over Corrie and crushing her to death.[35] Her family later sued both Caterpillar and the IDF, but judges in the United States and Israel threw out the lawsuits.

Through her job at a mental health clinic in Washington state, Corrie had been an active member of Service Employees International Union (SEIU) 1199NW. In the weeks after she was killed, the leadership of 1199NW issued a statement offering condolences to Corrie's parents and praising her for being a "worksite leader" who helped the union successfully lobby state legislators the year before to protect mental health care funding. AFL-CIO president Sweeney, who was the former president of SEIU, also issued a public message honoring Corrie. Calling her "a proud advocate of working families," Sweeney said, "[T]he labor movement is sincerely grateful for her contributions"—but he made no mention whatsoever of Palestine, Israel, or the circumstances of her death.[36]

In January 2004, a San Francisco chapter of SEIU Local 535—a 29,000-member health care union with chapters across California—passed a resolution calling on the statewide local and the California Public Employees' Retirement System to divest all pension holdings from Caterpillar "in honor and in memory of our SEIU sister Rachel Corrie." The measure was introduced and championed by Local 535 member Francesca Rosa, who worked at the Arc San Francisco, a nonprofit promoting the rights of people with intellectual and developmental disabilities. Several months after Rosa's chapter adopted the Caterpillar divestment resolution, it went before Local 535's civil and human rights committee, where it was unanimously passed in February 2005.[37]

The resolution next headed to SEIU Local 535's statewide executive board for final approval, accompanied by letters of support from Jewish Voice for Peace—a Jewish-led Palestine solidarity organization founded in 1996 in the Bay Area. But upon learning of the measure, the Jewish Labor Committee sprang into action, with its national staff and Los Angeles director seeking to convince Local 535's executive board to vote it down.

Besides the argument that any divestment activity aimed at Israel was "antisemitic," the JLC homed in on the fact that employees at Caterpillar were represented by the UAW, and thus the resolution would violate "an unwritten agreement in the labor movement that unions do not undertake positions that undermine the financial well-being of workers in a sister union." The JLC alerted the national headquarters of both UAW and SEIU about the resolution, telling them that if California's state retirement system divested from Caterpillar, it would have detrimental consequences on the company's unionized employees. "Officials from SEIU and UAW contacted the leadership of SEIU Local 535 and made clear their opposition to the resolution," the JLC later reported.[38]

Faced with this pressure from national union officials, along with the unfounded accusations of antisemitism, the Local 535 executive board voted thirty-four to twenty-six against passing the divestment measure in the summer of 2005.[39]

§

Also in 2005, the Teaching Assistants Association (TAA) at the University of Wisconsin-Madison—the longest-existing US union of graduate student workers and an American Federation of Teachers (AFT) local—advanced a resolution urging the university's board of regents to divest from all companies that did business with Israel, including Caterpillar. The resolution was introduced by Muslim American student workers involved in Al-Awda: The Palestine Right to Return Coalition.

Consisting of course instructors, teaching assistants, and research assistants working toward their master's degrees or doctorates, unions of graduate student workers at universities across the country would become some of American labor's most outspoken advocates for Palestinian freedom in the years to come. This was in part because of the tradition of left-wing, antiwar activism on university campuses, and because such unions included scholars in the humanities and social sciences—many of whom came from other countries to study in the United States—who tended to look critically at US propaganda about Israel and Zionism.

Deriding the TAA's divestment measure as a "negative, hate-filled" proposal that was aimed at "the destruction of the Jewish State of Israel," the JLC worked to undermine the resolution by organizing the TAA's pro-Israel members in partnership with the Milwaukee Jewish Council for Community Relations and the director of the Hillel Foundation-Madison, who together wrote a letter in the campus newspaper publicly objecting to the measure.

In the end, the TAA significantly amended and reworded the resolution to call on the university to divest from military contractors doing business with oppressive regimes around the world, but making no specific mention of Israel or Palestine. The JLC later noted that "fear that a large number of Jewish graduate students might quit the Teaching Assistants Association if the resolution passed" was a key factor in this decision.[40]

That same year, the AFL-CIO's director of international affairs, Barbara Shailor, distributed a policy statement to every AFL-CIO state federation and local labor council expressing the national federation's opposition to divestment from Israel. In laying out the AFL-CIO's official position on BDS, Shailor echoed the calls for "constructive engagement" with apartheid South Africa from the 1980s. She argued that divestment from Israel would economically harm Palestinians—while ignoring that it was Palestinian civil society organizations, including unions, who had issued the BDS call.

"The AFL-CIO does not support disinvestment into the region. On the contrary we favor increasing investment to the West Bank and Gaza, and to Israel itself, that would contribute to creating jobs, providing housing and other services, and in general contribute to strengthening the Israeli economy for all its citizens and building the economy of a future Palestinian State," she wrote. "This necessitates investment, not disinvestment, and requires greater cooperation between Israelis and Palestinians."[41]

§

Leaders of the AFL-CIO and its affiliated unions would further solidify their opposition to BDS in 2007 with the JLC's support and coordination. That year, as Israel's total blockade of Gaza began, more of the international labor movement started exploring support for BDS. Most noteworthy was a motion passed at the biennial conference of the UK Transport and General Workers' Union endorsing a consumer boycott of products from Israel.[42] (This was the same union once headed by Ernest Bevin, who—as UK Foreign Minister with the Labour Party in the late 1940s—presided over the violent end to the British Mandate in Palestine.)

Shocked by the apparent growing momentum of BDS among foreign trade unions, JLC president Stuart Appelbaum claimed that "the motivation behind these one-sided boycotts is less an authentic concern for human rights than it is a desire to bash Israel"—suggesting that BDS was simply motivated by antisemitism.[43]

Appelbaum, who also served as president of the AFL-CIO-affiliated Retail, Wholesale and Department Store Union, organized his fellow top US labor officials that year to sign onto a JLC-drafted statement condemning the BDS movement. The statement pointed out that with so many violent conflicts in the world, "we have to question the motives of these [BDS] resolutions that single out one country in one conflict."[44] Of course, the international labor movement frequently spoke out on wars and injustices in numerous countries, as it did with South Africa, so the framing of Israel being "singled out" was misleading at best.

"We notice with increasing concern that characterization of the Palestinians as victims and Israel as victimizer is a staple of such resolutions," the JLC statement continued, adding there were "victims and victimizers on all sides." This was also misleading as it obfuscated the gross power imbalances between Israel—which had the most well-equipped military in the Middle East and maintained an occupation and blockade over Palestinian territory—and the stateless, occupied Palestinians.

"Rather than divestment from Israel, we believe that investment of time, energy and material aid is the best means to alleviate the ongoing suffering of Palestinians and Israelis," the statement said, again echoing the "constructive engagement" argument that had attempted to undermine the South African anti-apartheid movement decades earlier. "Engagement, rather than disengagement, with the Israeli people and the Palestinian people is needed."

This statement was signed by AFL-CIO president John Sweeney, as well as the presidents of thirty-five national unions, including the UAW, United Mine Workers, AFSCME, AFT, International Association of Machinists, Teamsters, United Steelworkers, United Food and Commercial Workers, UNITE HERE, American Postal Workers Union, and International Brotherhood of Electrical Workers. Ironically, many of these same labor leaders had actively supported boycott and divestment campaigns against apartheid South Africa less than twenty years before. With the president of the AFL-CIO and the presidents of so many major US unions signing on, the JLC statement effectively served as US labor's formal stance on BDS.[45]

In 2008, the JLC's Appelbaum was honored at an Israeli bonds fundraiser attended by Democratic Senator Hillary Clinton. "We all know that unions and union pension funds hold more Israel Bonds than any other institution in this country," Appelbaum said at the event. He admitted that the bonds were not "the most lucrative investments out there," but explained that "the reason we buy Israel Bonds—and the reason why we enthusiastically encourage others to do the same—is because we share the Zionist dream."

He concluded, "Israel's enemies have often accused the Jewish Labor Committee of being a Zionist mouthpiece. Well, speaking as the president of the JLC, all I can say is: guilty as charged!"[46] Were they alive to hear it, this provocative declaration would surely have grated on the ears of the non-Zionist Bundists who had founded the JLC over seventy years earlier.

Also in 2008, the JLC produced a manual for pro-Israel organizations in the United States explaining how to strengthen their ties to unions, in part to ensure that support for Israel would remain strong within the US labor movement. To deliberately confound BDS organizers, the manual encouraged the American Zionist community not to disclose the amount of money unions held in Israeli bonds:

> Please DO NOT discuss with union members, representatives of the press or others, guesstimates of the value of State of Israel Bonds held by unions. "Divest from Israel" activists have used such information in their arguments and have quoted figures found in Jewish newspapers and/or provided by Jewish communal representatives.[47]

Indeed, since then, US unions, labor councils, and Zionist groups have tended to conceal labor's investments in State of Israel bonds. This ran counter to the common practice over the previous fifty years of unions openly boasting about their Israeli bond purchases to showcase their liberal bona fides—suggesting that investing in Israel was no longer considered something to brag about in labor circles. As a result, there are no publicly accessible estimates of how much money US labor currently holds in Israeli bonds.

§

Despite the efforts of pro-Israel labor officials like Appelbaum, US unionists continued organizing in favor of BDS. After the 2007 JLC statement signed by Sweeney and several national union presidents, which accused the BDS movement of unfairly targeting Israel, New York City Labor Against the War pushed back with a message of its own.

"It is no more unfairly selective or one-sided than the isolation of apartheid South Africa, a campaign in which we and many others actively participated," NYCLAW declared. "This boycott—many of whose supporters are Jewish—DOES NOT target Israel for its ethnicity, but for theft and colonization of Arab lands, denial of equality to Arab-Palestinians in Israel, and violation of Palestinian Refugees' right to return home."[48]

In late 2009, Labor for Palestine circulated a letter criticizing the AFL-CIO's incoming president, Richard Trumka, for his public opposition to BDS. At an event hosted by the Jewish Labor Committee that October, only weeks after succeeding Sweeney (who retired), Trumka declared that the AFL-CIO was "proud to stand with the JLC to oppose boycotting Israel" and equated anti-Zionism with antisemitism.[49] In response, hundreds of rank-and-file union members signed Labor for Palestine's open letter to Trumka expressing disagreement with his anti-BDS stance and encouraging US labor to divest from Israeli bonds, oppose US military aid to Israel, and break all ties with "the racist Histadrut."

As president of the United Mine Workers twenty years earlier, Trumka had been a leading advocate for boycotting and divesting from South Africa, a fact pointed out in Labor for Palestine's letter to him. "You rightly argued [in the 1980s] that, 'economic pressure and political isolation of the South African government can hasten the day when justice and freedom reign in that troubled land,'" the letter said, quoting Trumka's own words. "Two decades later, the cause of 'justice and freedom' for Palestinians requires no less of you as president of the AFL-CIO."[50]

Trumka did not respond, nor did the AFL-CIO reverse its opposition to BDS.

"YOU CAN'T NULLIFY AN IDEA WHOSE TIME HAS COME"

Trumka's anti-BDS speech came months after the first in a series of massive air and ground assaults on the besieged Gaza Strip by the Israeli military, ostensibly targeting Hamas militants. Beginning in late December 2008 and continuing into January 2009, Israel's so-called "Operation Cast Lead"—which consisted of relentless bombardment and an IDF ground invasion of the densely populated enclave—killed some 1,400 Palestinians in three weeks.[51]

Soon after this, in March 2009, Benjamin Netanyahu again became prime minister—a position he would remain in until 2021, and then return to yet again a year later. Under Netanyahu, Israel implemented a particularly belligerent policy toward Gaza known as "mowing the grass," which meant periodically launching new bombing campaigns supposedly meant to debilitate Hamas's military capacity before it grew too strong, but more likely designed to terrorize and kill Gaza's growing civilian population and make the coastal strip unlivable.

Besides "Operation Cast Lead" in 2008-2009, there was also the one-week "Operation Pillar of Defense" in 2012 and the fifty-day "Operation Protective Edge" in 2014. In these three military campaigns, Israel leveled entire neighborhoods, wiped out essential infrastructure, and killed a total of 3,804 Palestinians, almost 1,000 of them children. In contrast, because of Hamas rockets (and, to a lesser extent, friendly fire), a total of eighty-seven Israelis were killed during these conflicts, most of them military personnel.[52]

As this horrific violence sporadically unfolded—accompanied by the Israeli government's increasingly open embrace of far-right policies, the ongoing construction of illegal settlements in the West Bank, and the complete absence of peace talks—the United States under President Barack Obama increased military assistance to Israel to $3.8 billion per year.[53] But at the same time, a greater number of trade unionists, intellectuals, and artists around the globe joined the BDS movement.

In May 2010, a coalition of international activists organized the Gaza Freedom Flotilla. Six vessels sailed from Turkey to bring humanitarian aid and construction materials to the Gaza Strip in defiance of Israel's blockade. Claiming the flotilla was smuggling weapons for Hamas, Israeli forces raided it in the Mediterranean Sea before it could reach its destination, boarding one of the ships and killing nine activists because they allegedly attempted to resist by throwing chairs and plastic bottles. Turkish customs officials had thoroughly searched the ships before they departed and found no weapons. A UN investigation after the incident similarly found no evidence of arms onboard.[54]

A week after this deadly incident, a coalition of Palestinian trade unions, including the PGFTU and the Independent Workers Federation of Palestine, requested that dockworker unions around the world boycott Israeli cargo—a call quickly answered by such unions in South Africa, Turkey, Sweden, and India. In the United States, Local 10 of the International Longshore and Warehouse Union (ILWU) passed a motion that condemned Israel's raid on the Freedom Flotilla and called for "unions to protest by any action they choose to take."[55]

Based in the Bay Area, ILWU Local 10 had a proud tradition of standing up against oppression around the world. In 1984, Local 10 famously protested apartheid by refusing to unload a Dutch cargo ship carrying South African goods in the Port of San Francisco. In 2002, as the IDF attacked the West Bank during the Second Intifada, the local issued a statement demanding "an immediate cease-fire along with the immediate withdrawal of Israeli troops and settlers from occupied areas of Palestine."[56] Beyond Local 10, the larger ILWU also had a long history of protesting fascism and militarism dating back to the union's earliest days in the 1930s. During the First Intifada, the union had called on the US government to pressure Israel to end the occupation of the West Bank and Gaza; later, on May 1, 2008, the ILWU organized a one-day work stoppage at ports all along the West Coast demanding immediate US military withdrawal from Iraq and Afghanistan.[57]

Following Israel's attack on the Freedom Flotilla, on June 20, 2010, a group of around eight hundred Palestine solidarity activists picketed at the Port of Oakland to try stopping an Israeli cargo vessel operated by ZIM Lines from docking. Israel's largest shipping company, ZIM was reputed to carry weapons and military equipment in addition to consumer goods. The protest had been endorsed by the San Francisco Labor Council and Alameda County Labor Council. When they arrived for their shift, dockworkers with ILWU Local 10 refused to cross the picket line—ensuring the ship's cargo would not be unloaded. It was the most significant union-supported BDS action in the United States up to that point.[58]

That December, the Industrial Workers of the World (IWW) became the first US union to officially endorse the BDS movement following both a vote at its convention in Minneapolis and a membership referendum. Founded in 1905 by working-class radicals opposed to the AFL's more conservative brand of "pure and simple" trade unionism, the IWW had an almost legendary history in the US labor movement for its militant stances against capitalism, racism, and imperialism, especially when it was at its strongest in the first two decades of the twentieth century. The union had faced severe government repression as a result of its opposition to US involvement in World War I, with many of its key leaders at the time jailed, deported, or chased into exile.

Open to any and all workers dedicated to building a fighting labor movement oriented toward social justice, by the time it voted to support BDS in 2010, the IWW had roughly ten thousand members and remained independent of the AFL-CIO.

By endorsing BDS, the union committed to educating its members about Palestine and to not recognizing the legitimacy of the Histadrut until it called for an end to the occupation, accepted the right of Palestinian refugees to return, and supported an end to all racial and religious discrimination in Israel.[59]

§

A new jolt of BDS organizing within the US labor movement was prompted in 2014 after Israel's fifty-day air and ground attack on Gaza that summer, which killed some two thousand Palestinians. In the middle of the assault that July, Labor for Palestine again issued a statement calling on US unions to support BDS, which hundreds of union members signed onto.

As Israel bombed Gaza, a group of Bay Area activists sought to organize a mass community picket at the Port of Oakland to prevent a ZIM ship from being able to unload its cargo, just as had occurred in 2010. The grassroots Arab Resource and Organizing Center played a leading role in this effort, soon dubbed the "Block the Boat" campaign, and coordinated with ILWU Local 10. On August 16, around three thousand protesters marched to the port and delayed the docking of the ZIM Piraeus for the day.

When the cargo ship eventually docked the next day, picketers returned and ILWU Local 10 members refused to unload the vessel, forcing it to sail to Los Angeles instead. On September 27 and October 25, Block the Boat protesters again picketed at the Port of Oakland to prevent ZIM vessels from being able to unload their cargo, and the picket lines were again honored by the dockworkers.[60]

In December, UAW Local 2865, representing fourteen thousand graduate student workers throughout the University of California system, held a membership vote on whether to endorse BDS. A total of 2,168 union members cast ballots on the measure, with 65 percent of them voting in favor of urging the university administration and the UAW's national leadership to divest from companies "complicit in severe and ongoing human rights violations as part of the Israeli oppression of the Palestinian people." This made UAW Local 2865 the largest US union to date to formally support the BDS movement, as well as the first union affiliated with the AFL-CIO to do so.[61]

Unsurprisingly, the successful vote sparked backlash among Zionist organizations and pro-Israel labor officials. A group of Local 2865 members who had opposed the BDS measure appealed the vote results to the UAW's executive board. After an investigation spanning several months, in December 2015, the board determined that Local 2865's BDS vote had been fair and democratic, yet it nevertheless decided to formally nullify the measure.

The executive board argued in part that because BDS targeted companies with employees represented by the UAW and other unions—including Caterpillar and the major Pentagon contractors like Boeing, Lockheed Martin, Raytheon, and Northrop Grumman—it would "lead to a direct economic deprivation for members of the UAW, as well as other organized members by, categorically, interfering with the flow of commerce to and from earmarked companies." The board further contended that BDS "espouses discrimination and vilification against Israelis and UAW members of Jewish lineage" and thus violated the union constitution's ethical practices codes.[62]

The UAW leadership had been pressured to void the BDS resolution by officials from the Teamsters, some of whose members also worked at targeted companies. "We would find it difficult to ask our members to support your union in a labor dispute with the University of California so long as you are engaged in activities that are fundamentally hostile to their interests," said Teamsters vice presidents Randy Cammack and Rome A. Aloise in a letter addressed to Local 2865.[63] The letter also implied that as graduate workers, Local 2865's members had less of a stake in the labor movement than other workers: "Unlike the members of your union, who are graduate students and therefore union members for a short period of time, our members are working in jobs that must support them for a lifetime and it is our job to protect them for all of their working lives."[64]

J. David Cox, president of the American Federation of Government Employees—another AFL-CIO-affiliated union—had also beseeched UAW president Dennis Williams to "use your office to intervene and express in the strongest possible terms the UAW's opposition" to the "anti-Semitic" BDS measure.[65]

Local 2865 appealed the nullification decision to the UAW's public review board. In the meantime, in April 2016, the rank-and-file members of two more UAW-affiliated graduate worker unions—Local 2322 at the University of Massachusetts, Amherst (the Graduate Employee Organization) and Local 2110 at New York University (the Graduate Student Organizing Committee)—voted to endorse BDS resolutions of their own. Like the original resolution passed by Local 2865 in California, these measures called on the UAW's national leadership to divest from Israel, despite the fact that the union's top officers had already rejected such a move. "The [UAW executive board] has no power to stifle this movement," said Alyssa Goldstein, a Local 2322 member who helped organize the BDS vote at UMass Amherst. "You can't nullify an idea whose time has come." The following month, the union's public review board upheld the executive board's earlier nullification decision, effectively saying that the BDS resolutions democratically passed at UMass and NYU were void as well.[66]

Also that spring, the AFT-affiliated Teaching Assistants Association at the University of Wisconsin held its own membership vote on BDS—which passed with 81 percent approval. The TAA, which had unsuccessfully tried to pass an Israel divestment measure a decade earlier, now became the first AFT-affiliated local to endorse BDS. The resolution called on the national AFT to divest from Israel, although the union's president—Randi Weingarten—was a leading member of the JLC and one of the most pro-Israel figures in US labor.

But despite the national AFT's opposition to BDS, Weingarten did not move to stifle the TAA's vote, in line with the union's broader culture of allowing local autonomy. "We believe strongly in dialogue, debate and the free ability to express a range of viewpoints," she wrote to the Anti-Defamation League a few years later, explaining that "the national union does not override locals over differences or questions of policy."[67]

§

Meanwhile, on October 29, 2015, delegates at the Connecticut AFL-CIO's convention voted to approve a resolution calling on the national AFL-CIO to adopt a BDS strategy "in connection with companies and investments profiting from or complicit in human rights violations arising from the occupation of the Palestinian Territories by the state of Israel."[68] Like the measures passed by the graduate worker unions, this would mainly serve as a grassroots rebuke to labor officialdom's ongoing alliance with the Israeli state, since Trumka and the national AFL-CIO stuck by their anti-BDS policy.

The resolution was cosponsored by David Roche, president of the Connecticut Building and Construction Trades Council, and John Harrity, president of the Connecticut State Council of Machinists. Both men had traveled to the occupied West Bank on a delegation of statewide union leaders the month before and witnessed abuses carried out by settlers against the Palestinian population. "I went on this trip as what I considered the least informed person on this journey," Roche said. "As a unionist it didn't take long to realize the mistreatment of the Palestinian people that was going on. . . . I would challenge all labor leaders to take this journey and do as we did."[69]

Passage of Roche and Harrity's BDS measure was the culmination of years of organizing among Connecticut trade unionists, much of it led by schoolteacher and AFT member Stanley Heller. In 2006, Heller and a group of other union members in the state had learned that the Connecticut AFL-CIO held $25,000 in State of Israel bonds. With backing from the New Haven Central Labor Council, they convinced the state federation not to purchase any additional Israeli bonds once the existing ones matured in 2010, which Heller called "a small but satisfying victory."[70] In 2013, they brought PGFTU official Mahmoud Abu Odeh to speak at the Connecticut AFL-CIO's convention, where he received a warm reception and spoke about how Palestinian workers had to spend hours every day at security checkpoints just to get to their jobs.[71]

An additional labor victory for the Palestine solidarity movement came in August 2015, when delegates at the national convention of the United Electrical Workers (UE) voted to approve a resolution endorsing BDS and calling for an end to US military aid to Israel as a way of pressuring the Zionist state "to end the occupation of the West Bank and East Jerusalem and the siege of Gaza and negotiate a peace agreement on the basis of equality, democracy and human rights for the Palestinian and Israeli people, including Palestinian self-determination and the right of return for refugees."[72]

A national union of around thirty thousand members working in a wide variety of sectors, UE had a history of class-conscious, antiwar, progressive unionism and was independent of the AFL-CIO. "We reached a breaking point when Israel launched the war on Gaza in 2014, killing over 2,000 people including 500 children," said UE Western Region president Carl Rosen after the resolution was passed. (Rosen would later become the union's general president.) He added that supporting BDS was "a necessary step for labor to take in order to bring about a peaceful end to the conflicts there."[73]

In a letter to UE, leaders of the Palestinian Postal Workers Union expressed "our deepest appreciation for the courageous resolution . . . in support of our right as Palestinians to live in peace and dignity as equals on our lands." They added, "We sincerely hope that other national unions in the US and many other countries will follow in your footsteps."[74]

ONGOING RESISTANCE, GROWING SOLIDARITY

By the centennial of the Balfour Declaration in 2017, two million Palestinians were confined to the 140-square-mile Gaza Strip, roughly half of them children. With the Israeli military maintaining a total land, air, and sea blockade, Gaza was frequently referred to as "the world's largest open-air prison"—with its population guilty only of being Palestinian.

Another three million lived in the occupied West Bank, where their homes and communities were continuously demolished to make room for more Israeli settlements in blatant contravention of international law. Most of the West Bank and Gaza's residents were refugees, including survivors of the Nakba and their descendants. Approximately six million other Palestinian refugees lived beyond the borders of historic Palestine, still banned from returning to their homeland after seven decades of displacement.

In December 2017, the US government under President Donald Trump officially recognized Jerusalem as the capital of

Israel and moved the American Embassy there from Tel Aviv—a deliberately provocative move because of the city's religious significance and disputed status as a potential capital for both Israel and a future Palestinian state. Eight months later, the Israeli Knesset passed the controversial "Jewish Nation-State Law," which served as a slap in the face to the country's roughly two million Palestinians citizens. The legislation codified the long tradition of discrimination they suffered by explicitly stating that only the country's Jewish population had a right to self-determination.[75]

Faced with these humiliations—only the latest in a century marked by constant dispossession and colonization—Palestinians continued resisting. From March 2018 to November 2019, tens of thousands of Gazans staged weekly marches to the boundary fence with Israel to nonviolently demand an end to the blockade and call for the right of return for all Palestinian refugees. The Great March of Return, as these weekly demonstrations were collectively called, was organized from the grassroots by civilians from all walks of life, and soon received the backing of Hamas, Fatah, and other political factions.

In marching to the militarized boundary fence, the unarmed protesters were confronted by heavily armed Israeli soldiers who attacked them with tear gas, rubber-coated bullets, and live ammunition—which was "justified" by reports that a miniscule number of demonstrators threw rocks and Molotov cocktails. At least 214 Palestinians were killed in the marches, including 46 children. Another 36,000 were wounded, including 8,800 children.[76]

§

In May 2021, new protests erupted in occupied East Jerusalem after Israeli courts ordered the forced eviction of several Palestinian families from the neighborhood of Sheikh Jarrah to make space for Zionist settlers. Swarms of Israeli police in riot gear attacked the demonstrators—mostly young people—using stun grenades, rubber-coated bullets, and "skunk water" (a chemical irritant that leaves a repulsive odor, frequently used by Israeli occupation forces against Palestinians).

Israeli police had already blocked the nearby Damascus Gate and stormed the al-Aqsa Mosque compound to ban mass gatherings there during Ramadan a few weeks earlier. That affront, combined with the planned evictions in Sheikh Jarrah, caused protests to swell across the West Bank, with hundreds of Palestinians injured by Israeli security forces.[77] Gazans and Palestinian citizens of Israel also demonstrated in support of the West Bank protests. Spanning historic Palestine and endorsed by Fatah, Hamas, and other parties, the uprising was dubbed the "Unity Intifada."

Perhaps the most powerful action of the Unity Intifada came on May 18, when hundreds of thousands of Palestinians held a daylong general strike from the Jordan River to the Mediterranean Sea. The Karameh ("Dignity") Strike highlighted how, despite increasingly bringing in foreign workers from parts of Asia and Eastern Europe, the Israeli economy still depended on exploited Palestinian workers. According to the Israeli newspaper *Haaretz*, the Israel Builders Association reported that only 150 out of 65,000 Palestinian construction workers showed up to the job that day, causing an estimated $40 million in losses. Israel's transportation ministry noted that 10 percent of all bus drivers in the country also observed the strike, leading to three hundred journeys being canceled. And in Israeli cities like Modi'in, there was no municipal garbage pickup that day.[78]

As part of the work stoppage, shops in East Jerusalem, the West Bank, and Gaza were shuttered for the day. "In this strike, Palestinians are emerging unified, regardless of the colonial space that they are permitted to exist in," political analyst Bilal Shweiki told the news site *Middle East Eye*. "The idea of a unified strike constitutes a lever for joint Palestinian national action. It is also a declaration of rejection against all agreements that divide the land."[79]

Meanwhile, Hamas and Palestinian Islamic Jihad fired rockets into Israel's pre-1967 boundaries to pressure occupation forces to withdraw from Sheikh Jarrah and the al-Aqsa complex. In a familiar refrain of disproportionate reprisals, Benjamin Netanyahu's government ordered a fresh round of massive airstrikes on the Gaza Strip from May 10 to 21. At least 256 Palestinians, including 66 children, were killed in the assault, with another 1,900 injured. Thirteen Israelis were killed by the rockets.[80]

In the months immediately before this unrest, the Israeli human rights group B'Tselem and the international organization Human Rights Watch each issued detailed reports alleging that the State of Israel's oppressive treatment of Palestinians amounted to the crime of apartheid—confirming what Palestinians and their allies had been saying for decades. A year later, Amnesty International issued a report of its own reaching the same conclusion.[81]

§

Building off of the organizing of the previous decades, many in the US labor movement responded to the events surrounding the Unity Intifada by expressing support for Palestinians. Throughout the month of May 2021, several union locals posted Palestine solidarity statements on social media, including Roofers Local 36 in Los Angeles, Teamsters Local 804 in New York City, and UNITE HERE Local 17 in Minnesota and Local 23 in cities across the South and Southwest.

On May 15, the national officers of the UE released a statement reiterating the union's support for BDS and calling on the US government to "end military aid to Israel and pressure Israel to end the occupation of the West Bank and East Jerusalem and the siege of Gaza."[82]

After the Israeli military intentionally bombed a Gaza tower housing the offices of the Associated Press and Al Jazeera, the NewsGuild—the union of twenty-four thousand journalists across North America (formerly called the Newspaper Guild)—called the bombing "a blatant attack on press freedom that was clearly intended to prevent independent reporting on the [Israeli] government's actions." NewsGuild president Jon Schleuss said on social media that "Israel's attacks on Palestine need to stop now."[83]

Even more significant than these statements, on May 19, the general assembly of United Educators of San Francisco, a union of 6,200 teachers and school staff, voted to approve a resolution endorsing BDS—making it the first K–12 teacher union in the United States to do so. The Seattle Education Association followed suit one month later by endorsing a BDS resolution of its own.

Five chapters of United Teachers Los Angeles (UTLA)—the second-largest local teacher union in the country—also passed pro-Palestine motions, two of them explicitly supporting BDS. One such motion, calling for BDS and urging an end to US military aid to Israel, then headed to UTLA's top decision-making body for final approval. But desperate to prevent the normalization of BDS, pro-Israel groups including the Jewish Federation of Greater Los Angeles, Anti-Defamation League, and StandWithUs organized a vocal opposition campaign and recruited numerous teachers and parents to the cause. Fearful of alienating large swaths of the union membership and local community, UTLA leaders eventually shelved the BDS measure in favor of an amendment calling for more discussions on Palestine and Israel.[84]

Members of the San Francisco Labor Council—the local body of the AFL-CIO—also introduced a BDS resolution in June 2021, which was to be debated and voted on at the council's meeting that fall. But before that could happen, the national leadership of the labor federation intervened by pointing to an obscure rule explaining that, as chartered organs of the AFL-CIO, central labor councils must conform to the policies of the national federation. Since the national AFL-CIO was opposed to BDS, "the San Francisco Labor Council may not hold a vote on a resolution to support boycott, divestment, and sanctions against Israel and thus any debate is not germane at your meeting," AFL-CIO president Liz Shuler wrote in a memorandum to the labor council's leaders. Consequently, the BDS measure was scrapped.[85]

Although some union members' attempts to express support for BDS were stopped during this period, West Coast dockworkers with the ILWU helped put BDS into practice in June 2021. As they had in 2010 and 2014, ILWU Local 10 members in the Bay Area refused to cross a community picket blocking a cargo vessel operated by the Israeli shipping company ZIM. On June 4, the ship was forced to leave the Port of Oakland without unloading its goods—which pro-Palestine organizers viewed as a concrete victory. Another Block the Boat picket was simultaneously happening at the Port of Seattle, respected by ILWU Local 19 members, that prevented a different ZIM vessel from docking for two weeks. It was only after Seattle police forcibly broke the picket line and arrested eleven people on June 17 that the ship was able to unload its cargo.[86]

§

By the early 2020s, Palestinians were continuing to assert their dignity and freedom despite the ever-intensifying violence of settler colonialism, imperialism, occupation, and apartheid. Inspired by their courage, many unionists in the United States continued to organize in solidarity with Palestinians—especially by supporting the nonviolent BDS movement—despite the constant obstruction of many top AFL-CIO officials who stubbornly remained dedicated to US empire while clinging to nostalgia around the purported achievements of Labor Zionism.

The growing Palestine solidarity activism within the labor movement coincided and overlapped with an uptick in workplace organizing and shopfloor militancy driven by younger generations of American workers fed up with decades of unchecked corporate greed, especially after the COVID-19 pandemic revealed just how much the US economy depended on highly exploited labor. Many of the same young baristas, warehouse workers, teachers, health care workers, retail workers, higher ed workers, library and museum workers, tech workers, and writers bringing renewed vitality to the labor movement through their tireless organizing were also highly sympathetic to the Palestinian cause and disturbed by union officialdom's general hostility toward BDS and reluctance to stand in solidarity with Palestine.

When the Israeli government used the Hamas attack of October 7, 2023, as a pretext for launching a genocidal assault on Gaza's population with Washington's full support, the newly reenergized US labor movement would be forced to reckon with its century-long alliance with Zionism. As the genocide unfolded, Palestinian trade unionists and working-class people of conscience around the world—including hundreds of thousands of activists in the United States, many of them Muslims, Arab Americans, and anti-Zionist Jews—pushed the US union movement to confront the same question posed by a classic labor ballad: which side are you on?

CONCLUSION

From the start of the Gaza genocide in October 2023, many US unions at the local, state, and national level called for a ceasefire at the urging of rank-and-file members and a handful of progressive labor leaders. The following July, seven major unions associated with the National Labor Network for Ceasefire—representing roughly half of all union members in the United States—formally called on President Joe Biden to impose an arms embargo on Israel.[1] Much of this was met with backlash from both inside and outside the labor movement, with detractors contending that it is inappropriate for unions to weigh in on thorny questions of war, peace, international law, and human rights—and especially to take a stand on the so-called Israel-Palestine conflict, which, they claim, is totally irrelevant to the US labor movement.

American unions, these critics suggest, have up until now been exclusively focused on narrowly defined bread-and-butter issues that "impact [their] members the most" and "not foreign policy." They argue that "unions should stay out of politics" and pursue only their members' material interests, which do not include "broader and more abstract" subjects like the Gaza genocide. Venturing into controversial matters that supposedly hold no relevance whatsoever to US workers, they say, is a newfangled and foolhardy experiment being forced onto the labor movement by radical leftists and out-of-touch intellectuals like newly unionized academic workers.[2]

But as the preceding chapters of this book have demonstrated, there is absolutely nothing novel about the US labor movement getting involved in foreign affairs, least of all in the century-long struggle for Palestine. Far from being silent or neutral, American unions and their top officials—motivated by their admiration for Labor Zionism and their devotion to US global power—have long been among the State of Israel's most stalwart champions. What is different now, and what the critics likely find so objectionable, is that some unions are expressing sympathy for Palestinians and questioning Israel's US-sponsored occupation, apartheid, and ethnic cleansing.

§

Eager to demonstrate their loyalty to President Woodrow Wilson's international agenda as he brought the United States into World War I, leaders of the AFL first expressed support for the Zionist goal of establishing a "Jewish homeland" in Palestine in November 1917, mere days after the fateful Balfour Declaration. A few years later, the Labor Zionist organization Histadrut began actively seeking the financial and political backing of US unions for its settler-colonial activities in Palestine, initially by trying to court Jewish American labor leaders. To overcome the traditional anti-Zionism of Jewish American unionists, the Histadrut found success by couching its appeals in the language of international worker solidarity. Support for the Histadrut quickly expanded in the 1920s from a handful of Jewish labor leaders to the more powerful, non-Jewish leaders of the AFL who had earlier endorsed Zionism as part of their pro-war posturing.

Thus, by the 1930s and 1940s—the decades when US unions experienced their most significant growth thanks in part to an alliance with the federal government—labor officialdom was already committed to aiding the colonization of Palestine. During this same period, Zionism gained newfound legitimacy and urgency as the United States and United Kingdom refused to take in Jewish refugees attempting to escape the persecution and mass murder of Germany's genocidal Nazi regime. When Zionist settlers founded the State of Israel in 1948 by brutally uprooting Palestine's Indigenous population, American labor leaders used their newfound status to lobby Washington on the young state's behalf well before the US political establishment reached a consensus view that Israel would serve as an indispensable proxy.

In the first decades of Israel's existence, top officials from both the American Federation of Labor (AFL) and Congress of Industrial Organizations (CIO), and eventually the merged AFL-CIO, generously donated huge sums of money to the Histadrut and the Israeli government to help build the basic infrastructure of the new Zionist state on lands that had just been violently taken from native Palestinians. At the height of their power in the 1950s and 1960s, AFL-CIO leaders—who could claim to speak on behalf of one in three nonagricultural US workers at the time—also lent their considerable political support to Israel each time the state became embroiled in another armed conflict with its Arab neighbors.

Although Jewish American union leaders like David Dubinsky were often crucial players in these efforts, it was the more influential, non-Jewish labor officials whose pro-Israel voices and actions carried the most weight—men like William Green, Philip Murray, George Meany, Walter Reuther, and Lane Kirkland. To them, Israel and its ostensibly worker-centric society represented a solution to multiple geopolitical and domestic challenges posed by the Cold War.

Substituting class struggle and proletarian revolution with class collaboration and nation-building, Israel's Labor Zionist movement was ideologically indistinguishable from the AFL-CIO's own brand of nonradical and patriotic trade unionism.

By dominating Israel's political and economic system in the mid-twentieth century, it seemed to these men that Labor Zionist vehicles like the Histadrut and Mapai offered a successful model for workers' movements in the newly independent countries of the Third World to emulate, rather than embrace anti-capitalism and anti-imperialism. Labor Zionism also served, in the AFL-CIO's view, as a positive example of noncommunist trade unionism to hold up at home in response to right-wing politicians and business executives exploiting anticommunist hysteria to crack down on American labor.

US union leaders' enthusiastic support for Israel was also an extension of their broader support for the American empire. As a reliable US proxy capable of militarily defeating Soviet-backed Arab states in the oil-rich Middle East, Israel repeatedly proved to be a valuable Cold War ally—which naturally appealed to the AFL-CIO's cold warriors. Besides being ardent anticommunists, labor officials were convinced that the future survival of their unions depended on the continued survival of the postwar, US-managed international capitalist system. What's more, like their AFL predecessors during World War I decades earlier, they remained eager to prove their jingoistic loyalty to Washington's foreign policy agenda. They therefore believed that if a strong and prosperous Israel was strategically beneficial to the US empire, then it was strategically beneficial to US labor as well.

In the 1970s and 1980s—after American imperialism and anticommunist orthodoxy suffered a stinging defeat in Vietnam and, simultaneously, political and economic forces became less favorable for US industrial workers—AFL-CIO leaders like Meany and Kirkland clung ever tighter to their hawkish foreign policy positions, often with less nuance than Washington. Such labor officials seemed to believe that the decline in US union density (caused most immediately by factory closures and corporate attacks) could be reversed only if the defeat in Vietnam could symbolically be undone through the full-fledged revival of US imperial power and the return to a broad anticommunist consensus in Western society.

This meant doubling down on the AFL-CIO's Cold War alliance with Israel, particularly by lambasting the anti-imperial, anticolonial Palestine liberation movement as it started gaining international sympathy. But this all became increasingly difficult as the US labor movement lost influence at home and as Israel's Labor Zionist movement was gradually supplanted by the right-wing Likud Party.

This book has also highlighted the history of working-class resistance to Zionism and imperialism. From as early as the 1880s, revolutionary Jewish workers in Eastern Europe rejected Zionism as a nationalist distraction from class struggle that would only lead to the violent dispossession of Palestine's Indigenous Arab population. Although the early Palestinian nationalist movement was formally led by wealthy notables, between the 1920s and 1940s a dynamic Palestinian Arab workers' movement developed that took on Zionist colonization, British imperialism, and workplace exploitation—most famously by leading a six-month general strike in 1936 that sparked a wider revolt and would inspire future generations of Palestinian workers.

In the United States, Bundists who had immigrated in the early 1900s and helped build thriving unions resisted the steady pressure to get behind Zionism for many years, until the depravity of the Holocaust served to finally break down their opposition. In 1949, despite Palestinians having virtually no voice in US society at the time, a group of rank-and-file members of the International Ladies' Garment Workers' Union—mostly Arab Americans—convinced their pro-Israel union president to make a small donation to assist Nakba refugees.

Twenty-four years later, Arab American autoworkers in Detroit, with inspiration and support from the League of Revolutionary Black Workers, organized the first major Palestine solidarity action in US labor history when they went on a one-day wildcat strike demanding that their union, the UAW, divest from Israeli state bonds. The Arab Workers Caucus that was born as a result of this action fought for workplace dignity and respect and was successful in getting some UAW locals to dump their Israel bonds in the 1970s.

Working-class Palestinians were at the forefront of the First Intifada in the late 1980s to early 1990s, demanding freedom from Zionist colonial rule and economic exploitation not only by taking to the streets in protest, but by collectively withholding their labor through a series of general strikes that crippled the Israeli economy. Moved by this resistance and incensed at the AFL-CIO's longtime complicity in Palestinian oppression, left-wing, antiwar, and anti-apartheid trade unionists in the United States formed groups like the Labor Committee on the Middle East and the Palestine Labor Action Network to mobilize union support for the Intifada. Coming in the period of deindustrialization and declining union power, such efforts were part of a larger rank-and-file rebuke to an increasingly ossified and ineffective US labor officialdom that often seemed to be more interested in serving Washington's imperial interests overseas than fighting corporate interests at home.

The rank-and-file activism during the First Intifada opened up space for more consistent Palestine solidarity organizing within US labor beginning in the early 2000s. Drawing parallels between Israel's destructive response to the Second Intifada and President George W. Bush's so-called war on terrorism, groups of American union members again spoke up in favor of Palestinian freedom and self-determination by demanding an end to US labor's support for Zionism. With the founding of Labor for Palestine in 2004 and the launching of the international Boycott, Divestment, and Sanctions movement in 2005, there were now permanent grassroot networks and a defined set of demands that could rally working-class Palestine solidarity activists on a steadier basis than ever before.

By the 2010s and early 2020s, a younger, more diverse, more class-conscious generation of American workers began bringing new energy and militancy to the US labor movement. In those same years, Israel abandoned the earlier charade of a "peace process" by escalating its murderous occupation and apartheid policies, only to receive increased military aid from Washington. Rank-and-file US workers who tried getting their unions to express solidarity with Palestinians and adopt BDS resolutions were frequently met with resistance from labor officialdom, which—in lockstep with the American political establishment—encouraged continued, unconditional support for Israel and equated any opposition to Zionism with antisemitism, while occasionally mouthing empty platitudes about the long-dead "peace process."

With a latent showdown over the Palestine question already brewing within organized labor, the US-fueled Gaza genocide and its impact on American society have brought unions to an inflection point linked to a host of other issues concerning the future of the US labor movement. In grappling with whether and how to respond to the genocide—including the systematic crackdown on dissent at home—US unions are also wrestling with questions of internal democracy, political allegiances, organizing strategies, resource allocation, and the meaning of solidarity in a nation and world increasingly dominated by unaccountable multibillionaires, ecologically destructive corporations, and fascist warmongers.

§

After Imperial Japan invaded China in 1937 and massacred civilians by the tens of thousands, the United States continued exporting scrap iron to Tokyo, which was recycled into armaments and other war material used by the Japanese military to slaughter

Chinese men, women, and children. But between December 1938 and July 1939, US dockworkers with the International Longshore and Warehouse Union (ILWU) repeatedly refused to load scrap iron onto ships bound for Japan. All along the West Coast, at the ports of San Francisco, Astoria, Seattle, and elsewhere, thousands of Chinese American community members—including children and seniors—would picket such ships for several days at a time, and sympathetic ILWU members refused to cross their picket lines.[3]

At the time, ILWU president and radical leftist Harry Bridges admitted, as relayed by an Associated Press reporter, that "the longshoremen might not be in strict conformity with union contracts by refusing to load the vessels because of the Chinese pickets, but he said the problem was a 'social' one."[4] Indeed, the employers and the US government condemned the union for apparently skirting the rules of collective bargaining and labor law, with federal marshals and arbitrators eventually intervening to put an end to the protests. But to Bridges and many others in the ILWU, demonstrating solidarity with a people and a nation under brutal military assault took precedence over cooperating with bosses and the state. The dockworkers and the Chinese American picketers would soon be vindicated when, in September 1940, President Franklin Roosevelt ordered an embargo on further scrap iron exports to Japan.[5]

In a television interview with Bridges over thirty years later, journalist Bill Moyers asked the labor leader how he felt "about using your strength as a union to affect foreign policy." Bridges answered, "Why, that's what unions are for, to help make foreign policy in the interest of the majority of the people in this and other countries." He continued, "When we shut down ships and we refused to ship oil and scrap iron to Japan when it invaded China, it was a very radical, revolutionary thing. I got a telegram from Mr. Roosevelt saying, 'hey, quit interfering in the good diplomatic relationships between two nations.' But we still shut down the ships."

Moyers then pointed out that "what you're doing when you do that is to interfere with the foreign policy of your country."

"Sure as hell are," Bridges replied unapologetically. "That's our job. That's our privilege. That's our right. And that's our duty."[6]

§

The ILWU's brave stance in the late 1930s, as well as Bridges's notion of the role unions should play in matters of foreign policy, are instructive for today's US labor movement as it grapples with the question of Palestine.

Ultimately at issue is whether US labor will stick to the AFL-CIO's traditional style of unionism—which has generally prioritized class conciliation, patriotic loyalty, and a cautious approach to new organizing—or embrace a different kind of unionism that emphasizes class struggle, anti-imperialist internationalism, and a bold vision of organizing tens of millions of unorganized workers.

A labor movement animated by such principles, and situated in the heart of a global empire, would be a powerful ally to oppressed peoples around the world. It would not hesitate to mobilize the collective strength of US workers to hinder the production and transportation of weapons, equipment, and technology used to massacre and repress fellow workers abroad, nor would it tolerate any union resources being used to bolster apartheid and genocide or the politicians who further such crimes.

Between the urgency of Palestinian calls for international worker solidarity and the legacy of US labor's complicity with empire and settler colonialism, today's labor movement is challenged to consider whether union membership and collective bargaining are ends in themselves, or if they are means to greater ends like freedom, justice, and dignity for all humanity.

ACKNOWLEDGMENTS

It is fitting to first acknowledge all of those who daily resist the systematic and depraved efforts by the United States and Israel to violently subjugate, uproot, and eradicate the Palestinian people. During the same years that I was working on this book, as countless Palestinians were being martyred or experiencing unimaginable trauma and grief, millions of workers and students in Palestine and across the globe were risking their safety and livelihoods in the struggle for liberation and dignity. Their courage and determination have been a constant source of inspiration to me.

I'm grateful to the entire team at Haymarket for their hard work and commitment to this book, particularly Charlotte Heltai, John McDonald, Rachel Cohen, Rory Fanning, and Jamie Kerry. Charlotte consistently provided helpful editorial guidance throughout the writing process and incredibly valuable feedback on multiple drafts of the manuscript.

Sai Englert generously read through an early draft and offered highly insightful and constructive suggestions. Michael Letwin also kindly took the time to read an early draft and provided detailed comments that tremendously strengthened the manuscript. Of course, I alone am responsible for any shortcomings or errors in the book.

I owe special thanks to Ari Bloomekatz for being an early and enthusiastic advocate for this book's publication. I'm also thankful to Aparna Gopalan, Nora Caplan-Bricker, Sarah Lazare, Miles Kampf-Lassin, Jessica Stites, Shawn Gude, Micah Uetricht, Anita Palathingal, Manny Ness, Julie Greene, and Gabe Winant for supporting, editing, and publishing my previous writing on US labor and Palestine. Thanks also to Robin D. G. Kelley for encouraging my research and writing on this history, and to my supportive colleagues at the Harry Van Arsdale Jr. School of Labor Studies at SUNY Empire State University.

Over the years—and especially since the Gaza genocide—I've had the privilege to meet, learn from, collaborate with, and be challenged and inspired by numerous trade unionists, organizers, and intellectuals interested in uniting the labor movement with the Palestine solidarity movement. They include many of the individuals mentioned above, as well as Amira A., Olivia Katbi, Sumaya Awad, Dylan Saba, Indigo Olivier, Nastaran Mohit, Aminah Sheikh, Yasemin Zahra, Taher Dahleh, Ghina Abi Ghannam, Charmaine Chua, Marcie Pedraza, Steve Zeltzer, Kim Scipes, Gene Bruskin, Frank Hammer, Mimi Rosenberg, Chris Townsend, George Mavrikos, Peter Cole, Katy Fox-Hodess, Riya Al'sanah, Rafeef Ziadah, Alice R., Greg Waldman, Kayla Hoskinson, Andrew Knox, Christopher Hutchinson, Rachael Stryker, Lucy Griswold, Joe Iosbaker, Dennis Kosuth, Jessica Cook-Qurayshi, Nina Woodsum, Alyssa Goldstein, Leah Fried, and Carl Rosen, among many others.

Lastly, I'm forever grateful to my family for their lifetime of support and love.

NOTES

INTRODUCTION

1. "An Urgent Call from Palestinian Trade Unions: End All Complicity, Stop Arming Israel," *Progressive International*, October 16, 2023, https://progressive.international/wire/2023-10-16-an-urgent-call-from-palestinian-trade-unions-end-all-complicity-stop-arming-israel/en.
2. "TLMCLC Resolution on the War in Gaza," October 17, 2023, quoted in Jeff Schuhrke, "The AFL-CIO Squashed a Council's Cease-Fire Resolution. What Does It Say About Labor Right Now?," *In These Times*, November 2, 2023, https://inthesetimes.com/article/afl-cio-israel-palestine-ceasefire-resolution-gaza.
3. Schuhrke, "The AFL-CIO Squashed."
4. Schuhrke, "The AFL-CIO Squashed."
5. Elizabeth Shuler to Principal and Secondary Officers of State Federations and Area and Central Labor Councils, Reminder Concerning Policy Positions on Matters of National Importance, October 31, 2023.
6. National Labor Network for Ceasefire, https://www.laborforceasefire.org/.
7. Jeff Schuhrke, "Unions Must Go Beyond Calling for a Cease-Fire in Gaza," *Jacobin*, February 13, 2024, https://jacobin.com/2024/02/us-labor-movement-gaza-cease-fire-action.
8. Current and Former Grad Workers at UC Santa Cruz, "From the Camp to the Picket: Reflections from the UC Strike for Palestine," *Long-Haul*, no. 2 (Spring 2025), https://longhaulmag.com/uc-strike-for-palestine/.
9. Schuhrke, "Unions Must Go Beyond."
10. International Longshoremen's Association, "ILA Will Maintain Pledge to Handle Military Cargo During Strike; Passenger Cruise Ships to Be Unaffected by 10/1 Strike," September 25, 2024, https://ilaunion.org/ila-will-maintain-pledge-to-handle-military-cargo-during-strike-passenger-cruise-ships-to-be-unaffected-by-10-1-strike/.

11. Christians United for Israel, "CUFI Reaches 10 Million Members," December 22, 2020, https://cufi.org/press-releases/cufi-reaches-10-million-members/; Matt Spetalnick et al., "'I Am a Zionist': How Joe Biden's Lifelong Bond with Israel Shapes War Policy," *Associated Press*, October 21, 2023; Michael Williams and Sam Fossum, "Biden Says He Considers Himself a Zionist," *CNN*, July 15, 2024.
12. "Solidarity Forever: Song by Ralph Chaplin, 1915," Zinn Education Project, https://www.zinnedproject.org/materials/solidarity-forever/.
13. See Jeff Schuhrke, *Blue-Collar Empire: The Untold Story of US Labor's Global Anticommunist Crusade* (London and New York: Verso, 2024); Anthony Carew, *American Labour's Cold War Abroad: From Deep Freeze to Détente*, 1945–1970 (Edmonton: Athabasca University Press, 2018); Kim Scipes, *AFL-CIO's Secret War Against Developing Country Workers: Solidarity or Sabotage?* (Lanham: Lexington Books, 2010); Beth Sims, *Workers of the World Undermined: American Labor's Role in US Foreign Affairs* (South End Press: Boston, 1992); Ronald Radosh, *American Labor and United States Foreign Policy* (New York: Random House, 1969).
14. Dylan Saba, "Democrats Are Helping Make the US Border Look More and More Like Gaza," *Nation*, February 15, 2024; Laura Gamba Fadul, "'What We See in Gaza Is the Rehearsal of the Future': Colombian President at UN Climate Summit," *Anadolu Agency*, February 12, 2024.

CHAPTER 1: LAYING THE FOUNDATIONS

1. Jewish Virtual Library, "Zionist Congress: First Zionist Congress & Basel Program," https://www.jewishvirtuallibrary.org/first-zionist-congress-and-basel-program-1897.
2. Melech Epstein, *Jewish Labor in U.S.A.: An Industrial, Political and Cultural History of the Jewish Labor Movement, 1882–1914* (New York: Trade Union Sponsoring Committee, 1950), 23–30, 38.
3. Alain Brossat and Sylvia Klinberg, *Revolutionary Yiddishland: A History of Jewish Radicalism* (London: Verso, 2009/1983), 30–31; Sharon Rudahl, Paul Buhle, and Michael Kluckner, *The Bund: A Graphic History of the Jewish Labour Resistance* (Toronto: Between the Lines, 2023), 1–3.
4. Abraham Brumberg, "Anniversaries in Conflict: On the Centenary of the Jewish Socialist Labor Bund," *Jewish Social Studies* 5, no. 3 (Spring/Summer 1999): 198.
5. Brossat and Klinberg, *Revolutionary Yiddishland*, 33.
6. Library of Congress, "Immigration and Relocation in U.S. History: A People at Risk," https://www.loc.gov/classroom-materials/immigration/polish-russian/a-people-at-risk/.
7. Epstein, *Jewish Labor in U.S.A.*, 318–323, 348.

8. Steven Fraser, *Labor Will Rule: Sidney Hillman and the Rise of American Labor* (New York: Free Press, 1991), 13–23.
9. Fraser, *Labor Will Rule*, 87.
10. Fraser, *Labor Will Rule*, 87.
11. Fraser, *Labor Will Rule*, 81–91.
12. Zachary Lockman, *Comrades and Enemies: Arab and Jewish Workers in Palestine, 1906–1948* (Berkeley: University of California Press, 1996), 27.
13. Fayez Sayegh, *Zionist Colonialism in Palestine* (Beirut, Lebanon: Research Center-Palestine Liberation Organization, 1965), 1–2.
14. Ilan Pappé, *Ten Myths About Israel* (London: Verso, 2017), 25–31.
15. Quoted in Rudahl et al., *The Bund*, 29; Brossat and Klinberg, *Revolutionary Yiddishland*, 48–50.
16. Brumberg, "Anniversaries in Conflict," 201–202; Adam M. Howard, *Sewing the Fabric of Statehood: Garment Unions, American Labor, and the Establishment of the State of Israel* (Urbana: University of Illinois Press, 2017), 6–7.
17. Edward W. Said, *The Question of Palestine* (New York: Vintage Books, 1979), 10–12; Rosemary Sayigh, *The Palestinians: From Peasants to Revolutionaries* (London and New York: Zed Books, 1979), 1–35; James Reilly, "The Peasantry of Late Ottoman Palestine," *Journal of Palestine Studies* 10, no. 4 (1981); Muhammad Y. Muslih, *The Origins of Palestinian Nationalism* (New York: Columbia University Press, 1988), 22–23, 37–38, 60–61; Rashid Khalidi, *The Hundred Years' War on Palestine: A History of Settler Colonialism and Resistance, 1917–2017* (New York: Picador, 2017), 18–19.
18. Justin McCarthy, *The Population of Palestine: Population History and Statistics of the Late Ottoman Period and the Mandate* (New York: Columbia University Press, 1990), 10.
19. Khalidi, *Hundred Years' War*, 19.
20. Muslih, *Origins of Palestinian Nationalism*, 71.
21. Ran Greenstein, "Class, Nation, and Political Organization: The Anti-Zionist Left in Israel/Palestine," *International Labor and Working-Class History* 75 (Spring 2009): 86.
22. Greenstein, "Class, Nation, and Political Organization," 85–86; Lockman, *Comrades and Enemies*, 36; Alan Dowty, "Much Ado About Little: Ahad Ha'am's 'Truth from Eretz Yisrael,' Zionism, and the Arabs," *Israel Studies* 5, no. 2 (2000): 162.
23. Khalidi, *Hundred Years' War*, 6–7.
24. Quoted in Khalidi, *Hundred Years' War*, 4.
25. Khalidi, *Hundred Years' War*, 4–5.
26. Khalidi, *Hundred Years' War*, 6–7.
27. Library of Congress, "Immigration and Relocation in U.S. History."

28. Library of Congress, "Immigration and Relocation in U.S. History," 27; Said, *Question of Palestine*, 97.
29. Amos Perlmutter, "Dov Ber-Borochov: A Marxist-Zionist Ideologist," *Middle Eastern Studies* 5, no. 1 (1969): 34–35.
30. Brossat and Klinberg, *Revolutionary Yiddishland*, 26–27, 261; Lockman, *Comrades and Enemies*, 48; Musa Budeiri, *The Palestine Communist Party, 1919–1948: Arab and Jew in the Struggle for Internationalism* (Chicago: Haymarket Books, 2010/1979), 4–5.
31. Sayigh, *The Palestinians*, 45.
32. Khalidi, *Hundred Years' War*, 26–27.
33. Stuart Bruce Kaufman, *Samuel Gompers and the Origins of the American Federation of Labor, 1848–1896* (Westport: Greenwood Press, 1973); Julie Greene, *Pure and Simple Politics: The American Federation of Labor and Political Activism, 1881–1917* (New York: Cambridge University Press, 1998); Paul Buhle, *Taking Care of Business: Samuel Gompers, George Meany, Lane Kirkland, and the Tragedy of American Labor* (New York: Monthly Review Press, 1999).
34. Sheila Stern Polishook, "The American Federation of Labor, Zionism, and the First World War," *American Jewish Historical Quarterly* 65, no. 3 (1976): 234.
35. Elizabeth McKillen, *Making the World Safe for Workers: Labor, the Left, and Wilsonian Internationalism* (Urbana: University of Illinois Press, 2013), 147–148.
36. Richard Ned Lebow, "Woodrow Wilson and the Balfour Declaration," *Journal of Modern History* 40, no. 4 (1968): 521.
37. Philip S. Foner, *History of the Labor Movement in the United States, Vol. 7* (New York: International Publishers, 1987), 119–120.
38. *Report of Proceedings of the Thirty-Seventh Annual Convention of the American Federation of Labor, Held at Buffalo, New York, November 12 to 24, Inclusive, 1917* (Washington, DC: The Law Reporter Printing Company, 1917), 100.
39. Polishook, "American Federation of Labor," 231, 238–242.
40. Jonathan Schneer, "How Anti-Semitism Helped Create Israel," *Foreign Policy*, September 8, 2010.
41. Said, *Question of Palestine*, 27–29.
42. Memorandum of Edwin Montagu on the Anti-Semitism of the Present (British) Government, Submitted to the British Cabinet, August 1917, Jewish Virtual Library, https://www.jewishvirtuallibrary.org/montagu-memo-on-british-government-s-anti-semitism.
43. Quoted in Khalidi, *The Hundred Years' War*, 24.
44. Quoted in Khalidi, *The Hundred Years' War*, 24.

45. Polishook, "American Federation of Labor," 231–232; McKillen, *Making the World Safe*, 149; Howard, *Sewing the Fabric*, 14; "Labor Indorses Gompers on War," *New York Times*, November 20, 1917.
46. *Report and Proceedings, Fourteenth Convention of the International Ladies' Garment Workers' Union* (Boston: ILGWU, May 20–June 1, 1918), 201.
47. *Report and Proceedings*, 201.
48. *Proceedings of the Third Biennial Convention of the Amalgamated Clothing Workers of America* (Baltimore: ACWA, May 13–18, 1918), 193.
49. "Oppose a Jewish Republic: Labor Congress Favors Equal Rights for Inhabitants of Palestine," *New York Times*, January 20, 1919; "To Ask Wilson's Aid for European Jews," *New York Times*, September 6, 1915.
50. Khalidi, *Hundred Years' War*, 20–22, 26–33; Sayigh, *The Palestinians*, 50.
51. Khalidi, *Hundred Years' War*, 40.
52. Khalidi, *Hundred Years' War*, 31–32.
53. National Committee for Labor Israel, "Histadrut: General Federation of Jewish Labor in Israel," February 1954, RG18-001, International Affairs Department, Country Profiles, box 10, folder 10, George Meany Memorial Archive, University of Maryland (GMMA).
54. Lockman, *Comrades and Enemies*, 53–55; Jonathan Preminger, *Labor in Israel: Beyond Nationalism and Neoliberalism* (Ithaca: Cornell University Press, 2018), 4–6; Steven A. Glazer, "Language of Propaganda: The Histadrut, Hebrew Labor, and the Palestinian Worker," *Journal of Palestine Studies* 36, no. 2 (2020).
55. Budeiri, *Palestine Communist Party*, 1–30; Brossat and Klinberg, *Revolutionary Yiddishland*, 245–247.
56. Lockman, *Comrades and Enemies*, 66–80.
57. Eric Foner, *Free Soil, Free Labor, Free Men: The Ideology of the Republican Party Before the Civil War* (London: Oxford University Press, 1970); Carlos A. Schwantes, "The Concept of the Wageworkers' Frontier: A Framework for Future Research," *Western Historical Quarterly* 18, no. 1 (January 1987); Mark A. Lause, *Young America: Land, Labor and the Republican Community* (Urbana: University of Illinois Press, 2005); Antonina Griecci Woodsum, "'Get First the Freedom of the Soil': Settler Colonialism and the Politics of Justice in the Land Reform Movement of the 1840s-1850s" (unpublished master's thesis, University of Massachusetts Amherst, 2013).
58. Greg Grandin, *The End of the Myth: From the Frontier to the Border Wall in the Mind of America* (New York: Metropolitan Books, 2019), 77; Sean Wilentz, *Chants Democratic: New York City and the Rise of the American Working Class* (Oxford: Oxford University Press, 1984/2004), 372.
59. Grandin, *End of the Myth*, 95.
60. Grandin, *End of the Myth*, 110.

61. Quoted in Alexander Saxton, *The Indispensable Enemy: Labor and the Anti-Chinese Movement in California* (Berkeley: University of California Press, 1971), 271.
62. Bernard Mandel, "Samuel Gompers and the Negro Workers," *Journal of Negro History* 40, no. 1 (1955): 34–60; Priscilla Murolo and A. B. Chitty, *From the Folks Who Brought You the Weekend: A Short, Illustrated History of Labor in the United States* (New York: The New Press, 2001), 130; Philip S. Foner, *Organized Labor and the Black Worker: 1619 to 1981* (Chicago: Haymarket Books, 1974/2017), 64–102.
63. Howard, *Sewing the Fabric*, 17–19; Fraser, *Labor Will Rule*, 88.
64. Howard, *Sewing the Fabric*, 20–21.
65. David Montgomery, *The Fall of the House of Labor: The Workplace, the State, and American Labor Activism, 1865–1925* (Cambridge: Cambridge University Press, 1987), 460–462.
66. Albert Waldinger, "Abraham Cahan and Palestine," *Jewish Social Studies* 39, no. 1.5 (Winter-Spring 1977): 76, 83.
67. Quoted in Waldinger, "Abraham Cahan and Palestine," 77.
68. Howard, *Sewing the Fabric*, 21.
69. Howard, *Sewing the Fabric*, 21–23; Melech Epstein, *Jewish Labor in U.S.A.: An Industrial, Political and Cultural History of the Jewish Labor Movement: New Edition* (New York: Ktav Publishing House, 1969), 411–412.
70. Quoted in Howard, *Sewing the Fabric*, 23.
71. Howard, *Sewing the Fabric*, 27–29; Brossat and Klinberg, *Revolutionary Yiddishland*, 248–249.

CHAPTER 2: HOLOCAUST AND NAKBA

1. Robert D. Parmet, *The Master of Seventh Avenue: David Dubinsky and the American Labor Movement* (New York: New York University Press, 2005), 4–12; Irving Bernstein, *The Turbulent Years: A History of the American Worker 1933–1941* (Chicago: Haymarket Books, 2010/1969), 84–89, 709–712; Gail Malmgreen, "Comrades and Kinsmen: The Jewish Labor Committee and Anti-Nazi Activity, 1934–41," in *Jews, Labour and the Left, 1918–48*, ed. Christine Collette and Stephen Bird (Aldershot: Ashgate, 2000), 8.
2. Quoted in Adam M. Howard, *Sewing the Fabric of Statehood: Garment Unions, American Labor, and the Establishment of the State of Israel* (Urbana: University of Illinois Press, 2017), 31.
3. Tom Segev, *A State at Any Cost: The Life of David Ben-Gurion* (Picador: New York, 2019), 19–23.
4. Segev, *A State at Any Cost*, 73–74.
5. Segev, *A State at Any Cost*, 165, 171, 182–185.
6. Avi Shlaim, *The Iron Wall: Israel and the Arab World* (New York: W. W.

Norton and Company, 2001), 17–18; Zachary Lockman, *Comrades and Enemies: Arab and Jewish Workers in Palestine*, 1906–1948 (Berkeley: University of California Press, 1996), 72–77.

7. Quoted in Howard, *Sewing the Fabric*, 20.
8. Shlaim, *Iron Wall*, 18.
9. Quoted in John J. Mearsheimer and Stephen M. Walt, *The Israel Lobby and the US Foreign Policy* (London and New York: Penguin Books, 2007), 95.
10. Jane Power, "'Real Unions': Arab Organized Labor in British Palestine," *Arab Studies Quarterly* 20, no. 1 (Winter 1998): 15–17; Musa Budeiri, *The Palestine Communist Party, 1919–1948: Arab and Jew in the Struggle for Internationalism* (Chicago: Haymarket Books, 2010/1979), 40–41; Lockman, *Comrades and Enemies*, 145, 160.
11. Power, "'Real Unions'," 17; Lockman, *Comrades and Enemies*, 196–197, 246.
12. Yf'aat Weiss, "The Transfer Agreement and the Boycott Movement: A Jewish Dilemma on the Eve of the Holocaust," *Yad Vashem Studies* 43 (1998): 129–171; Joseph Massad, "Zionism, Anti-Semitism, and Colonialism," *Al Jazeera*, December 24, 2012.
13. Samuel Halperin, *The Political World of American Zionism* (Detroit: Wayne State University Press, 1961), 20.
14. Ghassan Kanafani, *The 1936–39 Revolt in Palestine* (New York: Committee for a Democratic Palestine, 1972), 12–14.
15. Lockman, *Comrades and Enemies*, 223–224, 235–236.
16. Kanafani, *1936–39 Revolt*, 35–38; Lockman, *Comrades and Enemies*, 234–235.
17. Lockman, *Comrades and Enemies*, 238–239.
18. Quoted in Lockman, *Comrades and Enemies*, 241.
19. Kanafani, *1936–39 Revolt*, 42–43; Budeiri, *Palestine Communist Party*, 63–65.
20. Kanafani, *1936–39 Revolt*, 39.
21. Kanafani, *1936–39 Revolt*, 16, 45; Lockman, *Comrades and Enemies*, 240–246, 250; Rashid Khalidi, *The Hundred Years' War on Palestine: A History of Settler Colonialism and Resistance, 1917–2017* (New York: Picador, 2017), 42–43.
22. Khalidi, *Hundred Years*, 44
23. Shlaim, *Iron Wall*, 21.
24. Kanafani, *1936–39 Revolt*, 49; Khalidi, *Hundred Years' War*, 44–47; Lockman, *Comrades and Enemies*, 240.
25. Kanafani, *1936–39 Revolt*, 55.
26. Shlaim, *Iron Wall*, 18–19.
27. Quoted in Shlaim, *Iron Wall*, 13.
28. Quoted in Khalidi, *Hundred Years' War*, 51.

29. Quoted in Catherine Collomp, *Rescue, Relief, and Resistance: The Jewish Labor Committee's Anti-Nazi Operations, 1934–1945* (Detroit: Wayne State University Press, 2016), 35.
30. Malmgreen, "Comrades and Kinsmen," 6–10; Catherine Collomp, "The Jewish Labor Committee, American Labor, and the Rescue of European Socialists," *International Labor and Working-Class History*, no. 68 (Fall 2005): 112–118.
31. "Labor Group Maps Policy on Hitler," *New York Times*, April 5, 1934; Collomp, *Rescue, Relief, and Resistance*, 33; Halperin, *Political World*, 21.
32. Ben-Gurion quoted in Howard, *Sewing the Fabric*, 43.
33. Benjamin Balthaser, "When Anti-Zionism Was Jewish: Jewish Racial Subjectivity and the Anti-Imperialist Literary Left from the Great Depression to the Cold War," *American Quarterly* 72, no. 2 (June 2020): 451–454.
34. Quoted in Howard, *Sewing the Fabric*, 32.
35. Howard, *Sewing the Fabric*, 32–39.
36. George Antonius, *The Arab Awakening: The Story of the Arab National Movement* (London: Hamish Hamilton, 1938), 411.
37. Lockman, *Comrades and Enemies*, 261; S. Shamir Hasan, "Zionism and Terror: The Creation of the State of Israel," *Proceedings of the Indian History Congress* 62 (2001): 867; Jewish Virtual Library, "Irgun Tz'va'i Le'umi (Etzel): Background & Overview (1931–1948)," https://www.jewishvirtuallibrary.org/background-and-overview-of-the-irgun-etzel.
38. Howard, *Sewing the Fabric*, 41.
39. Collomp, "The Jewish Labor Committee," 119–127; Malmgreen, "Comrades and Kinsmen," 13.
40. Daniel A. Gross, "The U.S. Government Turned Away Thousands of Jewish Refugees, Fearing That They Were Nazi Spies," *Smithsonian Magazine*, November 18, 2015.
41. Khalidi, *Hundred Years' War*, 60; Shlaim, *Iron Wall*, 23.
42. Samuel Halperin, "Zionism and Christian America: The Political Use of Reference Groups," *Southwestern Social Science Quarterly* 40, no. 3 (December 1959): 230–233.
43. Halperin, "Zionism and Christian America," 225–226.
44. Howard, *Sewing the Fabric*, 51; Halperin, *Political World*, 165–166, 174.
45. Quoted in Howard, *Sewing the Fabric*, 58.
46. Quoted in Howard, *Sewing the Fabric*, 62.
47. Quoted in Howard, *Sewing the Fabric* (emphasis added), 61–64.
48. Anglo-American Committee of Inquiry, *Report to the United States Government and His Majesty's Government in the United Kingdom*, Lausanne, Switzerland, April 20, 1946.
49. Khalidi, *Hundred Years' War*, 91; Lockman, *Comrades and Enemies*, 314.

50. Howard, *Sewing the Fabric*, 66–68.
51. Philip Mattar, "Amin Al-Husayni and Iraq's Quest for Independence, 1939–41," *Arab Studies Quarterly* 6, no. 4 (1984): 267–181; Basheer M. Nafi, "The Arabs and the Axis: 1933–1940," *Arab Studies Quarterly* 19, no. 2 (1997): 1–24; Rashid Khalidi, *The Iron Cage: The Story of the Palestinian Struggle for Statehood* (Boston: Beacon Press, 2006), 62; Khalidi, *Hundred Years' War*, 66.
52. Abigail Jacobson, "Between National Liberation and Anti-Colonial Struggle: The National Liberation League in Palestine," Working Paper 3, Crown Center for Middle East Studies, Brandeis University, August 2012.
53. Budeiri, *The Palestine Communist Party*, 98–108, 119–123; Jacobson, "Between National Liberation and Anti-Colonial Struggle."
54. Quoted in Lockman, *Comrades and Enemies*, 323.
55. Power, "'Real Unions,'" 18–19.
56. Lockman, *Comrades and Enemies*, 324–341.
57. Khalidi, *Hundred Years' War*, 71; Ilan Pappé, *The Ethnic Cleansing of Palestine* (London: Oneworld Publications, 2006), 29–32.
58. Quoted in Pappé, *Ethnic Cleansing*, 33–34.
59. Pappé, *Ethnic Cleansing*, 36.
60. Bruce J. Evensen, "The Limits of Presidential Leadership: Truman at War with Zionists, the Press, Public Opinion and His Own State Department over Palestine," *Presidential Studies Quarterly* 23, no. 2 (1993): 269–287; "United States Proposal for Temporary United Nations Trusteeship for Palestine: Statement by President Truman, March 25, 1948," United Nations—The Question of Palestine (UNISPAL), https://www.un.org/unispal/document/auto-insert-194247/.
61. Shlaim, *Iron Wall*, 35; Gita Zbavitelová, "The Czech Arms That Saved Israel," *Jerusalem Post*, November 30, 2020.
62. Khalidi, *Hundred Years' War*, 72–74; Shlaim, *Iron Wall*, 30–31; Pappé, *Ethnic Cleansing*, 40.
63. Pappé, *Ethnic Cleansing*, 111–112, 133–136.
64. Pappé, *Ethnic Cleansing*, 95.
65. Pappé, *Ethnic Cleansing*, 103; Khalidi, *Hundred Years' War*, 73.
66. Khalidi, *Hundred Years' War*, 75–77; Shlaim, *Iron Wall*, 30–34.
67. Khalidi, *Hundred Years' War*, 75–77; Shlaim, *Iron Wall*, 30–34.
68. Pappé, *Ethnic Cleansing*, 196–197.
69. Quoted in Pappé, *Ethnic Cleansing*, 190.
70. Rashid Khalidi, "'A New Abyss': Gaza and the Hundred Years' War on Palestine," *Guardian*, April 11, 2024; "The Nakba Did Not Start or End in 1948," *Al Jazeera*, May 23, 2017.
71. Pappé, *Ethnic Cleansing*, 188–89.

72. Institute for Palestine Studies, Interactive Encyclopedia of the Palestine Question, "The Nakba-Stages of a Forced Displacement," https://www.palquest.org/en/highlight/160/nakba; "The Nakba Did Not Start or End in 1948."
73. Marjorie N. Feld, *The Threshold of Dissent: A History of American Jewish Critics of Zionism* (New York: New York University Press, 2024), 33–34.
74. Joseph Spriznak to Philip Murray, May 6, 1947, RG18-002, CIO International Affairs, Michael Ross Files, box 13, folder 22, George Meany Memorial Archive, University of Maryland (GMMA).
75. Howard, *Sewing the Fabric*, 76.
76. Howard, *Sewing the Fabric*, 71–73.
77. Quoted in David Slucki, *The International Jewish Labor Bund After 1945: Toward a Global History* (New Brunswick, NJ: Rutgers University Press, 2012), 185.
78. Slucki, *The International Jewish Labor Bund*, 179–187; Collomp, *Rescue, Relief, and Resistance*, 233–234.
79. Quoted in Parmet, *Master of Seventh Avenue*, 239.
80. Quoted in Parmet, *Master of Seventh Avenue*, 240.
81. M. Nemirovsky to Philip Murray, December 26, 1947, RG18-002, CIO International Affairs, Michael Ross Files, box 13, folder 22, GMMA.
82. Joseph Breslaw, Max Zaritsky, Joseph Schlossberg to Philip Murray, January 22, 1948, RG18-002, CIO International Affairs, Michael Ross Files, box 13, folder 22, GMMA.
83. "Unions Urge U.N. and Jewish State," *New York Times*, March 2, 1948; Howard, *Sewing the Fabric*, 86.
84. Howard, *Sewing the Fabric*, 87–88.
85. Minutes, Special Executive Committee Meeting, American Trade Union Council—National Committee for Labor Palestine, April 9, 1948, ILGWU David Dubinsky Correspondence, Collection #5780/002, box 121, folder 2, Kheel Center for Labor-Management Documentation & Archives (KC), Cornell University.
86. "30,000 Here Hold Palestine Rally," *New York Times*, April 15, 1948.
87. David Dubinsky to Joseph Breslaw, April 14, 1948, ILGWU David Dubinsky Correspondence, Collection #5780/002, box 121, folder 2, KC.
88. "30,000 Here Hold Palestine Rally."
89. Howard, *Sewing the Fabric*, 88–93; Peter L. Hahn, "The Influence of Organized Labor on U.S. Policy Toward Israel, 1945–1967," in *Empire and Revolution: The United States and the Third World Since 1945*, ed. Peter L. Hahn and Mary Ann Heiss (Columbus: Ohio State University Press, 2001), 161.
90. "Union Head Scores Bevin as Betrayer," *New York Times*, May 22, 1948.
91. Howard, *Sewing the Fabric*, 98–99.

92. David Dubinsky and A. H. Raskin, *David Dubinsky: A Life with Labor* (New York: Simon and Schuster, 1977), 330–331.

CHAPTER 3: BONDING WITH ISRAEL

1. See Jeff Schuhrke, *Blue-Collar Empire: The Untold Story of US Labor's Global Anticommunist Crusade* (London and New York: Verso, 2024); Anthony Carew, *American Labour's Cold War Abroad: From Deep Freeze to Détente*, 1945–1970 (Edmonton: Athabasca University Press, 2018); Kim Scipes, *AFL-CIO's Secret War Against Developing Country Workers: Solidarity or Sabotage?* (Lanham: Lexington Books, 2010); Beth Sims, *Workers of the World Undermined: American Labor's Role in US Foreign Affairs* (Boston: South End Press, 1992); Ronald Radosh, *American Labor and United States Foreign Policy* (New York: Random House, 1969).
2. Yoav Fromer, "The 'Other' Pro-Israel Lobby: The AFL-CIO and Israel (1952–1960)," *Modern American History* 7, no. 2 (Spring 2024): 232–234.
3. "Peace in the Middle East: A Statement by the Presidents of the CIO and AFL," 1950, RG18–002, CIO International Affairs, Michael Ross Files, box 13, folder 22, George Meany Memorial Archive, University of Maryland (GMMA).
4. Peter L. Hahn, "The Influence of Organized Labor on U.S. Policy Toward Israel, 1945–1967," in *Empire and Revolution: The United States and the Third World Since 1945*, ed. Peter L. Hahn and Mary Ann Heiss (Columbus: Ohio State University Press, 2001), 163–164.
5. Hahn, "The Influence of Organized Labor."
6. "Israel Gets AFL Promise," *New York Times*, October 30, 1948.
7. "Palestine Labor Seeks $3,000,000," *New York Times*, November 25, 1945; Adam M. Howard, *Sewing the Fabric of Statehood: Garment Unions, American Labor, and the Establishment of the State of Israel* (Urbana: University of Illinois Press, 2017), 100–101.
8. "ILGWU Will Lend $1,000,000 to Israel," *New York Times*, June 11, 1948.
9. David Dubinsky to David Ben-Gurion, June 13, 1951, David Dubinsky Correspondence, Collection #5780/002, box 431, folder 2B, Kheel Center for Labor-Management Documentation & Archives (KC), Cornell University.
10. "$20,000,000 Corporation Formed to Provide Housing in Israel; Backed by Unions," *Jewish Telegraphic Agency*, March 9, 1950; Howard, *Sewing the Fabric of Statehood*, 104–105; Memo to David Dubinsky, July 28, 1952, #5780/002, box 251, folder 3D, KC.
11. Memo to David Dubinsky, July 28, 1952, Correspondence, box 251, folder 3D, KC; Howard, *Sewing the Fabric*, 105.
12. David Ben-Gurion to David Dubinsky, October 30, 1951, and Dubinsky

to Ben-Gurion, November 28, 1951, #5780/002, box 431, folder 2B, KC.

13. Aba Khoushy to David Dubinsky, November 12, 1953, #5780/002, box 251, folder 3C, KC.
14. "Dubinsky Expresses Enthusiasm About Israel Upon Return to U.S.," *Jewish Telegraphic Agency*, June 29, 1955.
15. Quoted in Fromer, "The 'Other' Pro-Israel Lobby," 248; "Labor Does Not Support U.S. Middle East Policy, Leader Says," *Jewish Telegraphic Agency*, August 24, 1954.
16. Pappé, *Ethnic Cleansing of Palestine*, 195, 217.
17. Quoted in Histadrut, "David Dubinsky: A Mission to Histadrut in Israel," 1960, Collection #5780/002, box 253, folder 3A, KC.
18. Agreement between ILGWU and Histadrut, December 19, 1955, #5780/002, box 253, folder 4B and Histadrut, "David Dubinsky: A Mission to Histadrut in Israel," 1960, #5780/002, box 253, folder 3A, KC; Shifra Shvarts, *Health and Zionism: The Israeli Health Care System, 1948–1960* (Rochester: Boydell and Brewer, 2008), 249–260; Simha Flapan, "The Palestinian Exodus of 1948," *Journal of Palestine Studies* 16, no. 4 (Summer 1987): 14.
19. George M. Harrison and Jacob S. Potofsky, "Ten Years of Progress: A Report on Israel," December 1, 1958, RG18-001, International Affairs Department, Country Files, box 10, folder 10, GMMA.
20. Jonathan Preminger, *Labor in Israel: Beyond Nationalism and Neoliberalism* (Ithaca: Cornell University Press, 2018), 5–6.
21. "Delegation of Top U.S. Trade Union Leaders Leaves Today for Israel," *Jewish Telegraphic Agency*, August 16, 1955.
22. "Delegation of Top U.S. Trade Union Leaders"; "Reuther, in Israel, Dedicates Center," *New York Times*, September 6, 1955; George M. Harrison and Jacob S. Potofsky, "Ten Years of Progress: A Report on Israel," December 1, 1958, RG18-001, International Affairs Department, Country Files, box 10, folder 10, GMMA.
23. Hahn, "The Influence of Organized Labor," 159–160; "Cornerstone for Walter Reuther Youth Center Laid in Israel," *Jewish Telegraphic Agency*, May 18, 1961; National Committee for Labor Israel, Presentation to Walter P. Reuther, June 17, 1958, UAW President's Office: Walter P. Reuther Collection, box 457, folder 1, Walter P. Reuther Library of Labor and Urban Affairs, (Reuther Library), Wayne State University; "Walter Reuther Cited," *New York Times*, June 18, 1958; National Committee for Labor Israel, Presentation to David J. McDonald, March 16, 1963, Reuther Collection, box 507, folder 7, Reuther Library.
24. Calev Ben-David, "How Hoffa Helped Forge an Unlikely Union with Israel," *Jerusalem Post*, February 12, 2008; "James ('Jimmy') Hoffa

(1913–1975)," *Jewish News Syndicate*, May 1, 2018; Robert Rockaway, "Gangsters for Zion," *Tablet*, April 19, 2018; "Eyewitnesses to History," *New Jersey Jewish News*, June 3, 2019; Ricky-Dale Calhoun, "Arming David: The Haganah's Illegal Arms Procurement Network in the United States, 1945–49," *Journal of Palestine Studies* 36, no. 4 (Summer 2007): 28; Joe Allen, "The Teamster Connection: Apartheid Israel and the IBT," *CounterPunch*, December 29, 2023.

25. Damon Stetson, "Hoffa Is Honored for Aid to Labor," *New York Times*, April 21, 1956; Kimberly Lifton, "Teamster Connection: Jimmy Hoffa and His Labor Union's Help to Be Cited by Israel," *Detroit Jewish News*, January 24, 2008.
26. Lifton, "Teamster Connection"; "Hoffa and Group Will Go to Israel," *New York Times*, August 8, 1956; "Israel Children's Home Named for Teamsters' Chief," *New York Times*, August 20, 1956.
27. Abba Eban to David Dubinsky, December 13, 1950; Dubinsky to Henry Montor, January 5, 1951; David Ben-Gurion to Dubinsky, May 30, 1951; Dubinsky to Ben-Gurion, June 13, 1951; Benjamin Dzick to Dubinsky, July 1, 1955; Dzick to Dubinsky, January 31, 1956; Dubinsky to Dzick, February 21, 1956, #5780/002, box 431, folder 7, KC.
28. Leo Bernstein to city managers and supervisors, February 20, 1967, ILGWU Louis Stulberg Correspondence, Collection #5780/004 (Stulberg Correspondence), box 32, folder 6B, KC.
29. "State of Israel Bonds: A Legacy of Achievement" and "Labor's Bond with Israel," Development Corporation for Israel, 1994, UAW President's Office: Owen Bieber Records, LR001270, box 130, folder 3, Reuther Library.
30. Philip S. Foner, *Organized Labor and the Black Worker: 1619 to 1981* (Chicago: Haymarket Books, 1974/2017), 294; Dan Georgakas and Marvin Surkin, *Detroit: I Do Mind Dying: A Study in Urban Revolution* (Chicago: Haymarket Books, 1998/1975), 32–34.
31. Pamela E. Pennock, *The Rise of the Arab American Left: Activists, Allies, and Their Fight Against Imperialism and Racism, 1960s–1980s* (Chapel Hill, NC: University of North Carolina Press, 2017), 7–8.
32. Roger Keeran, *The Communist Party and the Auto Workers' Unions* (New York: International Publishers, 1980), 44.
33. Vickie Karadashly to David Dubinsky, April 19, 1949, #5780/002, box 353, folder 2A, KC.
34. Vickie Karadashly to David Dubinsky, April 19, 1949, #5780/002, box 353, folder 2A, KC.
35. Vickie Karadashly to David Dubinsky, April 19, 1949, #5780/002, box 353, folder 2A, KC.
36. David Dubinsky's secretary to Vickie Karadashly, June 22, 1949, David

Dubinsky to Clarence E. Pickett, July 5, 1949, Clarence E. Pickett to David Dubinsky, July 7, 1949, George M. Barakat to David Dubinsky, July 26, 1949, #5780/002, box 353, folder 2A, KC; "ILGWU Gift for Arabs," *New York Times*, July 6, 1949.

37. Jay Lovestone to Hannah Haskel (n.d., summer 1955), #5780/002, box 353, folder 2B, KC.
38. Jonathan Cook, "'Visible Equality' as Confidence Trick," in *Israel and South Africa: The Many Faces of Apartheid*, ed. Ilan Pappé (London: Zed Books, 2015), 126; Marjorie N. Feld, *The Threshold of Dissent: A History of American Jewish Critics of Zionism* (New York: New York University Press, 2024), 75; Mohammad H. Fadel, "The 'Miraculous' Nature of the Israel Exception in International Law: Israel's Nationality Laws," *Contending Modernities*, June 4, 2024, https://contendingmodernities.nd.edu/global-currents/miraculous-israel-exception/.
39. Hani al-Hourani, *The Jordanian Labor Movement: History, Structure, and Challenges* (Bonn, Germany: Friedrich-Ebert-Stiftung, 2001), https://library.fes.de/fulltext/iez/01144002.htm.
40. Rashid Khalidi, *The Hundred Years' War on Palestine: A History of Settler Colonialism and Resistance, 1917–2017* (New York: Picador, 2017), 88–91.
41. Khalidi, *Hundred Years' War*, 90–91; Avi Shlaim, *The Iron Wall: Israel and the Arab World* (New York: W. W. Norton and Company, 2001), 90–92.
42. Quoted in Shlaim, *Iron Wall*, 93.
43. No. 695 Department of State Press Release, S/PRS files, lot 77 D 9, Foreign Relations of the United States, 1952–1954, the Near and Middle East, Volume IX, Part 1, https://history.state.gov/historicaldocuments/frus1952-54v09p1/d695.
44. Quill and Carey quoted in Fromer, "The 'Other' Pro-Israel Lobby," 236.
45. Shlaim, *Iron Wall*, 92; Jewish Labor Committee, Memorandum on Israel-Arabic Tensions, 1953, #5780/002, box 253, folder 3A, KC.
46. George Meany remarks at the JLC Chicago chapter, April 1955, RG1-027, AFL-CIO Office of the President, George Meany Files, box 31, folder 20, GMMA.
47. Cook, "'Visible Equality," 126–127.
48. Quoted in Feld, *Threshold of Dissent*, 75–77.
49. Quoted in Daniel Maier-Katkin, *Stranger from Abroad: Hannah Arendt, Martin Heidegger, Friendship and Forgiveness* (New York: W. W. Norton, 2010), 153.
50. Report on Israel, 1954, AFL-CIO Office of the President, George Meany Files, box 31, folder 21, GMMA; George M. Harrison and Jacob S. Potofsky, "Ten Years of Progress: A Report on Israel," December 1, 1958, RG18-001, International Affairs Department, Country Files, box

10, folder 10, GMMA.

51. Quoted in "Labor Leaders to Seek Change in U.S. Policy Toward Israel," *Jewish Telegraphic Agency*, August 27, 1954.
52. Report on Israel, 1954, AFL-CIO Office of the President, George Meany Files, box 31, folder 21, GMMA; George M. Harrison and Jacob S. Potofsky, "Ten Years of Progress: A Report on Israel," December 1, 1958, RG18-001, International Affairs Department, Country Files, box 10, folder 10, GMMA; Pappé, *Ethnic Cleansing*, 219–220; Zachary Lockman, *Comrades and Enemies: Arab and Jewish Workers in Palestine*, 1906–1948 (Berkeley: University of California Press, 1996), 197; Preminger, *Labor in Israel*, 7.
53. Fromer, "The 'Other' Pro-Israel Lobby," 247.
54. Rashid Khalidi, *Sowing Crisis: The Cold War and American Dominance in the Middle East* (Boston: Beacon Press, 2010), 191.
55. Khalidi, *Hundred Years' War*, 90–92; Shlaim, *Iron Wall*, 124–126; "Reuther Says Israel Has Moral Duty to Defend Itself from Attack," *Jewish Telegraphic Agency*, August 31, 1955.
56. Khalidi, *Hundred Years' War*, 92; Shlaim, *Iron Wall*, 126–129.
57. "Reuther Bids U.S. Aid Middle East," *New York Times*, November 27, 1955.
58. Khalidi, *Sowing Crisis*, 182; Salim Yaqub, *Containing Arab Nationalism: The Eisenhower Doctrine and the Middle East* (Chapel Hill, NC: University of North Carolina Press, 2004), 47.
59. Khalidi, *Hundred Years' War*, 92–94; Shlaim, *Iron Wall*, 181.
60. David Dubinsky to Pinhas Lavon, November 5, 1956, #5780/002, box 251, folder 3B, KC.
61. Quoted in Hahn, "The Influence of Organized Labor," 165–166.
62. Avi Shlaim, "Israel Between East and West, 1948–1956," *International Journal of Middle East Studies* 36, no. 4 (November 2004): 660–664.
63. Report on Israel, 1954, AFL-CIO Office of the President, George Meany Files, box 31, folder 21, GMMA.
64. George M. Harrison and Jacob S. Potofsky, "Ten Years of Progress: A Report on Israel," December 1, 1958, RG18-001, International Affairs Department, Country Files, box 10, folder 10, GMMA.
65. George Meany remarks at Histadrut's 40th anniversary, Washington, DC, June 4, 1961, Reuther Collection, box 457, folder 2, Reuther Library.
66. Eliahu Elath, "Afro-Asian School Teaches Progress Under Democracy," *AFL-CIO American Federationist*, June 1961, box 328, folder 28, Communications Workers of America Records, Tamiment Library and Robert F. Wagner Labor Archives, New York University; "The Afro-Asian Institute for Labour Studies and Cooperation," and Ben-Zion Ilan to Meany, April 18, 1963, box 10, folder 8, RG18-001, GMMA.

67. Ben-Zion Ilan to George Meany, April 18, 1963;"The Afro-Asian Institute for Labor Studies and Cooperation," n.d., 1964–65, RG18-001, International Affairs Department, Country Files, box 10, folder 8, GMMA.
68. UAW Contributions to Histadrut Afro-Asian Institute, January 10, 1969, Victor G. Reuther Papers, LP000002, box 39, folder 11, Reuther Library.
69. Howard, *Sewing the Fabric*, 113.
70. Khalidi, *Sowing Crisis*, 18, 22; Yaqub, *Containing Arab Nationalism*, 2, 5, 117.
71. Khalidi, *Hundred Years' War*, 116; Shlaim, *Iron Wall*, 230–231.
72. Rashid Khalidi, *The Iron Cage: The Story of the Palestinian Struggle for Statehood* (Boston: Beacon Press, 2006), 142.
73. Shlaim, *Iron Wall*, 229–237; Khalidi, *Hundred Years' War*, 97–98.
74. Victor Riesel, "Waterfront Unions on Israel's Side," *Indianapolis Star*, June 1, 1967; Shlomo Sapir, "The Trade Unions Have Passed the Test," *Davar*, June 22, 1967, RG18-001, International Affairs Department, Country Files, box 10, folder 11, GMMA.
75. "Lyndon Johnson Administration: Statement Supporting Independence and Integrity of All Nations in the Middle East," Jewish Virtual Library, May 23, 1967, https://www.jewishvirtuallibrary.org/president-johnson-statement-supporting-independence-and-integrity-of-all-nations-in-the-middle-east-may-1967.
76. Shlaim, *Iron Wall*, 239–240; Khalidi, *Hundred Years' War*, 97; John J. Mearsheimer and Stephen M. Walt, *The Israel Lobby and the US Foreign Policy* (London and New York: Penguin Books, 2007), 41, 55.
77. Louis Stulberg to Aharon Becker, May 26, 1967; Becker to Stulberg, May 26, 1967, Stulberg Correspondence, box 32, folder 6B, KC; "Labour's Support Voiced Abroad," *Jerusalem Post*, May 26, 1967.
78. Hahn, "The Influence of Organized Labor," 168–169.
79. George Meany statement, June 1, 1967, RG18-001, International Affairs Department, Country Files, box 10, folder 12, GMMA.
80. "UAW Officers Support U.S. Peace Efforts in Mid-East Crisis," June 1, 1967, Reuther Collection, box, 457, folder 5, Reuther Library.
81. Shlaim, *Iron Wall*, 240–241; Khalidi, *Hundred Years' War*, 104; Mearsheimer and Walt, *Israel Lobby*, 41–42, 368n97.
82. Shlaim, *Iron Wall*, 241; Khalidi, *Hundred Years' War*, 97.
83. "A Near Riot Erupts at Rally for Israel," *New York Times*, June 6, 1967.
84. American Trade Union Council for Histadrut, June 1, 1967, Stulberg Correspondence, box 32, folder 6B, KC; Hahn, "The Influence of Organized Labor," 169.
85. Shlaim, *Iron Wall*, 242–248.
86. Walter Reuther to Aharon Becker, June 9, 1967, Reuther Collection, box 457, folder 5, Reuther Library.

87. Khalidi, *Sowing Crisis*, 117.
88. Khalidi, *Hundred Years' War*, 102–107.
89. Quoted in Hahn, "The Influence of Organized Labor," 170.
90. Louis Stulberg to All Organizations, Officers and Staff of the ILGWU, June 16, 1967, #5780/002, box 431, folder 8, KC.
91. Pennock, *Rise of the Arab American Left*, 110.
92. M. T. Mehdi to Moe Salikman [*sic*], June 19, 1967, Stulberg Correspondence, box 32, 6B, KC.

CHAPTER 4: STRAINED FRIENDSHIP

1. Robin D. G. Kelley, "Apartheid's Black Apologists," in *Apartheid Israel: The Politics of an Analogy*, ed. Jon Soske and Sean Jacobs (Chicago: Haymarket Books, 2014), 129–134.
2. "A Near Riot Erupts at Rally for Israel," *New York Times*, June 6, 1967; "Randolph Rallies Negroes' Support to Israel's Cause," *Chicago Daily Defender*, June 7, 1967; Shlomo Sapir, "The Trade Unions Have Passed the Test," *Davar*, June 22, 1967, RG18-001, International Affairs Department, Country Files, box 10, folder 11, George Meany Memorial Archive, University of Maryland (GMMA).
3. Kelley, "Apartheid's Black Apologists," 135–136.
4. George Meany, "The Shambles of Detente," April 8, 1975, box 18, folder 42, RG34-002, GMMA; Les Finnegan, "Close Kinship: American Labor Has Huge Stake in Israel and Its Very Survival," Press Associates, Inc., published in the Congressional Record, November 12, 1973, Victor G. Reuther Papers, box 67, folder 21, Walter P. Reuther Library of Labor and Urban Affairs (Reuther Library), Wayne State University; Les Finnegan and Margaret L. Plunkett, *Country Profile: Israel*, US Department of Labor, Bureau of Int'l Labor Affairs, 1979.
5. Finnegan, "Close Kinship."
6. "Israeli Agency Struck," *New York Times*, September 7, 1961; "Bond Strike Settled," *New York Times*, September 11, 1961; "Israel Bond Offices Are Struck by 500," *New York Times*, May 16, 1967; "Pact Settles Bonds Strike" *Jewish Exponent*, May 26, 1967.
7. "Israel Bond Employees Strike, Picket 'Dinner of State' Here," *Jewish Exponent*, May 23, 1969; "Pickets Delay Humphrey, Tate at Bonds Dinner," *Philadelphia Inquirer*, May 19, 1969.
8. "450 Israeli Bonds Employees Out on Strike Across U.S." *New York Times*, May 15, 1971; "Israel Bond Employees Strike Continues," *Jewish Advocate*, June 3, 1971; "Central Labor Council Tells Members Not to Buy Israel Bonds Until Strike Settled," *Jewish Telegraphic Agency*, June 16, 1971; "Israel Bond Organization Employees Picket," *Jewish Exponent*, June 11, 1971.

9. "Accord Found in Strike of Israel Corporation," *Washington Post*, June 20, 1971.
10. Avi Shlaim, *The Iron Wall: Israel and the Arab World* (New York: W. W. Norton and Company, 2001), 289–310.
11. Shlaim, *Iron Wall*, 318–319.
12. Shlaim, *Iron Wall*, 319–322.
13. Quoted in Ed Townsend, "U.S. Labor Weighs in Behind Israel," *Christian Science Monitor*, October 25, 1973.
14. Philip Shabecoff, "Labor Delegates Are Not Satisfied," *New York Times*, October 24, 1973; Ed Townsend, "U.S. Labor Firmly on Israel's Side," *Christian Science Monitor*, November 15, 1973.
15. Sol Chick Chaikin speech at the Fiftieth Anniversary of the National Committee for Labor Israel, November 4, 1973, ILGWU Sol Chaikin Papers, Collection #5780/004, box 47, folder 5, Kheel Center for Labor-Management Documentation & Archives (KC), Cornell University.
16. Townsend, "U.S. Labor Firmly on Israel's Side."
17. "U.S. Labor Team Comes to Show Its Support," *Jerusalem Post*, January 22, 1974; "Labor Group Vows Support for Israel," *Washington Post*, January 29, 1974; Carl Gershman, *The Foreign Policy of American Labor* (Beverley Hills: Sage Publications, 1975), 64.
18. Rashid Khalidi, *The Hundred Years' War on Palestine: A History of Settler Colonialism and Resistance, 1917–2017* (New York: Picador, 2017), 109–116.
19. Khalidi, *Hundred Years' War*, 121–125.
20. Arab World for Research and Development, *Palestine Workers: A Comprehensive Report on Work Conditions, Priorities and Recommendations* (Palestine General Federation of Trade Unions, 2013), 6–7.
21. Joost R. Hiltermann, "The Emerging Trade Union Movement in the West Bank," *MERIP Reports* No. 136/137 (October-December 1985): 27.
22. Dan Georgakas and Marvin Surkin, *Detroit: I Do Mind Dying: A Study in Urban Revolution* (Chicago: Haymarket Books, 1998/1975), 63–65.
23. Pamela E. Pennock, *The Rise of the Arab American Left: Activists, Allies, and Their Fight Against Imperialism and Racism, 1960s–1980s* (Chapel Hill: University of North Carolina Press, 2017), 180–182.
24. Georgakas and Surkin, *Detroit*, 52–53, 65–66; Pennock, *Rise of the Arab American Left*, 180–182; Jeff Schuhrke, "When Arab-American Detroit Auto Workers Struck for Palestinian Liberation," *Jacobin*, August 3, 2020.
25. "Woodcock Condemns Unprovoked Attack on Israel; Calls for Peace in the Middle East," UAW, October 11, 1973, UAW International Affairs Department: Herman Rebhan Records, box 3, folder 5, Reuther Library.
26. Ismael Ahmed, "Organizing an Arab Workers Caucus," *MERIP Reports*, no. 34 (January 1975): 19.

27. Pennock, *Rise of the Arab American Left*, 186.
28. Tim McNulty, "B'nai B'rith Fetes Woodcock as Arabs Stage a Protest," *Detroit Free Press*, November 29, 1973; Ahmed, "Organizing," 19–20; Pennock, *Rise of the Arab American Left*, 182–187; "Arab Workers Shut Down Dodge Main," *Workers Vanguard*, December 7, 1973.
29. "Mazey Criticizes Unfounded Attacks on UAW Purchase of Israel Bonds," UAW, December 9, 1973, UAW International Affairs Department: Herman Rebhan Records, box 14, folder 7, Reuther Library; Russell Mokhiber, "Bonds of Affections," *Multinational Monitor*, April 1988.
30. Ahmed, "Organizing an Arab Workers Caucus," 21.
31. Ahmed, "Organizing an Arab Workers Caucus," 21.
32. Ahmed, "Organizing an Arab Workers Caucus," 20–21.
33. United Nations General Assembly Resolution 3379, "Elimination of All Forms of Racial Discrimination: Zionism as Racism – GA Resolution," adopted November 10, 1975, United Nations, The Question of Palestine (UNISPAL), https://www.un.org/unispal/document/auto-insert-181963/.
34. Seth Anziska, *Preventing Palestine: A Political History from Camp David to Oslo* (Princeton: Princeton University Press, 2018), 11.
35. Shlaim, *Iron Wall*, 330, 336; Khalidi, *Hundred Years' War*, 125–127; John J. Mearsheimer and Stephen M. Walt, *The Israel Lobby and US Foreign Policy* (London and New York: Penguin Books, 2007), 38.
36. Arnold Forster and Benjamin Epstein, *New Anti-Semitism* (New York: McGraw-Hill, 1974); Adam Haber and Matylda Figlerowicz, "Anatomy of a Moral Panic," *Jewish Currents*, May 2, 2024.
37. George Meany, "The Shambles of Detente," April 8, 175, box 18, folder 42, RG34-002, GMMA.
38. Schuhrke, *Blue-Collar Empire*, 205–207.
39. Finnegan, "Close Kinship"; Steven Brill, *The Teamsters* (New York: Simon and Schuster, 1978), 335.
40. Mark Segal, "U.S. Teamsters Union Strong for Israel," *Jerusalem Post*, December 8, 1972.
41. Donnie Radcliffe, "Teaming Up for Bonds for Israel," *Washington Post*, May 11, 1973.
42. Jack Nelson and Bill Hazlett, "Teamsters' Ties to Mafia—and to White House," *Los Angeles Times*, May 31, 1973.
43. Brill, *The Teamsters*, 335.
44. Stephen Lynton, "We Are Here to Pay Tribute," *Washington Post*, March 15, 1977; Ronald Sullivan, "U.S. Jury Indicts Four Union Aides," *New York Times*, August 20, 1971; Morton Mintz, "Racket-Probing Senators Get Few Answers," *Washington Post*, October 16, 1971; "Union Aide

Takes Fifth at Hearing," *Philadelphia Inquirer*, October 16, 1971.

45. Brill, *The Teamsters*, 335.
46. Jeff Black, "Staunch U.S. Ally," *Jerusalem Post*, May 26, 1989.
47. Walter Shapiro, "Lane Kirkland: Labor's New Leader Punches In," *Washington Post*, November 17, 1979; Kathy Sawyer, "Lane Kirkland: Made in America," *Washington Post*, July 14, 1984.
48. Quoted in Murrey Marder, "A 'Homeland' for Palestinians Seen as a Noteworthy Shift of Language," *Washington Post*, March 18, 1977.
49. Anziska, *Preventing Palestine*, 12; Shlaim, *Iron Wall*, 349–350.
50. "AFL-CIO Backs Israel," *Chicago Tribune*, December 10, 1978; "Labor Will Keep Backing Israel, Top AFL-CIO Official Declares," *The Sun*, December 10, 1978.
51. "AFL-CIO President Lauds Israel's Role," *The American Israelite*, January 24, 1980; "Kirkland Urges Support for Israel," *Jewish Exponent*, January 25, 1980.
52. Warren Brown, "Kirkland Urges Opposition to Any Palestinian State," *Washington Post*, March 31, 1980.
53. David A. Andelman, "Express Concern Over Israeli Settlements," *New York Times*, July 9, 1979; Jewish Labor Committee, Press Release, July 16, 1979, Jewish Labor Committee Records, Part III (JLC Records), box 444, folder 6, Tamiment Library and Robert F. Wagner Labor Archives (Tamiment), New York University.
54. Sol Chick Chaikin speech to Trilateral Commission, London, March 25, 1980, ILGWU Sol Chaikin Papers, box 48, folder 31, KC.
55. Anziska, *Preventing Palestine*, 176–177.
56. Muhammad Hussein, "Remembering the Zionists' Assassination of UN Palestine Mediator Count Bernadotte," *Middle East Monitor*, September 17, 2023; Jewish Virtual Library, "Modern History of Israel: The Assassination of Count Bernadotte," https://www.jewishvirtuallibrary.org/the-assassination-of-count-bernadotte.
57. Shlaim, *Iron Wall*, 354–361; Khalidi, *Hundred Years' War*, 135–136; Anziska, *Preventing Palestine*, 92–95.
58. Albert K. Herling, "Roar of Cheers Resounds When Meany Hails Labor Chiefs of Israel and Egypt," *New York Jewish Week*, December 18, 1977.
59. Wilfred Rodgers, "AFL-CIO Applauds Mondale," *Boston Globe*, December 10, 1977.
60. "Response by Sol C. Chaikin Honoree at the Histadrut Humanitarian Award Dinner," January 24, 1978, Sol Chaikin Papers, box 47, folder 5, KC.
61. Anziska, *Preventing Palestine*, 124; Shlaim, *Iron Wall*, 374–375; Khalidi, *Hundred Years' War*, 136.
62. Anziska, *Preventing Palestine*, 125.

63. "AFL-CIO Promotes Egypt-Israel Union Ties," *Jerusalem Post*, April 23, 1981.
64. Shlaim, *Iron Wall*, 342, 397; Khalidi, *Hundred Years' War*, 129–131.
65. Shlaim, *Iron Wall*, 395–412; Khalidi, *Hundred Years' War*, 128–156; Anziska, *Preventing Palestine*, 208; Geraldine Rosenfield, "U.S. Public Opinion Polls and the Lebanon War," *The American Jewish Yearbook, 1984*, Vol. 84 (1984): 105–116.
66. "Organized Labor Speaks Out on Lebanon," Display Ad 107, *New York Times*, August 15, 1982.
67. "AFL-CIO Supports Israel's Attack on PLO," *New York Jewish Week*, August 27, 1982.
68. Elaine Sciolino, "Kirkland Wins Acclaim for Success Abroad, but Faces Criticism at Home," *New York Times*, December 15, 1989.
69. Quoted in Anziska, *Preventing Palestine*, 219.
70. Shlaim, *Iron Wall*, 412–417 (Begin quoted on p. 416); Khalidi, *Hundred Years' War*, 154–161.
71. William E. Farrell, "Israelis, at Huge Rally in Tel Aviv, Demand Begin and Sharon to Resign," *New York Times*, September 26, 1982.
72. Victor Riesel, "When Labor Differs Sharply on Israel," *Indianapolis Star*, October 7, 1982.
73. Riesel, "When Labor Differs."
74. Gene Hoffman to El Al membership, January 10, 1984, JLC Records, box 419, folder "El Al Strike," Tamiment; "Israeli Airline Denounced on Strike Tactics," *AFL-CIO News*, April 7, 1984; Linda Pellizzi, "Another View of El Al Strike," *Newsday*, April 24, 1984; Elizabeth Weiner, "El Al Says Out All," *Village Voice*, July 10, 1984; "Israeli-Style Austerity Sparks an Angry U.S. Strike at El Al," *Business Week*, July 23, 1984; Arie Reichel and John F. Preble, "The El Al Strike in New York," *Journal of Management Case Studies* 3 (1987): 270–276.
75. Weiner, "El Al Says Out All."
76. Gene Hoffman to all members of the family of El Al employees, March 13, 1984, JLC Records, box 419, folder "El Al Strike," Tamiment.
77. "Israeli Airline Denounced on Strike Tactics"; Weiner, "El Al Says All Out"; "Israeli-Style Austerity."
78. Arieh Egozi, "Antisemitic Comments Against El Al in New York," *Yediot Ahronot*, April 13, 1984, and "Schneider: El Al Is Discriminated Against for Anti-Semitic Reasons," *Israel Shelanu*, May 30, 1985, JLC Records, box 419, folder "JLC Israel Statement," Tamiment.
79. Resolution passed by IAM Lodge 2656, District 100, April 24, 1984, JLC Records, box 419, folder "El Al Strike," Tamiment.
80. William Sapphire, "El Al Official Says AFL-CIO Call Will Not Affect

Airline, but Calls It Entirely, Absolutely Wrong," *Jewish Telegraphic Agency*, July 24, 1984; "Aiding Machinists, AFL-CIO Call for Boycott of El Al," *Labor Chronicle*, August 1984.

81. Martin Lapan, May 22, 1984, and Martin Lapan, November 15, 1984, JLC Records, box 419, folder "El Al Strike," Tamiment.
82. John Fox, Joseph Fisher, and Michael S. Perry, "On El Al's Labor Crisis," *Jewish Exponent*, September 28, 1984.
83. Herb Magidson letter to Knesset, September 12, 1984, JLC Records, box 419, folder "El Al Strike," Tamiment.
84. Michael Oreskes, "U.S. Labor Ties with Israel Are Strained by El Al Strike," *New York Times*, May 16, 1985; "Schneider: El Al Is Discriminated Against."
85. AFL-CIO Resolution: El Al Airlines, February 16, 1985, JLC Records, box 419, folder "El Al Strike," Tamiment.
86. Minutes of the AFL-CIO Executive Council, February 18–22, 1985, page 35, box 22, International Association of Machinists and Aerospace Workers Records, Georgia State University Library, Special Collections and Archives.
87. Oreskes, "U.S. Labor Ties with Israel Are Strained."
88. Lane Kirkland to Shimon Peres, September 13, 1985, reprinted in *Electrical Union World*, October 15, 1985, JLC Records, box 419, folder "JLC Israel Statement," Tamiment.
89. Quoted in "Machinists Get Jobs Back as Long El Al Strike Ends," *AFL-CIO News*, July 19, 1986.
90. "Tentative Settlement in 2-Year El Al Strike," *Associated Press*, May 31, 1986; "Machinists Get Jobs Back."

CHAPTER 5: INTIFADA

1. Joost R. Hiltermann, "The Emerging Trade Union Movement in the West Bank," *MERIP Reports* No. 136/137, (October-December 1985): 27–30.
2. Hiltermann, "The Emerging Trade Union Movement," 27–30; Marty Rosenbluth, "'No Commitment': Arab Workers and the Histadrut," *Middle East Labor Bulletin* (*MELB*) 1, no. 1 (Summer 1988).
3. Quoted in "Israeli Gov't Harasses Palestinian Unionists," *Labor Notes*, November 1987.
4. Quoted in "Israeli Gov't Harasses Palestinian Unionists."
5. "Israelis Crack Down on Gaza Unions," *Labor Notes*, May 1987.
6. Rosenbluth, "'No Commitment.'"
7. Quoted in "Gaza Strikes Spread to Israel, Two Million Palestinians in General Strike," *Labor Notes*, February 1988.

8. Rashid Khalidi, *Hundred Years' War on Palestine: A History of Settler Colonialism and Resistance, 1917–2017* (New York: Picador, 2017), 168–175; Avi Shlaim, *Iron Wall: Israel and the Arab World* (New York: W. W. Norton and Company, 2001), 450–459; John Kifner, "Islamic Fundamentalist Group Splitting Palestinian Uprising," *New York Times*, September 18, 1988.
9. "Gaza Strikes Spread to Israel."
10. "Gaza Strikes Spread to Israel"; Marty Rosenbluth, "Israel's Economy Suffering from Strike by Palestinian Workers and Shopkeepers," *Labor Notes*, April 1988.
11. John Kifner, "'Kill Us or Get Out!' Arabs Taunt as the Toll in Gaza Turmoil Rises," *New York Times*, December 16, 1987; John Kifner, "Israelis Reinforce Gaza Strip Troops," *New York Times*, December 17, 1987; "Israeli Troops Kill Gaza Protester in Clashes During General Strike," *New York Times*, January 10, 1988; Alan Cowell, "Israeli Troops Kill 2 Arabs; Palestinian General Strike Protests Shultz Visit," *New York Times*, February 26, 1988; Alan Cowell, "Strike Grips West Bank and Gaza as 2 More Palestinians Are Killed," *New York Times*, March 16, 1988; Joel Brinkley, "Palestinians Stage General Strike, But the Territories Remain Quiet," *New York Times*, May 16, 1988; "4,000 Gazans Shun Jobs for a Day as Israeli Permits Are Introduced," *New York Times*, August 19, 1989; Joel Beinin, "From Land Day to Peace Day . . . and Beyond," in *Intifada: The Palestinian Uprising Against Israel Occupation*, ed. Zachary Lockman and Joel Beinin (Boston: South End Press, 1989); Joel Beinin, "Palestinian Workers Have a Long History of Resistance," *Jacobin*, June 6, 2021.
12. Jeff Schuhrke, *Blue-Collar Empire: The Untold Story of US Labor's Global Anticommunist Crusade* (London and New York: Verso, 2024), 241–248; Peter Cole, *Dockworker Power: Race and Activism in Durban and the San Francisco Bay Area* (Urbana: University of Illinois Press, 2018).
13. Quoted in Sasha Polakow-Suransky, *The Unspoken Alliance: Israel's Secret Relationship with Apartheid South Africa* (New York: Vintage Books, 2010), 240–241.
14. Fayez Sayegh, *Zionist Colonialism in Palestine* (Beirut, Lebanon: Research Center-Palestine Liberation Organization, 1965), 27; Noura Erakat and John Reynolds, "Understanding Apartheid," *Jewish Currents*, November 1, 2022.
15. Quoted in Pamela E. Pennock, *The Rise of the Arab American Left: Activists, Allies, and Their Fight Against Imperialism and Racism, 1960s–1980s* (Chapel Hill, NC: University of North Carolina Press, 2017), 186.
16. See Polakow-Suransky, *Unspoken Alliance*.
17. Jack Hart, "To Hurt S. Africa, Israel Must Also Be Sanctioned," *Phila-*

delphia Tribune, August 26, 1986; Darrel Meyers, "Israel and South Africa," *Los Angeles Times*, September 2, 1985; Michael Ross, "Arabs Strike in Israel, Charge 'Apartheid,'" *Los Angeles Times*, June 25, 1987; Thomas L. Friedman, "A Forecast for Israel: More Arabs Than Jews," *New York Times*, October 19, 1987; Ned Temko, "Israel and South Africa: Some Similarities, Crucial Differences," *Christian Science Monitor*, January 22, 1988; Marjorie Olster, "Tutu Visits Palestinians in the West Bank: South Africa's Archbishop Compares Uprising with Anti-Apartheid Struggle," *St. Petersburg Times*, December 25, 1989.

18. "The Time Has Come: End All Aid to Apartheid Israel!" *New York Times*, March 13, 1988.
19. Statement by the AFL-CIO Executive Council on Israel, February 1988, Bal Harbour, FL, ILGWU Jay Mazur Papers, Collection #5780/203, box 12, folder 5, Kheel Center for Labor-Management Documentation & Archives (KC), Cornell University.
20. Ross, "Arabs Strike in Israel."
21. Statement by the AFL-CIO Executive Council on Israel, February 1988.
22. "Editorial: A Beginning," *MELB* 1, no. 1 (Summer 1988).
23. "Editorial: A Beginning"; Jeffrey Blankfort, "Unionists Picket Histadrut Benefit, Hit South African Connection," *Labor Notes*, December 1987; Steve Zeltzer, interview with author, September 29, 2024.
24. Souad Dajani, "Israel and South Africa: The U.S. Connection," *American-Arab Affairs* 24 (Spring 1988); Zeltzer interview with author.
25. "AFSCME Vote Says Bye to Histadrut, Israeli Bonds" and "Labor Council Says: 'Stop the Killings,'" *MELB* 1, no. 1 (Summer 1988).
26. "Steelworkers: 'End Aid to Israel,'" *MELB* 1, no. 1 (Summer 1988); "Steelworker Local Says Stop Aid, Sell Bonds," *MELB* 1, no. 4 (Summer 1989).
27. "ILWU: Israel Guilty of 'State Terror,'" *MELB* 1, no. 2 (Fall 1988); "Palestinian Statehood Called for by UE," *MELB* 1, no. 3 (Spring 1989).
28. "Guild Charges Israel with Press Violations," "AFSCME Cites Israel But Defends Histadrut," and "SEIU Condemns Use of Force, Expulsions," *MELB* 1, no. 2 (Fall 1988).
29. "UAW Condemns Israeli Violence as 'Unacceptable,'" *MELB* 1, no. 4 (Summer 1989).
30. "LCOME Brings Palestinian Union Leader to U.S.," *MELB* 1, no. 4 (Summer 1989).
31. Jeffrey Blankfort, "AFL-CIO Tries to Hide Palestinian Expulsions at Wash. Convention," *MELB* 2, no. 1 (Winter 1990).
32. Eugenia Kemble, "Trade and the Rights of Workers," *Freedom at Issue* (July–August 1988), Jewish Labor Committee Records, box 426, folder 2, Tamiment.

33. Gene Bruskin, interview with author, March 27, 2025; Marty Rosenbluth, "Attacking Labor," *Multinational Monitor*, April 1988; Simon Montlake, "Long Shot Lawyer: Defending Migrants in US's Toughest Immigration Court," *Christian Science Monitor*, April 22, 2019.
34. Quoted in Gene Bruskin, "Palestinians Face Repression & Discrimination, Say U.S. Unionists," *Labor Notes*, January 1989.
35. Bruskin interview with author.
36. Bruskin interview with author.
37. Bruskin, "Palestinians Face Repression,"; Gene Bruskin, "USTR Hears Evidence of Israeli Labor Violations," *MELB* 1, no. 3 (Spring 1989).
38. Presentation on Behalf of the American-Arab Anti-Discrimination Committee, Request for Review of the Status of Israel, Jewish Labor Committee Records, box 425, folder 1, Tamiment; Stuart Auerbach, "Arabs Assail Israel on Union Rights," *Washington Post*, November 18, 1988; "Israel's Trade Benefits to Continue," *Jewish Telegraphic Agency*, April 14, 1989; Judith Chomsky, "USTR Sidesteps Repression of Palestinian Workers," *MELB* 1, no. 4 (Summer 1989).
39. "Labor Defense Network Formed in Philly-PLAN," *MELB* 2, no. 3 (Summer 1990).
40. Resolution AFSCME, Social Service Local 1108, adopted May 19, 1990, Jewish Labor Committee Records, box 426, folder 3, Tamiment Library and Robert F. Wagner Labor Archives (Tamiment), New York University.
41. "Release of Palestinian Trade Unionist, Hani Beydoun," SEIU Local 600, 1990, JLC Records, box 426, folder 3, Tamiment.
42. "Solidarity Update: Hani Beydoun," *Labor Notes*, August 1990; Committee to Release Hani Baydoun, "U.S. Unionists Demand: Release Palestinian Trade Unionist Hani Beydoun!," 1990, JLC Records, box 426, folder 3, Tamiment; "American Trade Unionists Appeal for Release of Palestinian Trade Unionist Hani Baydoun," ALAA Roots, May 1, 1990, https://alaa2325.wordpress.com/1990/05/01/american-trade-unionists-appeal-for-release-of-palestinian-trade-unionist-hani-baydoun/.
43. Steven Slezak to Max Mont, August 1, 1990, JLC Records, box 426, folder 3, Tamiment.
44. Khalidi, *Hundred Years' War*, 186–188; Shlaim, *Iron Wall*, 485–488.
45. "AFL-CIO Makes Quick Adjustment, Supports Israel-PLO Agreement," *MELB* 4, no. 4 (Spring 1994).
46. Khalidi, *Hundred Years' War*, 178–204; Shlaim, *Iron Wall*, 485–544.
47. Marty Rosenbluth, "Palestinian Unions Reunify," *Labor Notes*, May 1990; Marty Rosenbluth, "Palestinian Trade Unions Demonstrate New Strength," *MELB* 2, no. 1 (Winter 1990); Rasem 'Abeidat, "A Critical

Study of the Current State of Palestinian Worker's Unity," *MELB* 4, no. 2 (Spring 1993).

48. Arab World for Research and Development, *Palestine Workers: A Comprehensive Report on Work Conditions, Priorities and Recommendations* (Palestine General Federation of Trade Unions, 2013), 7; Joel Greenberg, "West Bank Labour Federations Unite," *Jerusalem Post*, March 1, 1990; Michal Yudelman, "Histadrut Signs Accord with Arab Union," *Jerusalem Post*, November 14, 1994; Nina Sovich, "Stifling Democracy Within Palestinian Unions," *MERIP Reports* 215 (Summer 2000).
49. Sos Nissen, "Anything but Workers in the Palestinian Trade Unions," *News from Within*, April 1996; Barton Gellman, "PLO Leader Turns Tables to Break Teachers' Strike," *Washington Post*, April 27, 1997; Makhoul quoted in Sovich, "Stifling Democracy."
50. Harry Kelber, *The "Palace Revolution" That Changed the AFL-CIO* (New York: The Labor Educator, 1999).
51. Schuhrke, *Blue-Collar Empire*, 279–281, 287–288.
52. Bob Mattingly, "U.S. Unions Bankroll Israeli Aggression," *Socialist Action*, August 2002.
53. Jonathan Preminger, *Labor in Israel: Beyond Nationalism and Neoliberalism* (Ithaca: Cornell University Press, 2018), 8–9.
54. 16th Histadrut National Convention 1990, Resolutions on Peace and International Issues, UAW President's Office: Owen Bieber Records, box 130, folder 16, Walter P. Reuther Library of Labor and Urban Affairs (Reuther Library), Wayne State University.
55. NCLI, Israel Histadrut Campaign, General Outline, December 1990, Adam Klein to Jay Mazur, May 13, 1991, Jay Mazur Papers, box 17, folder 17 and folder 19, Kheel Center for Labor-Management Documentation & Archives (KC), Cornell University; "New Executive Director Appointed to NCLI," NCLI Notebook, May/June 1991, NCLI, "Who We Are/What We Do" (n.d., ca. 1992), ACTWU President Jacob Sheinkman Files, Collection #5619/004, box 149, folder 7, KC.
56. John Sweeney remarks at Israel Solidarity Rally, April 15, 2002, quoted in *Introduction to Labor: The U.S. Trade Union Movement and the Organized Jewish Community*, Israel Advocacy Initiative, 2008, 53.

CHAPTER 6: LABOR FOR PALESTINE

1. John J. Mearsheimer and Stephen M. Walt, *The Israel Lobby and US Foreign Policy* (London and New York: Penguin Books, 2007), 106.
2. Avi Shlaim, *The Iron Wall: Israel and the Arab World* (New York: W. W. Norton and Company, 2001), 575.
3. Shlaim, *Iron Wall*, 459, 556–557.

4. Mearsheimer and Walt, *Israel Lobby*, 105.
5. Rashid Khalidi, *The Hundred Years' War on Palestine: A History of Settler Colonialism and Resistance, 1917–2017* (New York: Picador, 2017), 207–213; Shlaim, *Iron Wall*, 564–601.
6. Ali Adam, "Palestinian Intifada: How Israel Orchestrated a Bloody Takeover," *Al Jazeera*, September 28, 2020.
7. Khalidi, *Hundred Years' War*, 212–215.
8. New York City Labor Against the War, Founding Statement, September 27, 2001, https://nyclaw01.wordpress.com/2002/10/26/2002-10-26-nyclaw-statement-1200-updated-signers/.
9. Deidre McFadyen, "'Justice, Not Vengeance': Some Union Heads Oppose 'Bush War,'" *Chief-Leader*, October 26, 2001; New York City Labor Against the War, "2001–2011: 10 Years of New York City Labor Against the War (NYCLAW)," September 27, 2011, https://nyclaw01.wordpress.com/2011/09/27/2001-2011-10-years-of-new-york-city-labor-against-the-war-nyclaw/.
10. Quoted in Bob Mattingly, "Middle East War Roils San Francisco Labor Council," *Labor Tuesday*, April 16, 2002.
11. Quoted in Mattingly, "Middle East War Roils."
12. Quoted in Joe Eskenazi, "S.F. Labor Council Passes Planck Condemning Israel," *Jewish Bulletin of Northern California*, March 29, 2002.
13. *Introduction to Labor: The U.S. Trade Union Movement and the Organized Jewish Community*, Israel Advocacy Initiative, 2008, 24.
14. Quoted in Tim Shorrock, "Toeing the Line? Sweeney and U.S. Foreign Policy," *New Labor Forum*, Fall/Winter 2002.
15. Quoted in Shorrock, "Toeing the Line?"
16. Vince Morris, "Bush Aide Booed at Rally for Israel," *New York Post*, April 16, 2002.
17. "Petition Protesting Sweeney AFL-CIO Support for Israeli Invasion," *Labor Standard*, May 6, 2002, https://laborforpalestine.net/2002/05/06/2346/.
18. *Forward* quoted in Bob Mattingly, "U.S. Unions Bankroll Israeli Aggression," *Socialist Action*, August 2002.
19. Letwin quoted in Mattingly, "U.S. Unions Bankroll Israeli Aggression"; "No Labor Money for Israeli War Crimes!," New York City Labor Against the War, May 21, 2002, https://laborforpalestine.net/2002/05/21/no-labor-money-for-israeli-war-crimes-new-york-city-labor-against-the-war/.
20. Quoted in Siobhan McGrath and Jordan Flaherty, "Palestinian Unionists Tour U.S. to Counter AFL-CIO's 'One-Sided' Stance on Conflict," *Labor Notes*, March 2003.

21. NYCLAW, "Report on the New York Visit by Representatives from the PGFTU," December 13, 2002, https://laborforpalestine.net/2002/12/13/report-on-the-new-york-visit-by-representatives-from-the-pgftu/; McGrath and Flaherty, "Palestinian Unionists Tour U.S."
22. Solidarity Center, "Delegation of Palestinian Trade Unionists Visits Solidarity Center," 2010, Wayback Machine, https://web.archive.org/web/20110106124414/http://www.solidaritycenter.org/content.asp?contentid=1032.
23. G. Nelson Bass, "Organized Labor and U.S. Foreign Policy: The Solidarity Center in Historical Context" (Ph.D. dissertation, Florida International University, 2012), 122.
24. Labor for Palestine Founding Statement, December 4, 2004, https://laborforpalestine.net/about/founding-statement/.
25. Michael Letwin, Suzanne Adely, and Jaime Veve, "Labor for Palestine: Challenging US Labor Zionism," *American Quarterly* 67, no. 4 (2015): 1049–1050.
26. Jimmy Carter, *Palestine: Peace Not Apartheid* (New York: Simon and Schuster, 2006), 192; B'Tselem, *Separation Barrier*, November 11, 2017, https://www.btselem.org/separation_barrier.
27. Avi Shlaim, "How Israel Brought Gaza to the Brink of Humanitarian Catastrophe," *Guardian*, January 6, 2009; Rashid Khalidi, *The Iron Cage: The Story of the Palestinian Struggle for Statehood* (Boston: Beacon Press, 2006), 205, 256–259.
28. Khalidi, *Hundred Years' War*, 218.
29. Khalidi, *Hundred Years' War*, 219.
30. Khalidi, *Hundred Years' War*, 215–221.
31. Omar Khalifa, "Palestinian Union Hit on All Sides," *Al Jazeera*, July 25, 2007.
32. Solidarity Center, "Palestinian Territories," 2007, Wayback Machine, https://web.archive.org/web/20070907074509/http://www.solidaritycenter.org/content.asp?contentid=425.
33. Omar Barghouti, *BDS: Boycott, Divestment, Sanctions: The Global Struggle for Palestinian Rights* (Chicago: Haymarket Books, 2011), 5, 7, 239–247.
34. Jeff Schuhrke, *Blue-Collar Empire: The Untold Story of US Labor's Global Anticommunist Crusade* (New York and London: Verso, 2024), 241–248, 269–271; United Mine Workers of America/Free South Africa Movement, "Why American Workers Have United to Boycott Shell," 1986, Elizabeth Ussher Groff Collection of Portland Anti-Apartheid Material, Michigan State University Libraries Special Collections, https://africanactivist.msu.edu/recordFiles/210-849-27803/african_activist_archive-a0b0o1-a_12419.pdf.

35. Tom Dale, "Rachel Corrie Gave Her Life for Palestine," *Jacobin*, March 16, 2024.
36. "Remembering Rachel Corrie," report by Jack Heyman, January 3, 2005, http://www.labournet.net/world/0502/rachel1.html; "Statement by AFL-CIO President John Sweeney on the Tragic Death of Rachel Corrie," March 21, 2003, Rachel Corrie Foundation, https://rachelcorriefoundation.org/multimedia/2017/07/March212003AFL-CIOLetter.pdf.
37. "Remembering Rachel Corrie."
38. *Introduction to Labor*, 23.
39. Hank Silver and Francesca Rosa, "SEIU Local 535 Members vs. Caterpillar Corporation and Union Bureaucracy," *LaborNet*, July 20, 2005, http://labornet.igc.org/news/0705/seiucat.htm; *Introduction to Labor*, 22–23.
40. *Introduction to Labor*, 21; Leon Cohen, "Divestment Vote Fails in Wisconsin," *Jewish Telegraphic Agency*, April 14, 2005.
41. Andrea Gregory, "City Rejects Divestment Signatures," *Somerville Times*, September 14, 2005; *Introduction to Labor*, 22, 52.
42. BDS Movement, "UK: The Transport and General Workers Union joins the Boycott Campaign," November 2, 2007, https://bdsmovement.net/news/uk-transport-and-general-workers-union-joins-boycott-campaign.
43. Jewish Labor Committee, "U.S. Labor Leaders Blast British Unions' 'Boycott Israel' Resolutions," 2007, http://www.jewishlaborcommittee.org/2007/07/us_labor_leaders_blast_british.html.
44. Jewish Labor Committee, "Statement of Opposition to Divestment from or Boycotts of Israel," 2007, http://www.jewishlaborcommittee.org/2007/07/statement_of_opposition_to_div.html.
45. Jewish Labor Committee, "Statement of Opposition."
46. Quoted in Henry Levy, "Israel Bonds Raises over $30 Million from Labor Division," *Jewish Post*, 2008.
47. *Introduction to Labor*, 17.
48. "NYCLAW Response to Anti-Boycott Attacks," *Chief-Leader*, October 19, 2007, https://nyclaw01.wordpress.com/2007/10/19/nyclaw-response-to-anti-boycott-attacks/.
49. Richard Trumka's Remarks at October 2009 JLC Dinner, Jewish Labor Committee, https://www.jewishlaborcommittee.org/2005/10/richard_trumkas_remarks_at_oct_1.html.
50. Open Letter from U.S. Trade Unionists to AFL-CIO President Richard Trumka: Boycott Apartheid Israel, December 4, 2009, Labor for Palestine, https://laborforpalestine.net/2009/12/19/trumka-letter/.
51. Amnesty International, *Israel/Gaza: Operation "Cast Lead": 22 Days of Death and Destruction*, July 2, 2009, https://www.amnesty.org/en/documents/mde15/015/2009/en/.

52. Khalidi, *Hundred Years' War*, 221–225; Efraim Inbar and Eitan Shami, "'Mowing the Grass': Israel's Strategy for Protracted Intractable Conflict," *Journal of Strategic Studies* 37, no. 1 (2014): 67–68.
53. Peter Baker and Julie Hirschfeld Davis, "U.S. Finalizes Deal to Give Israel $38 Billion in Military Aid," *New York Times*, September 13, 2016.
54. Geoffrey Palmet et al., *Report of the Secretary-General's Panel of Inquiry on the 31 May 2010 Flotilla Incident*, United Nations, September 2011.
55. Quoted in Letwin, Adely, and Vive, "Labor for Palestine," 1050.
56. ILWU Local 10, "For International Labor Solidarity to Stop Zionist Repression and Build a Just Peace," April 2, 2002, http://www.labournet.net/world/0204/palilwu.html.
57. Schuhrke, *Blue-Collar Empire*, 246–247; Peter Cole, "Don't Like War? Then Don't Work! Remembering When Dockworkers Shut Down the Ports on May Day," *In These Times*, April 26, 2008; Kim Kelly, "The Next Target for Protests Against Israel: Ports," *In These Times*, November 6, 2023; Sarah Lazare, "This Union Is Famous for Opposing South African Apartheid. Now It's Standing With Gaza," *Nation*, November 21, 2023.
58. Greg Dropkin, "Blockade: Dockers respond to Israel's Flotilla Massacre and Gaza Siege," BDS National Committee, July 9, 2010, https://archive.bdsmovement.net/news/blockade-dockers-respond-israel%E2%80%99s-flotilla-massacre-and-gaza-siege; Letwin, Adely, and Vive, "Labor for Palestine," 1050–1051.
59. IWW, "IWW supports Boycott, Divestment and Sanctions movement in support of Palestinian Rights," December 2, 2010, https://archive.iww.org/node/5282/; "IWW Friends of Palestinian Workers Group," https://archive.iww.org/projects/isc/palestine/.
60. Julia Wong, "Oakland Activists 'Block the Boat' for Three Days Running," *In These Times*, August 20, 2014; Murtaza Hussein, "A Small Band of Activists Is Humiliating and Israeli Shipping Giant," *Intercept*, October 31, 2014; Letwin, Adely, and Vive, "Labor for Palestine," 1051–1052.
61. Mario Vasquez, "California Campus Workers Become First Major Local Union to Endorse BDS Against Israel," *In These Times*, December 29, 2014.
62. UAW International Executive Board, Appeal of Stephen Brumbaugh vs. UAW Local Union 2865, December 15, 2015, 118.
63. UAW International Executive Board, Appeal of Stephen Brumbaugh, 45.
64. UAW International Executive Board, Appeal of Stephen Brumbaugh, 45.
65. UAW International Executive Board, Appeal of Stephen Brumbaugh, 46-47; Mario Vasquez, "UAW Overrules Academic Workers BDS Vote Against Israel Despite Finding Strong Turnout, No Misconduct," *In These Times*, January 6, 2016.

66. Jeff Schuhrke, "Univ. of Massachusetts Grad Student Workers Endorse BDS Against Israel," *In These Times*, April 21, 2016; Palestine Legal, "Union Officials Suppress Member Support for BDS," May 25, 2016, https://palestinelegal.org/news/2016/5/25/union-officials-suppress-member-support-for-bds.
67. "UW-Madison Union of Graduate Student Workers (TAA) Endorses BDS Movement," Labor for Palestine, May 19, 2016, https://laborforpalestine.net/2016/05/19/uw-madison-union-of-graduate-student-workers-taa-endorses-bds-movement-taaaft-local-3220/; Andrew Lapin and Gabriel Greschler, "US Teachers' Unions Increasingly Debate Israel, and in Some Places Back Boycotts," *Times of Israel*, July 17, 2021.
68. Quoted in Ali Abunimah, "Connecticut Labor Federation Backs Israel Boycott," *Electronic Intifada*, November 11, 2015.
69. Stanley Heller, "U.S. Union Support for Palestinian Rights Could Be a Game Changer," *Truthdig*, November 5, 2015.
70. Heller, "U.S. Union Support for Palestinian Rights."
71. Heller, "U.S. Union Support for Palestinian Rights"; Abunimah, "Connecticut Labor Federation Backs Israel Boycott"; Stanely Heller, "U.S. Labor, Boycotts, and BDS: Defending Workers' Rights" *New Politics*, December 26, 2018; Susan Webb, "Palestinian Union Leader Seeks Support from U.S. Unions," *People's World*, October 1, 2013.
72. Quoted in Ali Abunimah, "Gaza Attack Pushed US Electrical Workers' Union to Back Israel Boycott," *Electronic Intifada*, September 1, 2015.
73. Quoted in Abunimah, "Gaza Attack Pushed US Electrical Workers' Union."
74. Quoted in Abunimah, "Gaza Attack Pushed US Electrical Workers' Union."
75. Tamara Nassar, "Israel Passes Law Entrenching Apartheid," *The Electronic Intifada*, July 19, 2018; Ilene Prusher, "A New Law Shifts Israel Away from Democracy," *Time*, July 24, 2018.
76. "Two Years On: People Injured and Traumatized During the 'Great March of Return' Are Still Struggling," United Nations, The Question of Palestine (UNISPAL), April 6, 2020, https://www.un.org/unispal/document/two-years-on-people-injured-and-traumatized-during-the-great-march-of-return-are-still-struggling/.
77. "Hundreds Hurt as Palestinians Protest Evictions in Jerusalem," *Al Jazeera*, May 7, 2021, https://www.aljazeera.com/news/2021/5/7/al-aqsa-worshippers-protest-palestinian-evictions-in-jerusalem.
78. Lee Yaron, "General Strike Highlights Israel's Dependency on Palestinian Workers," *Haaretz*, May 19, 2021.
79. Quoted in Shatha Hammad, "Palestinians to Stage Nationwide General

Strike as Air Raids Pummel Gaza," *Middle East Eye*, May 17, 2021.

80. "Gaza Strip: One Year After the Bombing, Some Wounds Never Heal," Doctors Without Borders, May 31, 2022, https://www.doctorswithoutborders.ca/gaza-strip-one-year-after-the-bombing-some-wounds-never-heal/.
81. B'Tselem, *A Regime of Jewish Supremacy from the Jordan River to the Mediterranean Sea: This Is Apartheid*, January 12, 2021; Human Rights Watch, *A Threshold Crossed: Israeli Authorities and the Crimes of Apartheid and Persecution*, April 27, 2021; Amnesty International, *Israel's Apartheid Against Palestinians: A Look into Decades of Oppression and Domination*, February 1, 2022, https://www.amnesty.org/en/documents/mde15/5141/2022/en/.
82. Quoted in Jeff Schuhrke, "U.S. Unions Are Voicing Unprecedented Support for Palestine," *In These Times*, May 26, 2021.
83. Schuhrke, "U.S. Unions Are Voicing Unprecedented Support.".
84. Alex Schmaus and brian bean, "San Francisco Educators Endorse BDS," *Tempest*, May 24, 2021; Michael Arria, "Seattle Teachers Union Endorses BDS, Demands End to Police Partnership with Israel," *Mondweiss*, June 18, 2021; Isaac Scher, "How Israel Advocates Shut Down a Union's Motion to Endorse BDS," *Jewish Currents*, November 8, 2021.
85. Isaac Scher, "AFL-CIO Leadership Tries to Block Affiliate's Vote on Endorsing BDS," *Intercept*, October 21, 2021.
86. Alex N. Press, "Oakland Longshore Workers Say No to Israeli-Operated Cargo," *Jacobin*, June 8, 2021; Alex N. Press, "It Took a Police Crackdown to Get Israeli-Operated Cargo Unloaded in Seattle," *Jacobin*, June 20, 2021.

CONCLUSION

1. "Members of the National Labor Network for Ceasefire Send a Letter to Biden Demanding a Ceasefire in Gaza, End to Military Aid to Israel," National Labor Network for Ceasefire, July 23, 2024, https://drive.google.com/file/d/1ASKF012G-ZuMQ2cK0zePLm3PaXY72Q3Q/view; Adam Johnson, "Unions Demanding an End to Israel Military Aid Is a Welcome Escalation," *In These Times*, July 26, 2024, https://inthesetimes.com/article/labor-unions-israel-gaza-biden-harris.
2. Jonathan Chait, "Grad Students Furious United Auto Workers Endorses Biden," *New York*, February 2, 2024; Damien Fisher, "Progressives Push to Bring Far-Left Politics to Blue-Collar Unions," Association of Mature American Citizens, April 29, 2024, https://amac.us/newsline/society/progressives-push-to-bring-far-left-politics-to-blue-collar-unions/; Oren Cass, "When I Suggest Unions Should . . ." X (formerly Twitter), August 29, 2024, https://x.com/oren_cass/status/1829321307831275801;

Noam Sheiber, "Gaza Debate Reopens Divisions Between Left-Wing Workers and Union Leaders," *New York Times*, August 30, 2024; Will Sussman, "Letter to the Editor of the New York Times," *Where There's a Will*, September 7, 2024, https://willsussman.substack.com/p/letter-to-the-editor-of-the-new-york.

3. Charles P. Larrowe, *Harry Bridges: The Rise and Fall of Radical Labor in the United States* (New York: Lawrence Hill and Co., 1972), 131–133; Robert W. Cherny, *Harry Bridges: Labor Radical, Labor Legend* (Urbana: University of Illinois Press, 2023), 194.
4. Quoted in "Port Embargoes Scrap Iron After Chinese Picket Ship," *Daily Boston Globe*, March 5, 1939.
5. Robert W. Cherny, *Harry Bridges: Labor Radical, Labor Legend* (Urbana: University of Illinois Press, 2023), 194; Bruce Ramsey, "In 1930's Seattle Scrap Steel Was a Case for Trade Sanctions," ILWU Local 19, Seattle Waterfront History, https://www.ilwu19.com/history/1930; Oregon Historical Society, "Chinese Americans Picket Scrap Metal to Japan," Oregon History Project, https://www.oregonhistoryproject.org/articles/historical-records/chinese-americans-picket-scrap-metal-to-japan/.
6. "Harry Bridges," producer and director Jack Sameth (episode of *Bill Moyers Journal*, executive producer Jerome Toobin), WNET (PBS, January 29, 1974); Peter Cole, "Fighting Fascism, Writing Novels, and Preserving Radical History," *Process: A Blog for American History*, May 28, 2024, https://www.processhistory.org/fighting-fascism-writing-novels-and-preserving-radical-history-cole/.

INDEX

ABOUT THE AUTHOR

Jeff Schuhrke is a labor historian and assistant professor at the Harry Van Arsdale Jr. School of Labor Studies, SUNY Empire State University. He is the author of *Blue-Collar Empire: The Untold Story of US Labor's Global Anticommunist Crusade*. His writing appears frequently in *Jacobin*, *In These Times*, *Jewish Currents*, and *Labor Notes*.